The Nature of Vermont

The Nature of Vermont

Introduction and Guide to a New England Environment

Revised and Expanded Edition

by Charles W. Johnson

University Press of New England
Hanover and London

Published by University Press of New England
One Court Street, Lebanon, NH 03766
www.upne.com

Printed in the United States of America   5   4   3

CIP data appear at the end of the book

ISBN–13: 978–0–87451–856–6
ISBN–10: 0–87451–856–3

Reprint Permissions

Page 15: Skinner, Brian J. 1995. *The Dynamic Earth: An Introduction to Physical Geology*. John Wiley & Sons, New York. Copyright 1995 by John Wiley & Sons, Inc. Reprinted by permission of John Wiley & Sons, Inc.

Pages 22–24: Courtesy Jesse Bruchac.

Page 55: Udall, Stewart L. 1963. *The Quiet Crisis*. Avon Books, New York. Copyright 1963 by Stewart L. Udall. Reprinted by permission of Holt, Rinehart, and Winston. All rights reserved.

Page 65: Bradbury, Ray. 1957. *Dandelion Wine*. Doubleday & Company, New York. Copyright 1957 by Ray Bradbury. Reprinted by permission of the Harold Matson Company, Inc. All rights reserved.

Page 94: Forbush, Edward H. and May, John R. 1939. *A Natural History of American Birds of East and Central North America*. Houghton Mifflin Company. Boston. Copyright 1939 by Houghton Mifflin Company. Reprinted by permission.

Page 143: Densmore, Frances. 1910, "My Love Has Departed." *Smithsonian Institution Bureau of American Ethnology Bulletin* 45 (*Chippewa Music*), Washington, D.C. Reprinted by permission of the Smithsonian Institution Press.

Pages 144–45: Courtesy Jesse Bruchac.

Page 194: Trippensee, Reuben. 1953. *Wildlife Management*, Volume 2. McGraw-Hill Book Company, New York. Copyright 1953 by McGraw-Hill Book Company. Used with the permission of McGraw-Hill Book Company.

Page 221: *The Poems of Dylan Thomas*. New Directions Publishing Corp., New York. Copyright 1946 by New Directions Publishing Corporation. Reprinted by permission of New Directions.

Page 223: Thompson, Stith. 1996. *Tales of the North American Indians*. Indiana University Press. Reprinted by permission.

Page 247: Barnstone, Willis. 1965. *Sappho*. Anchor Books, Garden City, N.Y. Copyright 1965 by Willis Barnstone. Reprinted by permission of Doubleday and Co.

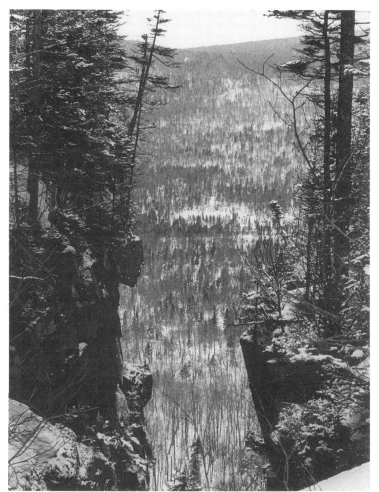

To my mother and father.
You opened my eyes
the first time.

Polyphemus Moth. Photo by Stephan Syz.

Contents

Preface

The image people have of Vermont is not beyond its reality. The descriptions of wild beauty interspersed with the purity of northern-New England villages need not be exaggerated. Residents of the state have always been proud of these attributes and are protective of their territory, and for outsiders who visit at any time of year, Vermont is a release from the intensity and sameness that grip many other parts of America.

Vermont doesn't have the vast wildernesses of a Minnesota or Alaska. It doesn't have the ten-thousand-foot peaks of the Sierras or open skies of prairies. Vermont is modestly grand, a softness over old ruggedness, blessed with diversity of land and wildlife. Within this small state lives an extraordinary array of plants and animals, and the reasons for this variety are many. Vermont lies within biological transition zones, from the southern deciduous forests to the northern boreal forests, from the eastern Atlantic region to the Midwest. Being so positioned, it has biological representatives from each area. It has a variety of landscapes—mountains, rivers, bogs, lakes, marshes, forests—and the unique associations of each. It lives under the stark polarities of the seasons. It has changed under the different uses to which humans have put it.

The landscape and natural resources here are tremendously important to Vermonters, in both economic and aesthetic terms. These are around us always and much of our income is in some way tied to them. Visitors come many miles to share in this special beauty. Residents and visitors alike are excited and curious about the state: its history, geology, plants, and wildlife, and people's relationship to them through the ages. For the student with time and means to research these topics, a wealth of information can be pieced together. But for the average person, there are few sources that give a panoramic view, that make sense of the diversity of Vermont.

For the latter group, this book is intended. It is neither a field guide nor a complete inventory of the flora and fauna of the state. Rather, it is an introduction to the nature of a state, placed into comprehensible components that reflect its natural character. It is history, natural history, and general discovery brought together in one package, to be opened by any interested person.

A book may be a disembodied teacher if it doesn't allow the reader direct contact with the subject matter. Anyone reading this book can get a mental picture of Vermont, but really to see, feel, and

Waits River. Photo courtesy of Vermont Department of Tourism and Marketing.

understand the words, one must experience the reality. Thus the book first looks at the state from a distance and then, after taking the reader closer, points the way for people to explore what has been discussed. Each chapter has a corresponding section in the appendix that lists areas of importance where the reader can inspect examples first hand.

Finally, this book is an attempt to capture some of the dynamics of ever-changing natural systems and to relate them to the present scenery. Some questions will be answered, many will go unanswered, and new ones will be outdated as soon as it is published. That is the point exactly: the book becomes what it is treating—embodying change, it serves as a catalyst for further exploration and reaction, rather than as an end in itself.

Preface to the New Edition

Since the initial publication of *The Nature of Vermont*, almost twenty years have passed. That is an insignificance in the awesome span of geologic time, but for us of human flesh and blood it is a noteworthy measurement, a milestone along our mortal path. It has been a generation more or less, clocking time enough for us to experience the full cycle of our seasons, time enough to see changes.

The changes have come in many forms.

There are the expected fluctuations and variations—though perhaps not exactly foreseen or anticipated—in all natural environments: increasing abundance of some species (e.g., moose, turkey vulture) and decreasing of others (wood turtle, butternut), and shifts in the composition of natural communities in response to climate, weather patterns, or unusual events. Of course, many of those changes may be directly or indirectly attributable to us humans (a formidable environmental force in our own right), such as from our growing numbers and the developments we bring, the side effects of our industrial way of life (e.g., pollution, acid deposition, global warming), the intentional or inadvertent introduction of nonnative plants and animals (zebra mussels, Eurasian watermilfoil).

There is more depth and detail to how we see the world, due to what science and technology reveal of what has been there all along but that we couldn't see, didn't understand, or only partially comprehended. The Natural Heritage inventories of rare species and natural communities, the ongoing measurement and monitoring of air and water quality, the new sophisticated geologic mapping, the archaeological discoveries, the long-term studies of forest health, all are examples of tools we use to pry open a little more the mysteries surrounding us.

Vermont's culture has shifted in subtle and not-so-subtle ways. Increasing urbanization in some parts of the state contrasts sharply with the strong rural traditions in others. The values coming out of these two sometimes clash, as witnessed in near decade-long debates on how to conserve the working Northern Forests of the state and region, the outcry against clear-cutting and the counterrebellion against government regulating or controlling it, the steady push for defining and practicing sustainable management of natural resources.

With losses of species and wildness, here as well as elsewhere in the world, has come a strong public desire for conservation not just of individual species or isolated natural areas, but the larger, more inclusive "biological diversity": the organisms, natural communities, ecological processes, and systems within which they all function together. This has gone hand in hand with the meteoric rise of "conservation biology" as a field of academic study and applied science—putting the theories of biodiversity conservation into practice on the ground.

Finally, change has come with the Information Age: more information available on lots of topics, more organizations to dispense it, more activities and techniques to pass it from one to another. The sheer volume and distribution of it can be bewildering at times.

Taken all together, these changes—the environmental, technological, cultural, and educational—are enough to warrant a new edition of this book, an attempt to document what has already happened here over the last two decades, keep pace with the process, and reset the stage for what is coming next.

At the same time, however, in writing this new edition I wanted to keep sight of the continuity of Vermont's nature, a legacy that endures through time, change, and the evolution of our knowledge. To do so, I have periodically included stories from the Abenakis, Vermont's Native Americans. Their stories, like those of other Native Americans, are passed from generation to generation, help bind them as a culture, and are ways to explain the wonders of their environment. In them, the Abenakis reveal how plants, animals, and even rocks and landforms are not just "things," but have animate spirit. They illustrate how people's fortunes are inextricably tied to those of nature.

What I have included here are only glimpses of a much bigger picture. As Abenaki storyteller Jesse Bruchac, who has contributed some of them, puts it:

> The Abenaki view of land, its history and geography can be illustrated in many ways within the traditional stories. The deepest views are woven into the stories and deserve more than a quote to understand. For it is only within the entire mythology that we can draw the truest and most ancient understandings of Abenaki world view.

In their stories, the Abenakis have much to say about respect, beauty, and identity with nature. Let us listen. We have much to learn.

Acknowledgments

My first debt is to the Vermont Department of Forests, Parks, and Recreation for allowing me the time to work on this book. I am grateful especially for the support and encouragement I received from Rodney Barber, Director of Parks, Robert DeForge, Park Operations Chief, and James Wilkinson, former Commissioner of Forests, Parks, and Recreation.

Friends, fellow workers, colleagues in the academic community, and family members have all been invaluable in untold ways. I would like to extend the deepest appreciation to my mother, Margaret Hunter Johnson, and to Gale Lawrence for the special effort they put into reviewing the manuscript. Both writers themselves, they were unselfish in sharing their skills with me and they encouraged me through both compliments and suggestions for improvement. Also, the guidance of Hub Vogelmann was welcome and valuable; he has been a source of inspiration for me as for so many others.

Other reviewers offered counsel in their particular fields of expertise, and to the following I owe a great deal: Ross Bell, Robert Candy, Benjamin Day, William Countryman, John Hall, Thomas Hudspeth, Angelo Incerpi, Stephen Loring, Giovanna Neudorfer, Charles Ratté, Robert Spear, James Stewart, Peter Thomas, James Wilkinson and Ian Worley. Several others read the first drafts of the book and gave me an early indication of how it was "coming across," and for their part in the completion of the work I would like to thank Rodney Barber, Robert DeForge, Brian Vachon, Jean Vissering, and Anne Winchester.

I pass on praise and gratitude to the people who contributed the various illustrative materials of the book, components that are essential companions to the written text. Among her many talents, Ann Pesiri shows here her fine, sensitive drawings. Jean Vissering provided the maps and diagrams, representing many hours taken from her free time. Numerous photographers were most gracious in donating their art, especially Robert Candy and John Hall.

Many organizations were generous in supplying photographs, maps, references, and other aids, and to them I extend appreciation: the Harvard University Forest, the Office of the Vermont State Geologist, the University of Vermont, the Vermont Department of Forests, Parks, and Recreation, the Vermont Fish and Game Department, the Planning Division of the Vermont Agency of Environmental Conservation, the Vermont Historical Society, the Vermont State Planning Office, and the Vermont Travel Division.

The many drafts of the manuscript took a great deal of time, forbearance of my near-illegible handwriting, and sacrifice on the part of Etta Gibson and Kathy Wheeler. Ann Boutin, Hope Davey, and Janet Greaves were also of great help as critical deadlines approached.

I have seen that most authors need images of inspiration, both past and present, upon which to look as they labor through the writing of a book. I have been lucky to have had several such sources. John Olsen, though long deceased, remains one of the most shining of my boyhood idols—his great sea still rolls within me. With a love of nature that permeates their knowledge of it, Robert Spear and Hub Vogelmann have in many ways been standards to guide my way of thinking. And in the background always have been my family, offering a foundation to rest upon: my aunt, Marjorie Plamenatz, is a kindred spirit and cherished friend; my parents are supports far beyond being parents; and the love, patience, and encouragement of my wife, Joanna, were the ties that bound the whole thing together.

Finally, to my young sons I tender both thanks and regret. To Hunter, I hope that one day, in your own way and time, you may share in the world I talk about. To Brendan and Graylyn, I know your joys outdoors are the real answers, and for every baseball game or hiking trip missed, I'm sorry—I never realized this would take so long. I'll make it up.

For the second edition

In addition to those already acknowledged (many of whom helped again on this second edition), I am grateful to these others: Cedric Alexander, Larry Becker, Lou Borie, Jesse Bruchac, Paul Carnahan, Charles Cogbill, Ken Cox, Barry Doolan, John Dudley, Chris Fichtel, Marjorie Gale, Trish Hanson, Ken Hollmann, David Laing, Rick Levey, Tom Luther, Brian MacDonald, Everett Marshall, Susan Morse, Ron Regan, and William "Nate" Thayer. I am especially indebted to Lou Borie, John Hall, Ted Levin, Brian MacDonald, and Susan Morse for sharing their wonderful art.

I also wish to recognize organizations not previously mentioned for the information they provided: U.S. Fish and Wildlife Service, U.S. Forest Service, Vermont Agency of Transportation, Vermont Chapter of The Nature Conservancy, Vermont Institute of Natural Science, and the Vermont Nongame and Natural Heritage Program (part of the Fish and Wildlife Department). My good fortune continues, too, in the long and satisfying associations I have had with both the Vermont Department of Forests, Parks and Recreation and University Press of New England.

I must single out a few who helped in ways they likely never realized. Nona Estrin, best friend and loving critic, for seeing nature as the touchstone of beauty, truth, and honesty. Stephan Syz, for always having a child's delight in poking around outside, and a child's thrill of

Bobcat. Photo by Susan C. Morse.

discovery. Mark DesMeules, for leaving me an indelible memory of small creatures in obscure places. Conrad Motyka, who does the unheralded, unseen hard work that conservation really is. Mollie Beattie, a brilliant star I know is still shining, there, just over the horizon.

A behind-the-hand whisper to Steven Wallach, who chided me for not having said a word about snow fleas: Well, what else should I have mentioned?

Finally, to my family—a circle ever widening, a pool ever deepening—I thank you, once again. For everything.

The Nature of Vermont

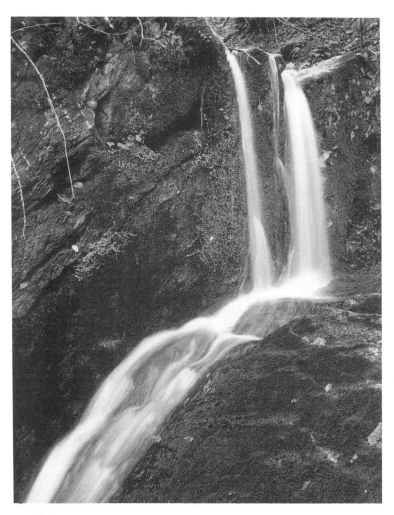

Waterfall. Photo by Louis Borie.

I   The Setting

*Only that day dawns to which we
are awake. There is more day to dawn.
The sun is but a morning star.*

—Henry David Thoreau, *Walden* (1854)

Introduction

As we hike on one of Vermont's wooded trails, or swim in one of its lakes, or simply gaze at its mountains, most of us are impressed with the solidity of what we see. We tend to assume that what is before us has been there forever. And many hope that it will continue in its natural beauty forever hence.

But we should stop and consider. No place on earth ever really stands still. The relentless actions of erosion and deposition, the massive movements of continents, the changes of climates and seasons, the interplay of living and nonliving things—all have shaped this world. And they continue to shape it.

By and large, this work proceeds slowly and imperceptibly. But over time—whether the ticking of minutes or the vast stretches measured by millions of years—the earth, landforms, and oceans change. Today's scenery is not the first or the final picture. We are seeing only the latest frame in the film of evolution, a movie that has no end.

Geological processes have set the stage and largely dictated what fragile beings can live on and in the soil, in the earth's thin skin of atmosphere, and in the waters of oceans, rivers, and lakes. Yet living things, too, modify the environment in which they live. And one most recent arrival, a phenomenon of nature, has superimposed changes on those built by eons of physical, chemical, and biological forces: humankind.

This species has had an inordinate effect on the world, not so much as a biological animal as in its power, multiplied by great numbers and extended by machines. The human strength and influence go far beyond the immediate area or nearby region or even country. They affect the world.

So as we serenely sit and absorb the moment's beauty, we should be mindful of what has taken place to bring it to us, from long ago to the recent past. It may be hard to visualize at times, or even to accept. But understanding the way Vermont has come to us is an important part of understanding its nature today.

1

To Move the World

The Bedrock

The hills, mountains, and valleys of Vermont are familiar to many through words and photographs; they are not easy to depict. In addition, there are other geological formations in the state that are not so well known but which are vital clues to Vermont's earlier form. For example, 500-million-year-old fossils of coral, the oldest in the world, and other organisms occur in limestone up and down the length of Lake Champlain. Since coral is an animal community of shallow tropical oceans, and limestone is a rock of marine origin, it is difficult to imagine how such organisms came to be in the interior of New England, some 200 miles from the ocean, in a climate that is far from tropical. Also, running north-south in the western part of the state, for almost its entire length, are great thrust faults, where huge chunks of land have been heaved up on top of themselves. These thrust faults were made by tremendous pressures from the side, but what those pressures were and where they came from remained for many years a mystery.

Until very recently, geologists could offer no convincing theories or mechanisms to account for the raising of mountains, the thrust-faulting of blocks of land, or the presence of coral thousands of miles from where it should be. Such features were all explained in a circular reasoning: "Mountains owe their origin to mountain-building processes . . . Thrust faults are caused by great stresses at right angles to the fault line . . . Coral indicates that this area was once under a warm ocean . . ." The underlying questions of *why?* and *how?* went unanswered.

In the late 1960s geologists and geophysicists came up with a revolutionary theory that began to give the answers. From a series of discoveries a grand and world-encompassing model was constructed that could explain mountains, earthquakes, volcanoes, thrust fault, and out-of-place fossils, all in the same breath. The theory had actually been proposed as early as 1915, but owing to the lack of solid evidence, it was never widely supported in scientific circles. The evidence has now come in, however, and it is still coming. The model of continental drift, or plate tectonics, is having an overwhelming impact on the earth sciences—and all natural sciences, as well.

Based on much corroborating evidence, the theory describes several global activities:

3

YOUNGEST

Granite from deep sources (200–100 MY)

Mudstone deposited during Acadian orogeny (405–390 MY)

Granite formed as mudstone melted in Acadian & Alleghanian orogenies (400–275 MY)

Lava (400–395 MY)

Limy sandstone in shallow sea (420–400 MY)

Brownsonian lavas and associated sediments (449–453 MY)

Lavas on west edge of Bronsonian plate (460 MY?)

Deep sea mudstone, lava, and sea floor, sheared in Taconian orogeny 455 MY ago

Deep sea mudstone (560–455 MY), thrust westward 455 MY ago

Beach sandstone and shallow marine limestone (560–455 MY)

Rift zone sediments and lavas (575–550 MY)

North American crust (1000 MY)

OLDEST

Geology of Vermont.
Compiled from many sources.
MY = million years old.
B = Burlington, M = Montpelier,
R = Rutland, W = Windsor
Copyright © David Laing 1992.

Vermont's Bedrock. A billion years of Vermont's complicated geologic history recorded in its rocks. In the legend at the right, the oldest formations are at the bottom, and the youngest at the top. Notice the compass direction alignment of Vermont 570 million years ago. See text for explanation. Map © David Laing; used by permission.

Vermont Fossils. Fossil evidence of events and life forms at various eras over the past half billion years. Clockwise from the top, oldest to youngest:

(1) Ripples (1 inch apart) made in the sands of tidal waters some 550 million years ago. They, along with mud cracks and raindrop pits, are visible in the red Monkton quartzite of the University of Vermont's Redstone Quarry Natural Area in Burlington. Photo by Kenneth Hollmann.

(2) Trilobite. This relative of the horseshoe crab and lobster crawled around the shallows of the ancient Iapetus Ocean over 500 million years ago. In existence for more than 150 million years, trilobites as a group became extinct over 400 million years ago. Photo by Kenneth Hollmann.

(3) Coral. The earliest known type of coral, in the 500-million-year-old limestone of Button Island, off Button Bay State Park, Vergennes. Photo by Brian MacDonald.

(4) Straight-shelled cephalopod, an extinct relative of the squid and chambered nautilus, preyed on trilobites, brachiopods, and other animals of the coral reef some 470 million years ago. Photo by Kenneth Hollmann.

(5) Large (2 inch diameter) sea snails, Maclurites magna, which preyed on corals 470 million years ago, appear in this polished slab of so-called black "marble" (really limestone) quarried in Isle La Motte. Tiles of this same black marble are in the main floor of the Vermont Capitol building in Montpelier (set in 1859). Photo courtesy Vermont Historical Society.

(6) Wood and seed pods of an extinct tree preserved in the 20-million-year-old lignite deposits near Brandon. Photo by Kenneth Hollmann.

(7) Mastodon tooth. Discovered in 1848 in a bog near Mount Holly, this upper molar (plaster cast of original) was from a mastodon that roamed the region some 11,000 years ago. It is one of many extinct Ice Age animals that once lived here. Photo by Kenneth Hollmann.

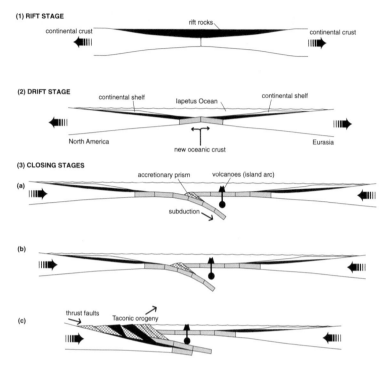

(1) RIFT STAGE

rift rocks

continental crust   continental crust

(2) DRIFT STAGE

continental shelf   Iapetus Ocean   continental shelf

North America   Eurasia

new oceanic crust

(3) CLOSING STAGES

accretionary prism   volcanoes (island arc)

(a)

subduction

(b)

thrust faults   Taconic orogeny

(c)

Origin of Vermont's Mountains. The diagrams illustrate the probable origin of the Appalachian Mountain system, including the Green Mountains of Vermont, and other deep-rock formations in the state. There have been at least three "Appalachian Mountain" systems in this region of the continent. The earliest we have evidence of—called the Grenville Mountains—was formed over a billion years ago, when continental collisions (predating Pangaea by some 800 million years) created mountains perhaps rivaling the present-day Himalayas in height. These mountains largely eroded away over the hundreds of millions of years, with the Adirondacks and portions of the southern Green Mountains the only remnants left. The diagrams pick up events beginning at that stage. See text for more complete explanation; mybp = millions of years before present. Sizes of features and distances are not to scale.

(1) Rift stage (late Precambrian to early Cambrian, 590–550 mybp). The ancient North American continental crust rifts (stretches, thins, and subsides), creating broad, deep valleys. The valleys fill with fluvial (water-borne) sediments from the adjacent uplands. Volcanoes are common in the New England region.

(2) Drift stage (early Cambrian to middle Ordovician, 555–440 mybp). The two continental masses "drift" apart, with subsidence between them increasing and the new Iapetus Ocean filling in between. A mid-ocean ridge supplies new ocean crust on either side. The Grenville Mountains continue to erode, with sediments accumulating on the shelves at the edge of the continents.

(3) Closing stages, or Taconic orogeny (middle to late Ordovician, 440–430 mybp).

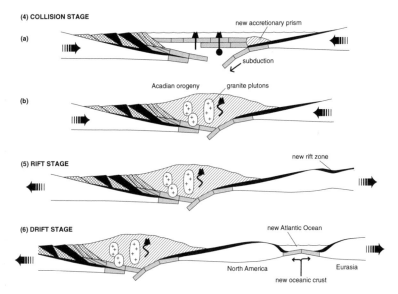

(4) COLLISION STAGE

(a)

new accretionary prism

subduction

(b)

Acadian orogeny   granite plutons

(5) RIFT STAGE

new rift zone

(6) DRIFT STAGE

new Atlantic Ocean

North America   Eurasia

new oceanic crust

(a) The Iapetus Ocean ceases to grow, with the continents beginning to move toward each other. The western crust plunges (is subducted) under the eastern continental crust as the continents converge. (b) The leading edge of the eastern mass acts like a bulldozer to scrape up sediments, ocean crust, and, eventually, continental crust, and pushes them into huge wedges (accretionary prism). (c) With increasing height, pressure, and heat, sediments and rocks in the prism undergo metamorphism. Thrust faults also develop. Finally, the prism—now the Taconic Mountains—is pushed up against the Adirondacks. An island arc of volcanoes, called the Bronson Hill formation, develops east of this zone, in the region of present-day New Hampshire.

(4) Collision Stage, or Acadian orogeny (middle Devonian, 360–345 mybp). (a) A new spreading center east of the present-day Green Mountains creates a long basin the length of New England and Gaspé Peninsula (called Connecticut Valley–Gaspé Basin), after which a new deep-ocean trench develops on the eastern side of what is left of the Iapetus Ocean, plunging to the west. The continents converge once again, with what will become eastern New England part of the leading edge of the eastern continental mass. (b) The collision. The eastern continental mass collides with the Taconic Mountains, with the sediments and rocks uplifting and metamorphosing into the Green Mountains. Melting and subsurface igneous (magma) activity continue under the crust, creating granite deposits (e.g., Barre). Pangaea is formed and will remain intact for 145 millions years.

(5) Rift Stage (Mississippian–lower Triassic periods, 345–200 mybp). Pangaea begins to pull apart. The North American plate rifts east of the Green Mountains, with subsidence and thinning of crust.

(6) Drift Stage (lower Triassic–present, 200 mybp–present). Pangaea splits apart. Eastern North America separates from Eurasia-Africa along the present-day east coast, as the Atlantic Ocean is born. The new mid-ocean ridge supplies ocean crust as the continents move away from each other. Over the last 200 million years, the Green Mountains may well have eroded down to half their original height.

Map by Barry Doolan, adapted by Brian MacDonald, from "The Geology of Vermont," *Rocks & Minerals*, July/August 1996 (vol. 71, no. 4).

- The earth's crust is not an unbroken sphere, but rather is made of several enormous "plates," which are moving (drifting) relative to one another. The plates are solid, but float in a semi-solid mobile zone far below the surface.

- Continents on the plates are made mostly of granite, whereas ocean basins are of a darker, denser rock, basalt. A plate may be made of continental crust only, ocean crust only, or both.

- As they drift, plates collide, separate, or slip parallel to one another, resulting in great disturbances deep within the earth.

- Where plates meet or separate, tremendous forces release untold amounts of energy. Where they meet, the plates are either "consumed" in abyssal trenches or crumpled up into mountains. Where they separate, new oceanic crust is added, in the form of midocean ridges: the new crust wells up as molten rock, mounds out on both sides, and solidifies. This perceptible addition of ocean crust, producing oceanic volcanoes that are relatively close to the earth's surface, bears witness to the movement of the plates. It also explains why the oldest ocean crust is much younger than the oldest continental crust—the continental crust is neither created nor destroyed, whereas ocean crust is continually being both created and destroyed.

- Where continental crust meets ocean crust, the denser basalt of the ocean plunges beneath the lighter continental granite, creating deep ocean trenches, volcanoes, and earthquakes. This also results in the rumpling up of continental crust—the process known as mountain building. (Where two continents collide, neither goes under the other and even higher mountains arise. This is what happened when India and Asia collided: the Himalayas became the world's greatest mountain range.)

- North and Central America and half of the North Atlantic Ocean are part of the so-called North American Plate. New ocean crust is being added at the Mid-Atlantic Ridge, and the entire plate is moving westward at a rate of 2 to 3 inches per year.

- The San Andreas Fault in California represents the zone where the North American Plate is slipping along and colliding with the northward-moving Pacific Plate. The regular, often intense, earthquakes along this line are a side effect of the prodigious forces in action. The Sierra and Rocky Mountain ranges are also a product of these two plates' activities; they are still being built.

- Since the North American Plate is moving west, the net result is that the Atlantic Ocean is getting larger while the Pacific is shrinking. Over a few years this amounts to but a minuscule change, but over millions of years it may involve thousands of miles.

Scientists estimate the earth to be about 4½ billion years old, but the oldest seafloor rock in the Atlantic is only about 200 million years old. As one might expect, the youngest Atlantic rock is at the Mid-Atlantic Ridge and the oldest is at the continental margins on either side of the ocean. These facts, combined with the measured rate and

Button Point Natural Area. The island and wooded peninsula of this 14-acre state natural area (within Button Bay State Park) are outcroppings of limestones of Ordovician age (between 500 and 440 million years ago). The western shore of the island is part of an ancient fossil coral reef. "Buttons," or concretions, of various sizes and shapes formed much later in the glacial clays elsewhere in the park (hence the name of Button Bay). The peninsula supports a mature stand of oaks, hickories, pines, maples, and other trees. The foothills of New York's Adirondacks are in the background. Photo by Brian MacDonald.

direction of plate movements, are evidence of a time 200 million years ago when the Atlantic Ocean did not exist. Europe, North Africa, and North America were fused as one. In fact, all the present continents were together then, in one vast landmass called Pangaea. Since then, the continents have been shifting around, separating, colliding, arriving at their present configurations and locations.

Since mountain building occurs in the area of plate collision, the Green Mountains of Vermont seem way out of place, far from the West Coast where such activity is now under way. But geological research has uncovered an even more complex history of the earth than the activity of 200 million years ago, which helps to explain the origin of our landscape.

The following account is based on the current interpretation of Vermont's ancient geologic history, as reconstructed from the evidence of plate tectonics and new mapping of the state's bedrock (see pages 6–7). Because so much activity has taken place over such a long period of time—more than a billion years—the story is complicated, difficult to decipher, and still unfolding. The diagrams will help the reader visualize what is discussed here.

At least three major mountain building events (*orogenies*, to geol-

Geologic Timetable

Era and Period	Began—Years Before Present	Vermont and Regional Events	World Events—Plate Tectonics
Cenozoic Era			
	0–2,000	Cooling trend.	Many large Ice Age mammals become extinct.
	4,000–6,000	Warming trend (hypsithermal interval). Rise of Native American cultures.	
	10,000	Last glacier leaves Vermont.	
Quaternary	3 million	Continental glaciers begin (Ice Age).	Origin of human beings.
Tertiary	65 million		Himalayas born (25 million years ago). Mammals at maximum. Rocky Mountains born (75 million years ago).
Mesozoic Era			
Cretaceous	136 million	Younger igneous intrusions, White Mountains formed.	Dinosaurs become extinct. Origin of birds. Origin of mammals.
Jurassic	195 million	Mountains continue to erode; new rifting east of Green Mountains.	Breakup of Pangaea. North America begins to move west.
Triassic	225 million		Rise of dinosaurs.

Paleozoic Era

Period	Age	Geologic Events	Life Events
Permian	280 million		Origin of reptiles.
Pennsylvanian	320 million	Alleghenian orogeny.	Vast swamps—origin of modern coal.
Mississippian	345 million	Older igneous intrusions (e.g., Barre). Acadian orogeny.	Continents collide, Pangaea formed.
Devonian	395 million		Origin of amphibians.
Silurian	440 million	Formation of Taconic and Green Mountains (Taconic orogeny).	Origin of fish. First vertebrates.
Ordovician	500 million	Corals and other marine life in Iapetus Ocean.	Continents begin to converge. No land life.
Cambrian	570 million		

Precambrian Era

Period	Age	Geologic Events	Life Events
	1.0 billion–4.5 billion	Grenville orogeny, Adirondacks formed. (1–1.3 billion years ago).	Archaic plate convergences and separations. Oldest fossils (3 billion years old). Oldest rocks (3.7 billion years old).

ogists) have profoundly affected the region we call Vermont, each modifying, moving, or, locally, obliterating structures of the previous. The first (or at least the first we know about), the *Grenville orogeny*, occurred about 1.3 to 1 billion years ago, in the Precambrian Era (4.5 billion to 570 million years before present, or mybp).

This was a major and widespread event in this region, where continental crust was buckled into what likely was a lofty, extensive range. The Adirondacks of New York are the most dramatic remains of this system, but the same mountains once covered the area of Vermont, as well. However, subsequent periods of erosion, deposition, and tectonic activity have all but worn away, concealed, or changed them here. Only the roots remain, mostly as foundation rock in the southern Green Mountains, exposed here and there in only a few locations (for example, at Killington and Pico Peaks). In fact, in the 400 million years following the Grenville orogeny, the Grenville Mountains apparently eroded to a relief of not much greater than 300 feet, with little tectonic activity accompanying their erosional history. (Since the Grenville orogeny, the Adirondacks, like the rocks of the Canadian Shield—the stable, largely granitic, continental land mass of much of Canada—have been more or less free from the massive, tectonically caused landform changes that took place in Vermont and areas to the east.)

About 590–550 mybp, the earth's crust (*lithosphere*) began to spread and thin (a process called *rifting*) in a long, broad belt along the axis east of the present-day Appalachian Mountains, including the Green Mountains of Vermont. Sediments from the eroding Grenville basement (by now they could no longer be called mountains) were transported by gravity and flowing water from both sides into the huge basin. At the same time, volcanic activity in the region added great quantities of basalt and other igneous rock, which broke through the crust thinned by rifting and came to rest in the basin. Eventually the basin became wide and deep enough to develop ocean "spreading centers" where molten magma from the earth's interior upwelled and continually added new rock on either side (similar to the Mid-Atlantic Ridge today). Coincident with the spreading and subsidence of the rift basin, a newly born ocean called Iapetus filled in the ever-widening gap.

It was the time before plants or animals had evolved on land. The Vermont region, within 30 degrees of the equator, was hot and located at the margins of or partly beneath a warm, shallow, tropical sea. Some of our earliest (Cambrian, 570–500 mybp) fossils of worms and trilobites are in the Monkton quartzites (former sands) dating back to this time. Features in the quartzites such as raindrop pits, ripples from currents, and mud cracks attest to an environment of periodically exposed tidal flats. With time, Vermont subsided more, and beach and tidal flat deposits gave way to marine shelf limestones containing fossils of animals living in the warm water shallows of what is now western Vermont: straight-shelled cephalopods, crinoids, brachipods, trilobites, bryozoans, gastropods, and corals.

During the middle Ordovician Period (440–430 mybp) dramatic changes took place on the ancient continental shelf. Mud in the form of fine silt and clay particles—later becoming shales and slates under compaction—began to blanket the carbonate platform which, over the previous hundred million years, had become two miles thick. This mud indicated not only a change from a shallow-water environment to a deep-water one, but also a new eroding source area for huge quantities of silt and clay that settled over the limestones. These observations led geologists to propose that in middle Ordovician time the continental edge of North America plunged to the east under the ocean crust, in a process called *subduction*.

With subduction, the Iapetus Ocean began to close, reversing what had been happening for more than a 100 million years and beginning what is known as the *Taconic orogeny*, the next great phase of mountain building here. As the western part of ocean crust was consumed in the trench, the eastern portion acted much like a giant bulldozer, scraping off and pushing before it stacked slices or wedges of the old rift sediments, continental shelf slope and rise sediments, and ocean crust, collectively called an *accretionary prism*. Also, an arc of active volcanoes popped up in the Ocean above the zone of subduction, along its entire length. By 430 mybp, some 60 million years after initial subduction began, the western part of the Iapetus Ocean closed, with the massive accretionary prism and volcanic arc overriding the land and remnants of the earlier Grenville Mountains.

The Taconic orogeny accounts for the most dominant mountains in Vermont—the main and secondary spines of the Green Mountains. Along the main range are most of the state's highest peaks, including, from north to south, Jay Peak, Mount Mansfield, Camel's Hump, Mount Ellen, Mount Abraham, Pico Peak, Killington Peak, Shrewsbury Peak, and Glastenbury Mountain. They display metamorphic schists and phyllites transformed within the gigantic accretionary prism—materials piled miles thick and eventually heated to temperatures exceeding 500 degrees Celsius. (In the southern part of the state, worn remains of the ancient Grenville Mountains sometimes are exposed as well.)

During this period of tremendous geologic compressive stresses, north-south trending thrust faults developed in the accretionary prism, providing evidence that slices were pushed over one another, often resulting in the anomaly of older rock lying atop younger; this phenomenon is well illustrated in the Champlain Trust at Lone Rock Point and in the Taconic Mountains themselves in southwestern Vermont. In other areas, the slices reveal their westward translocation from more

Champlain Thrust Fault. Lone Rock Point, north end of Burlington Harbor. The light-colored, 565-million-year-old dolostone (dolomitic limestone of former shallow ocean shelf) lies atop the darker, 430-million-year-old shale (former deeper ocean sediments). A topmost layer of shale has been eroded away. The light rocks in the water in the foreground are chunks of dolostone fallen from the cliffs. See text for explanation of thrust faulting. Photo by Rolfe Stanley.

distant places, such as the ultramafic rocks of Belvidere Mountain in northern Vermont representing the basaltic oceanic crust and mantle originating below the ancient Iapetus Ocean.

The last great mountain-building event took place in the Devonian Period (360–345 mybp), in what is known as the *Acadian orogeny*. It was preceded by another stretching and subsidence of land east of the Taconic and present-day Green Mountains, extending from southern New England to the Gaspé Peninsula and creating the Connecticut Valley–Gaspé Basin, which received erosional material from the highlands to the west and east. This was followed by a new subduction on the east side of the basin, its presumed west-plunging trench somewhere near the present Connecticut River. It was accompanied by a convergence of land masses east of there.

This convergence was geologically momentous for the region. It created great folds of land (nappes) in the Connecticut Valley–Gaspé Basin and Bronson Hill Province (the latter is the region of the former island arc of volcanoes, at and just east of the Connecticut River area). It also refolded the Green Mountains, reactivated thrust faults, elevated deeper rocks, and, in areas of melting, produced huge deposits of granite (plutons), including that of the renowned Barre granite quarries.

The remade mountains must have been high; erosional material from them made it far across New York and Pennsylvania, to be depos-

Tropical Vermont. The supercontinent Pangaea as it probably looked 200 million years ago before it broke apart into the present-day continents. The enormous, encircling ocean is called Panthalassa. Note that the area that is now Vermont (•) was positioned almost at the equator, next to Africa and not far from Eurasia. As the continents separated, the newly formed Atlantic Ocean filled the widening gap between North/South Americas and Eurasia/Africa. Map from Brian J. Skinner and Stephen C. Porter, *The Dynamic Earth: An Introduction to Physical Geology*, 3rd ed., Copyright 1995 John Wiley & Sons, Inc. Reprinted by permission of John Wiley & Sons, Inc. Adapted by Brian MacDonald.

ited over 100 miles away as a delta in the Catskill Mountains. Although the event thoroughly reheated and deformed the eastern parts of the earlier-formed Taconic Mountains, fossils east of the Champlain Valley escaped further degradation. These include echinoderms, brachiopods, bryozoans, sponges, corals, cephalopods, and trilobites.

A later great mountain-building event, the *Alleghenian orogeny*, was especially important in the southern Appalachians and southeastern part of New England during the Carboniferous Period (345–280 mybp). However, it apparently did not affect Vermont, or at least its effects are unknown. Certainly by the end of the Alleghenian orogeny the continents of the world had come together to form the giant supercontinent Pangaea; little Vermont was at its center, thousands of miles from any ocean. Later, beginning about 200 mybp (early Mesozoic Era), the continents broke apart, with a spreading center at the Mid-Atlantic Ridge and the Atlantic Ocean filling the widening gulf. The North American plate has been moving away from the Eurasian and African plates ever since at the rate of two or three inches a year, until now there is a sea of 3,000 miles between them. But the North American–Eurasian connection is forever preserved in the rocks of our respective shorelines.

So ends, for the time being, this abridged story of Vermont's foundation. Many other chapters are worthy of the telling, such as the

Mesozoic era (225–65 mybp) down-dropping of great blocks of land (*grabens*) to form the predecessors of Lake Champlain, or Cenozoic (30–25 mybp) lignite fossils of wood, seeds, and fruits preserved near Brandon. But, fascinating and helpful as they are in understanding the full dimension of Vermont's natural history, these stories must be left for others to relate.

Instead, we will jump ahead in time to the latest earth-moving event, one that by geologic clocks never even registers a tick. But for us who look at, travel through, or work upon the land, it makes a deep, long-lasting impression.

The Glaciers Pass

In 1848 workmen were excavating a new railroad bed near Mount Holly, in south central Vermont, when they unearthed large and strange bones. These were later studied by the famous Harvard zoologist and geologist Louis Agassiz, and were determined to be of a woolly mammoth, an elephant that lived in Arctic regions through the time of glaciation. Some scientists believe the bones were probably of a mastodon rather than a mammoth; mastodons lived in the scrubby spruce-fir forests of the north, whereas mammoths stayed more in the open tundra regions. Regardless, remains of both kinds of elephant were subsequently found in the American Northeast, proof that both had lived in the region at one time. The presence of the Vermont animal, buried in the earth, could mean but one thing: Vermont had a different look—owing to a different, colder climate—long ago, when these beasts were roaming the territory.

A year later, in 1849, other fossil bones were discovered in a railroad-bed excavation near Charlotte, on Lake Champlain. First thought to be of a horse, they were later determined to be of a small whale, also an extinct species but closely related to white beluga whales that live today in northern and Arctic waters. Along with this skeleton were found shells of clams and oysters, the same kind that now live in a cold marine environment. Other remains of cold-water marine mammals came to light as excavations uncovered them: a ringed seal (Brandon), hooded seal (Plattsburgh, New York), finback whale (Thetford), humpback whale (Quebec), and bowhead whale (Quebec). These facts suggest indeed a cold ocean here. But what ocean, and how did the animals get there?

These mammal species, whale, seals, and ancient elephant, could not have come from the time of Pangaea or the Iapetus Ocean, since no mammals had at that point even appeared on earth. There must have been a later restructuring of topography to account for them. These stories bring us to another great geological event that has profoundly affected Vermont: the Ice Age, the time of glaciation during the Pleistocene epoch, lasting from 3 million to 10,000 years ago.

Mount Ascutney. This peak is an isolated monadnock of igneous rock near the Connecticut River, an outlier of the White Mountains deposited more than 120 million years ago in an underground "cavern" (pluton), and left exposed after the surrounding Piedmont area was eroded away. The last glacier plucked rocks from the mountains and carried them south into Massachusetts—this line of strewn rocks, called the Mount Ascutney Train, is an important indication of the direction of glacial advance in this part of the country. Photo by Charles W. Johnson.

The prehistoric existence of glaciers has been established from the glacial remnants that survive in the Arctic, Antarctica, Alaska, Greenland, Switzerland, Austria, and Scandinavia. But only in the mid-1800s did powerful evidence indicate that glaciers once covered most of North America, including the northern half of what is now the United States. Foremost among proponents of the new and hotly debated theory of continental glaciation was the same Louis Agassiz mentioned above. Largely to him do we owe this landmark concept, now almost universally accepted as fact.

For us, the Arctic and even Vermont in winter may be cold indeed. But in the past 3 million years there have been even colder times, when the average yearly temperature was 5 to 25 degrees Fahrenheit lower than today's. Now, continental glaciers exist only in Greenland and Antarctica, but at that earlier time they covered both poles and extended down into what are now temperate regions of the continents. They were so extensive that it is estimated that enough water was bound in glacial ice to lower the sea level worldwide by 475 feet. Even today, with Greenland's ice cap up to 10,000 feet thick and Antarctica's 3 miles in places, about 77 percent of all the fresh water in the world is in continental glaciers, or 2.5 percent of all water on earth, including oceans.

Ice is normally thought of as a solid, and indeed on a glacial surface it may be brittle. But under the tremendous pressures within a glacial mass it becomes more mobile, exhibiting a slow, fluidlike movement. The glacier indeed "flows" from north to south (in the Northern Hemisphere) in slow motion, yet with great abrasive powers.

As they moved over the land, the glaciers reworked it in two different ways: first by eroding or gouging out existing formations, and then by transporting and depositing the eroded materials. This jumble of rocks, pebbles, sand, and clay—called *till*—was deposited in Vermont in various fashions. Some was forcibly plastered on the bedrock surfaces to form a relatively hard coating; some was merely dumped as the glacier melted, left in loose piles, mounds, or sheets, depending on the glacier's subsequent movements. These formations are called *moraines.* Where the till accumulates when the glacier reaches its farthest point, the formation is a terminal moraine; we have no terminal moraines of the last continental glacier in Vermont,

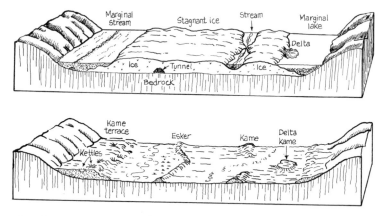

Glacial Features of the Landscape. Many of Vermont's physical features are products of the activity of glaciers. The upper picture shows the landscape while the Ice Age glaciers were present; the lower, depicting the same landscape, shows the modern results of that presence. Kames are large banks of sand and gravel that collected between the melting edges of two glaciers; the broader kame terraces formed when erosional material from the side of a hill or mountain and the melting edge of a glacier were deposited in a lake. Eskers are long, tall, sinuous mounds of similar composition that collected within "tunnels" melting inside the ice sheet, where long cracks allowed water to enter and flow. Kettles are ponds in the till (glacially deposited clay, sand, gravel, boulders) created when huge blocks of ice became separated from the receding glacier, were trapped, and melted. Deltas may be formed either off the land in a river, or off the glacier, as meltwater carries rocks, sand, and clay out into a lake or pond, building a wide fan-shaped terrace, called a delta kame. Drawing by Jean Vissering.

Postglacial Lakes. Various "pulses" or episodes of ice advance and retreat during the Wisconsin glaciation (20,000–10,000 years ago) created large bodies of water, long since vanished. In chronological order, the oldest to youngest are: Bennington Ice lakes; Shelburne Ice lakes; Connecticut Valley Lake (Lake Hitchcock); Burlington Ice lakes; and Lake Vermont. Lake Hitchcock, a long, narrow lake on the east side of the state (in the now Connecticut River valley), formed behind a moraine south, in Connecticut; later, the dam broke and the lake drained. Lake Vermont, meltwater impounded by the last waning ice sheet and with its surface 600 feet higher than today's Lake Champlain level, reached up the flanks of the Green Mountains and into the major east-west river valleys. As the ice sheet continued to retreat, the Atlantic Ocean flowed in from the St. Lawrence River area and created the Champlain Sea—smaller than Lake Vermont but still considerably larger than Lake Champlain. Present-day Lake Champlain and Lake Memphremagog are in black. From Surficial Geologic Map of Vermont, Vermont Geological Survey, adapted by Brian MacDonald.

but two extraordinary examples farther south are Long Island and Cape Cod (Martha's Vineyard and Nantucket are terminal moraines of an earlier glacier). If the glacier recedes for a period of time and then stops, it piles up another bank of till, called a recessional moraine. But if the glacier melts back quickly, these "hills" do not have time to form and the till spreads out like a blanket over the land, creating ground moraines. This kind of till is what we see as the predominant subsoil of Vermont.

The subsoil of sand, gravel, and boulders is what the glaciers left behind. But the work they did in Vermont when they were active is also obvious. Though the mountains, gaps, and valleys were here long before the Ice Age, the glaciers reshaped them—scouring and rounding off the peaks, broadening and smoothing the valleys, widening the gaps to notches.

The reshaped land and the rubble of till blocked former drainages, resulting in the creation of most of our ponds, lakes, bogs, and streams. Huge boulders (*erratics*) stand isolated in the most unlikely places, such as open fields and on the tops of mountains; these rocks were carried by the glaciers, occasionally over hundreds of miles, and then left behind when the ice receded. Sometimes the rock type of the erratic is quite different from that upon which it rests, and if these erratics were carried any distance from the parent material and in substantial numbers, geologists can trace the path the glacier took by mapping the erratics. Boulders that originated at Mount Ascutney, near Windsor, have been strewn well into Massachusetts and together make up the well-known "Mount Ascutney Train," which delineates exceptionally clearly the course of the last glacier. In addition, deep grooves and scratches in the bedrock show where erratics and other coarse materials were dragged over the landscape, and these grooves (*striae*) also help geologists record the direction glaciers took in their passage over the land.

But all was not ice and cold in times past. Interestingly, periods of glaciation alternated with long warmer intervals, often lasting hundreds of thousands of years, which caused the glaciers to retreat and expose bare ground. For the last 10,000 years or so we have been in an interglacial period, and at one stretch during this time, about 4,000 to 6,000 years ago, the climate was very much warmer than today's. This hypsithermal interval, or climatic optimum, had great influence not only on Vermont's vegetation, but also on human development, as we shall see later.

At least four glaciers have covered Vermont over the past 3 million years, but the last is the one we know most about, since it left the clearest signs and trails, as well as having obliterated the bulk of the evidence of the previous glaciers. This last is known as the Wisconsin glaciation and was at its maximum development in the northern

United States about 18,000 years ago. In the East it reached as far south as the Long Island region before retreating; it left Vermont about 10,000 years ago.

The mammoth of Mount Holly, the whale of Charlotte, and other species discovered (elk, caribou) are direct testimony to the existence of the glaciers. It is likely that the north-ranging mammoth populations moved steadily south ahead of the advancing glacier, and returned north when it receded. The mammoth found here was undoubtedly only one of many that roamed over Vermont in the preglacial and early postglacial times, feeding on the tundra lichens and facing the arrows and spears of Paleolithic natives.

The whale, however, gives no clue to other geologic events associated with the glaciers. Long before the Wisconsin glacier descended upon Vermont, the Champlain Valley had been in existence. It has been suggested that it was created when a long, massive block of bedrock (graben) dropped down between the Adirondack Mountains and the Green Mountains more than 200 million years ago; this deformation probably was due to crustal movement associated with plate collisions. The glaciers greatly modified the valley, and rivers have since brought down much silt and clay from higher adjoining areas to fill in hundreds of feet on the bottom. Millions of years after the valley's creation the Wisconsin glacier filled it. But in its retreat, about 12,500 years ago, the glacier cleared the Burlington area, the valley became exposed, all drainage to the north was blocked by ice, and the

Mount Philo. Fifteen miles south of Burlington, this 980-foot hill is a prominent landmark in the central Champlain Lowlands. It stood as an island above the surface of both postglacial Lake Vermont and the Champlain Sea. The rolling meadow represents old lake and sea floors. Photo by Brian MacDonald.

water melting from the glacier created a freshwater lake (called Lake Vermont), much larger than the present Lake Champlain. Lake Vermont extended up into the foothills of the Green Mountains, leaving such peaks as Mount Philo as islands and covering the lower hills and islands we see today. (A comparable lake was formed on the eastern side of Vermont and the western side of New Hampshire by the damming of the Connecticut River. This "Lake Hitchcock" reached as far west as Randolph and north beyond St. Johnsbury.)

The sheer weight of the ice had depressed the land 500 to 600 feet, so that Lake Vermont actually drained south into what is now the Hudson Valley. At the same time, the sea level was more than 400 feet lower than it is today, owing to water locked up as glacial ice. But as the ice melted, the land began to "spring back" and the oceans to rise. However, the oceans rose faster than the land rebounded, and salt water backed into the St. Lawrence River Valley and eventually crept around the southern and eastern edges of the shrinking glacier, and finally into Vermont. Lake Vermont became diluted with sea water and changed into the "Champlain Sea," as we have named it, an estuary of the ocean with about half its salinity.

During a later colder period of glacier advanced once more, re-creating a second Lake Vermont, then withdrew to allow formation of a second Champlain Sea. At last, some 10,000 years ago, the glacier withdrew for good. The land, relieved of its burden, rose high enough to block off the Atlantic Ocean. The southern Champlain basin, having been uncovered earlier than the northern, rose higher, giving a tilt north to the entire valley. This resulted in drainage to the north into the Richelieu River, which is the case today.

In one of the two Champlain Seas the marine mammals must have lived, having traveled from the ocean or been born there. They are undoubtedly among many animals that, after death, were buried in the sediments brought down by the rivers, only to become located on dry land when the Champlain Sea dropped to the present level of Lake Champlain.

We have many other reminders of this former "sea." Several species of fish today in Lake Champlain are ancestors of modern saltwater species. An Atlantic-coast dune plant, beach heath, is clinging to existence at a location near the shores of Lake Champlain. The sediments at such places as Sand Bar State Park, the Missisquoi River delta, and Button Bay State Park have the same blue clay that enveloped the Charlotte whale. Marine beach gravel lies at the foot of Mount Philo.

In the long view of geologic history, the glacier's presence was just a short while ago, and our closeness in time to it is still clear in many respects. We can measure the land's rebounding from its relieved stress, even though it be only a centimeter or two per year. The landforms and waters plainly show much of what the glacier did, and, as we shall see later, we know it erased former vegetation and associated wildlife, but in withdrawing it opened the way for new colonizations.

These are only some of the records of the glacier's passing—both living and nonliving records—and what it left behind has helped to make Vermont. We know that the glacier did come and go. But no one can say for sure that it has gone for good.

From the Abenaki story of creation:

We are told that Odzihozo (The One Who Shaped Himself) [from the leftover dust of creation] saw the world around him and, before he had finished shaping his body, wanted to see more. He became excited like a child and forgot the job at hand (finishing his own creation). You see, we are told that Tabaldak (The Owner) had already shaped the earth and all life on it. It was he who made plants and trees and fish and animals and birds, all who were the relations of Odzihozo. Tabaldak had also made the surface of the earth, and he had chosen to make it very flat so that it would be easy for all those he created to travel from one place to the next.

It was the flatness of the land that allowed Odzihozo to see far off into the distance, but he wasn't happy with this; he wanted to see more. And so he tried to move, but could not because he had forgotten to make legs and was still connected to the earth. However, he didn't give up. He pushed against the earth, so that he could slide along the ground. He traveled like this for some time and explored the world. He was so powerful that every time he pushed, he made great piles of earth, creating hills and mountains on either side of the trail he left behind. After traveling all over New England and making many mountains and hills, he no longer had the view he had once enjoyed. It was now blocked by the mountains he had created. So Odzihozo reached to the tops of these mountains and pulled, trying to stand. His fingers dug deep channels in the earth, but he couldn't stand.

It was only then that Tabaldak became curious about what was happening in New England and traveled to that country, only to find it covered with hills and mountains and deep ravines and channels. Tabaldak, who wanted the world to be flat, was very angry. When he found Odzihozo, he asked, "Awani kia?" (Who are you?) "I have shaped all things, but not you."

"I am The One Who Shaped Himself," Odzihozo said defiantly.

Odzihozo was then given the name Gluskabe by Tabaldak, a name that means "The Talker." Tabaldak scolded Gluskabe for being so foolish as to forget to shape his own legs before trying to venture out into the world and then told him that his sentence would be that his children and grandchildren would have to live in this land Gluskabe had shaped, and it would be hard for them to travel from one place to the next because of the ravines and the mountains. And so it is that this was called Nd'akinna (Our Land) [New England], and is still the home of Gluskabe's grandchildren, the Wabanaki peoples.

Gluskabe looked down and saw that indeed Tabaldak was correct: he had forgotten his own legs. And so he shaped them and stood. He, like Tabaldak, was now a giant. Gluskabe felt a bit foolish about forgetting to shape his legs, and so he immediately challenged Tabaldak to a contest to see whose power was the greatest. In two strides they walked to the top of the mountains. Gluskabe threw his leg over Camel's Hump and made it his seat, Dawabodiiwadzo (The Seat Mountain). In the contest both tried to make the wind blow. Gluskabe made the wind blow so hard he flattened the trees, and was very proud of this. Tabaldak was not impressed and in return made the wind bird Wadzosen first tangle Gluskabe's hair into balls of knots, which stood straight up on top of his head. Then Tabaldak offered Gluskabe some help getting them untangled and blew every last hair off his head, leaving him bald. Finally, to seal his victory Tabaldak made the wind blow in such a way that it lifted all the trees which Gluskabe had blown over and covered their roots with soil. However, some trees could not be straightened and while they stand, they remain twisted to this day.

Gluskabe, being defeated by Tabaldak, wandered the world. He hunted a great moose and, after a chase all over Nd'akinna, he killed it. The moose was so great that its body, now covered with soil, can still be seen and is called Mozondebiwadzo (Moose Head Mountain) [Mt. Mansfield].

2

Physiographic Regions of Vermont

The geologic processes of plate tectonics and glaciation have shaped the foundation of Vermont and made or affected most of the landforms we see today. Of course, a closer look at the state's 9,609 square miles yields more details of those and other events, most of which have sooner or later to do with rocks.

Geologists classify rocks in three categories, according to their manner of origin. Vermont has good examples of all three.

1. *Igneous rocks*, from molten material (*magma*), cooling and solidifying either at or below the earth's surface.
2. *Sedimentary rocks*, eroded from other rocks, the particles compacted and cemented, or chemically combined, under pressure from above or the sides.
3. *Metamorphic rocks*, "changed" from preexisting sedimentary, igneous rocks, or metamorphic rocks by intense pressure and heat associated with plate tectonics or other crustal movements.

Obviously, the three types are so closely related that they can be diagrammatically represented in the "rock cycle":

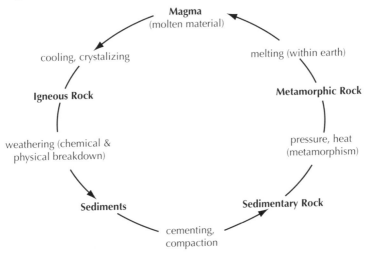

This is a simplified picture, as there are many crossovers and shortcuts.

Physiographic Regions of Vermont. Map by Charles W. Johnson, based on Jacobs (1969).

Canada

Swanton
St. Albans
Newport
Island Pond

Morrisville
Burlington
St. Johnsbury

Lake Champlain

New Hampshire

Montpelier
Barre

Bristol

White River
Junction

Rutland

Poultney

Green Mountains

Taconic Mountains

Springfield

Champlain Lowlands

Manchester

Valley of Vermont

Vermont Piedmont

Connecticut River

Northeastern Highlands

New York

Bennington
Brattleboro

Massachusetts

Though the list of the kinds of rocks in each category is long, a few common ones in Vermont illustrate the processes in action.

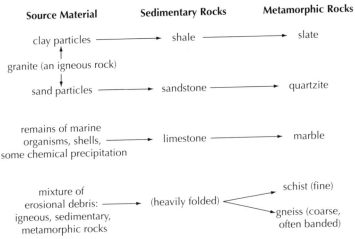

The great pressures and heat associated with plate collisions are now believed to be responsible for widespread regional metamorphism in mountain building. Fossils are usually destroyed by metamorphism, so any that may have existed are no longer evident. Fortunately, the limestone of the Champlain Valley escaped this metamorphism, so that we have a fine record of fossil history there.

The three basic rock types differ from one another in many respects—physical appearance, resistance to erosion, the kinds of minerals they release upon weathering, and so on. Their presence in a region may be reflected in any number of ways, whether directly, as a scenic feature, or indirectly, as indicated by the kinds of plants growing on or near them.

For purposes of characterizing the state's regional differences, geographers and geologists often divide Vermont into six zones, called physiographic regions, each of which has a distinctive combination of topography, climate, and vegetation. These differences are largely attributable to geologic features (both bedrock and surface deposits) and latitude.

The Green Mountains

This chain runs north-south the length of Vermont. It is part of the very long Appalachian Mountain system that extends from Alabama to the Gaspé Peninsula, in Canada, where it plummets into the St. Lawrence River Valley. In fact, as the supercontinent Pangaea is reconstructed, the Appalachian system continues even farther, lining up perfectly with the Caledonian range of Scotland and Scandinavia, and exhibiting the same folding patterns and rock types as its European relatives.

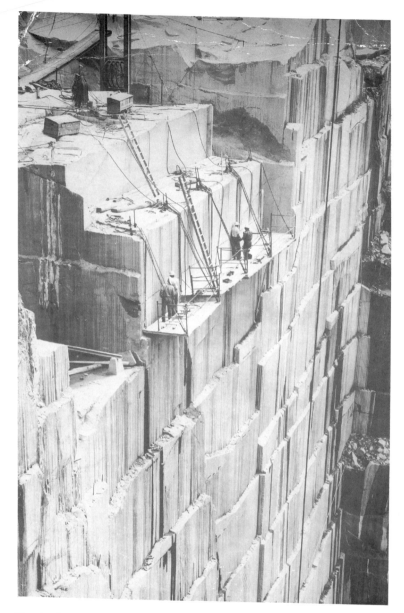

Granite Quarry, Barre. Extracting a famous natural resource of Vermont. The granite here was deposited as molten rock in huge subsurface spaces (plutons) in the already formed surrounding bedrock. This quarry, belonging to the Rock of Ages Corporation, is the largest in the world, more than 350 feet deep. It is made wider at the top than the bottom to prevent the walls from collapsing.
Photo courtesy Rock of Ages Corporation.

The Green Mountains are 160 miles long and fairly uniform in width, 21 miles at the Canadian border and 36 at the Massachusetts line. They are the dominant feature of Vermont, and until the automobile brought momentous road improvements, they presented a real obstacle to east-west travel and communication. When Zadock Thompson, nineteenth-century naturalist and historian, referred in 1853 to "going over the mountain," he meant a very difficult journey. This barrier blocked more than human beings, as we shall see later, in that it helped prevent populations of plants and animals from mixing freely throughout the state, thus setting up different botanical and zoological zones on either side of the mountains.

The highest peaks in Vermont are in the Green Mountain range. Mount Mansfield is the tallest, at 4,393 feet, followed in order by Killington Peak, Mount Ellen, and Camel's Hump. The substance of the Green Mountains is by and large metamorphic rock. Most abundant is the schist form, with its green-gray color and often wavy appearance due to heavy folding. It is exposed on the higher summits and in many outcroppings throughout the region. Just east of the backbone of the Green Mountains are parallel subsidiary ranges: north of the Winooski River Valley are the Lowell and Worcester ranges, south of it is the Northfield range.

Belvidere Mountain. This 3,360-foot mountain near Lowell and Eden in the northern Green Mountains is a wedge of ancient oceanic crust pushed up during the latter stages of the Taconic orogeny (445 million years ago). It contains unusual minerals related to its origin, including serpentine and asbestos (the now-defunct asbestos mines are at the base, on the other side). The Long Trail traverses the mountain's summit. Photo by Louis Borie.

In addition to the dominant metamorphic rocks, important igneous mineral deposits occur in the Green Mountains, especially on the eastern flanks, and help make the range an economically important region. Talc and asbestos have been quarried here in such quantities as to put Vermont high on the list of total United States production.

The Green Mountains to some extent influence the climate of the whole state. They are high enough to intercept the prevailing west winds, forcing them to move up and then over, which cools the air masses and causes them to release precipitation regularly throughout the year, as rain in summer, snow in winter. In the mountains themselves are recorded the greatest snowfall and overall wetness—and on north-facing slopes, the shortest growing season, coldest temperatures, heaviest precipitation, and severest winter weather—of any place in the state.

The Taconic Mountains

The Taconic range runs from near Lake Bomoseen 75 miles south to the Massachusetts line, and west from the Valley of Vermont to the New York line. They are low, rounded, mature mountains, and strange as it sounds, they appear to be upside down. That is, whereas in the usual sequence of rock deposition younger layers lie on top of older, in the Taconics just the reverse is true. A puzzle, indeed, until plate tectonics provided an explanation.

The Taconics are about the same age as the Green Mountains—perhaps slightly older—but the bedrock of the Taconics is unlike that of the Green Mountains or any area north, west, or south of them. Near the surface they are mostly a mixture of shale and slate, and have a geologic affinity with the area southeast of the Green Mountains. This affinity has led geologists to speculate that the Taconics were originally thrust over from somewhere east of the area that was to become the Green Mountains. The clay-based shales and slates indicate that the original material of the Taconics was deep-ocean sediment beyond the continental shelf, the fine particles of which drifted far out to sea from the rivers that emptied into it. Plate collisions thrust huge chunks of this land on top of itself, and eons of time have eroded away the topmost layers of shale, revealing the older stratum of limestone. Below this limestone, however, is another layer of shale. Therefore since the uppermost layers of shale have disappeared, the mountains give the illusion of being upside down.

The Taconics are the slate-producing center of Vermont. Quarries, both active and inactive, are spotted all over this region, especially near Lakes Bomoseen and St. Catherine; the area around Poultney is perhaps the most productive still being mined. Indeed, the slate here is famous the world over, and in total United States production Vermont is second only to Pennsylvania. Much marble has been quarried here, too, especially in the vicinity of Proctor.

The Taconics. The ridgeline of Big (right) and Little Equinox Mountains (3,816 and 3,315 feet, respectively), in the Taconic Mountains of southwestern Vermont, curls around steep-sided Skinner Hollow. Though appearing much like a cirque (carved by an isolated, local glacier following the retreat of the main ice sheet), the Hollow is probably much older, a giant "sink hole" created in the calcium-based bedrock by water percolating down for eons. Photo by Brian MacDonald.

The Valley of Vermont

The Valley of Vermont is a narrow strip of land nestled between the Green Mountains to the east and the Taconic Mountains to the west. It is about 85 miles long, reaching from Massachusetts to near Brandon. It varies in width from a few hundred yards near Emerald Lake to 8 miles in the Bennington area. U.S. Route 7 travels straight through the Valley, testifying to its flatness. It is essentially a long, skinny extension of the Champlain Lowlands.

The Valley is underlaid by sedimentary and metamorphic rock. The bulk of the rock, however, is of a different kind from that in the mountains. Much of it is limestone, the sedimentary rock of oceanic origin, and marble, its metamorphosed counterpart. The surrounding area is famous for its marble, producing some of the finest in the world. The calcium-rich environment of the Valley fosters an interesting flora; many species here are unusual calciphilic ("calcium-loving") plants, not found with such frequency at low elevations elsewhere in the state.

Because of its flatness and fertility, this region is heavily agricultural, with few forested areas remaining.

The Champlain Lowlands

Lake Champlain, its basin and islands, the rivers that drain into it, and the neighboring wetlands make up the complex character of the

Champlain Lowlands. This region is cradled by the Adirondack Mountains to the west and the Green Mountains to the east. Its greatest width is 20 miles, but it narrows to about 5 miles in the southern end, at the Taconics. It is about 109 miles long. The focal point, Lake Champlain, is, after the Great Lakes, the largest lake in the United States, being 109 miles long and 11 miles across at its widest, and comprising 440 square miles.

Owing to the protection offered by mountain ranges on three sides and to the moderating effect of Lake Champlain, the climate in this region is the mildest in the state: the frost-free season is longer, the precipitation less, and the temperatures not so extreme as in the other regions.

This area is important geologically not only for the stories it tells in thrust faults, fossils, and glacial evidences, but also for its clay soils and flat topography, further testimony to the Ice Age: thick silt and clay deposits brought down year after year by rivers to the large ancient Lake Vermont and Champlain Sea, after the glacier had left the area.

This is a fertile region. Human inhabitants have transformed it into one of the prime agricultural domains of the state. The white-pine forests that originally grew here in great abundance were clear-cut, their stumps pulled out by horses and drawn to the field edges, where they made the tangled fences still occasionally seen today. Animal inhabitants make the large marshes at the union of flatland,

The Valley of Vermont. Just north of Emerald Lake State Park in southern Vermont, the Valley of Vermont narrows to a few hundred yards between the Taconics on the left and Green Mountains on the right. The valley ecologically is an extension of the Champlain Lowlands. Photo by Brian MacDonald.

Stump Fence. The large remains of white pines that were cut down, these stumps were pulled by horses out of the fields and left as effective fences. They give an indication of the formerly wooded appearance of the landscape. This fence is near Addison, in the Champlain Valley. Photo by Charles W. Johnson.

major tributaries, and Lake Champlain important breeding, spawning, and nesting grounds for multitudes of species; these are also major oases for migrating waterfowl, which stop to feed and rest during their treks up and down the continent.

The Vermont Piedmont

Piedmont literally means "foot-mountain" or "foot-hill," and that is exactly what the Vermont Piedmont comprises: foothills of the Green Mountains, running the length of the state just east of the higher range. Extensive erosion has removed much of the metamorphic and sedimentary rocks that were originally here, and what remains is a mixture of limestone, schist, and granite. Generally, the landscape is mellow, with gentle hills, broad valleys, and quiet lakes.

An occasionally higher peak emerges from the Piedmont's topography. But these are mountains of a different origin from those described earlier. They are monadnocks (named after New Hampshire's famous mountain), or mounds of resistant rock that have been exposed after the softer outer "coats" of metamorphic rock have been eroded away all around them. Such granite peaks as Mount Ascutney and Burke Mountain, both more than 3,000 feet high, were once hidden below the surface of the land, to be exposed only after the land surrounding them was carried away. These mountains, then, serve as a measuring stick of the quantity of land eroded in the region.

Monadnocks are large-scale *intrusions* of younger rock into pre-existing rocks, having squeezed into cracks, pockets, or caverns in a molten state, then solidifying. Most monadnocks are much younger than the host rock into which they have flowed. This is illustrated in the Vermont Piedmont by Mount Ascutney, which is only about 120 million years old, or three to four times younger than the bedrock around it.

Other kinds of geologic intrusions here are of substantial economic importance. Great volumes of granite are quarried in East Barre; some of the quarries here are the largest anywhere, and Vermont granite is world-famous. Veins of copper ore were once mined heavily in the area around Vershire and Strafford, but have since been abandoned.

Because the region is in the lee of the Green Mountains, its climate is generally less severe than in some other places in the state. But a great deal of regional variation is experienced in cold pockets and valleys up and down its length. Lakes are a frequent and attractive resource of the Piedmont drawing many visitors every year.

The Northeastern Highlands ("The Northeast Kingdom")

The Northeastern Highlands are the wild corner of Vermont, totaling more than 600 square miles. The region is different from any other part of the state in that it is in fact an extension of the White Mountains of New Hampshire and Maine, and the Whites are not at all like the Green Mountains.

Like one immense monadnock, the White Mountains originated as a huge subsurface reservoir of magma. As this molten material slowly cooled, it eventually formed granite. The surface has long since been worn away and the light-colored granite mountains stand out clearly. The White Mountains and the granite peaks of the Northeastern Highlands are both relatively young, being 135 million to 180 million years old.

In the Northeastern Highlands—commonly called the Northeast Kingdom—schists, other metamorphic rocks, and glacial till hide some of this ancestral relationship to the White Mountains, but large areas of igneous rock do outcrop throughout the region. Indeed, an older name of the Northeastern Highlands is the Granite Hills.

The area has some very thick glacial deposits, which are the result, it is believed, of repeated local advances and recessions—"stutters," as one author has called them. This is most evident in the fields and forests (Maidstone State Forest has striking examples) and as indicated by the many ponds, bogs, and black-spruce swamps.

Owing to the northerly location and the absence of any softening effect from a large body of water, this region's climate ranks second in severity only to some high peaks and north slopes of the Green Mountains.

3

Before We Came

The passage of the glaciers over Vermont eradicated the former forests here. Down to Long Island Sound, across Pennsylvania, Ohio, Indiana, Illinois, and farther west everything was crushed under the enormous ice sheets. No soil to warm in the sun. No spring flowers, or trees to color the fall. No mammals, no birds. It was, in effect, a biological desert.

Mostly through analysis of pollen grains preserved in bogs and lake sediments scientists have been able to reconstruct a picture of what our land looked like long ago. Even 200 million years before the Ice Age, a great broad-leaved (deciduous) forest spread over most of North America, including Alaska and Greenland, as well. It is likely that this forest also covered much of the entire land mass of Pangaea. Experts believe that the Great Smoky Mountains of North Carolina and Tennessee are the place of origin of *all* modern deciduous forests in the eastern half of the United States. These mountains—especially a small ancient, undisturbed section within them called the "cove forest"—contain the greatest variety of deciduous-tree species on the continent. More than 45 species grow there: tulip poplar, maples, beech, white ash, basswood, oaks, and other trees are amassed in this patriarch of forests. From this focal region, the deciduous forest radiated out to other regions. But with the shifting of continents, raising of mountains, disruption of tracts of land, formation of oceans, and later changes wrought by the Ice Age, the picture changed dramatically. The vast forest system was wiped out in some areas and reshaped in others, and the Smoky Mountain cove forest was left as a fraction of a once grander forest.

As continents and sections of continents acquired increasingly different environment characteristics, their forests changed in response. In any given region, the more stringent conditions demanded by new topographies, climates, and soils meant that not all the species of the original continental forest could survive. Replacing the complex and uniform Eastern Deciduous Forest formation of the Smokies were simplified local "associations," dominated by a few species.

For example, on dry, glaciated sites in the Midwest, species of oak and hickory dominate in the oak-hickory association. Northward, the deciduous forest in Minnesota and Wisconsin belongs to the maple-basswood association, and in glaciated regions of southern New England and New York the beech-maple association exists. In the Northeast, in areas where deciduous forest manages to grow, it belongs

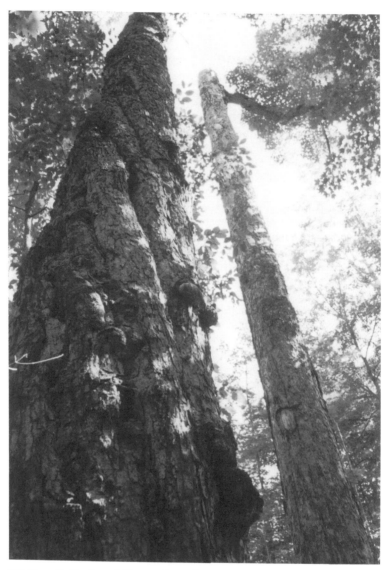

Old-Growth Hardwood Forest. A small tract of old-growth forest at Gifford Woods Natural Area, Gifford Woods State Park, not far from Rutland. Here large sugar maples are part of a mixed forest that includes beech, hemlock, yellow birch, elm, and basswood. "High-snaps"—large, dead trees broken off well above the ground (shown here on the tree to the right)—are typical in old-growth hardwoods. Although the understory is quite open, the rich and deep soils support a variety of woodland wildflowers and ferns. Some trees here have been recorded as more than 400 years old. Photo by Brian MacDonald.

mostly to the hemlock–northern-hardwood association, typically consisting of a mixture of sugar maple, beech, yellow birch, basswood, red oak, white ash, and hemlock (a coniferous, or softwood, member). But regardless of the variations across the continent, the reservoir from which all deciduous-tree species come is the archaic forest of the Great Smoky Mountains.

The northern forests, however, have a deeper green than the forests elsewhere: over much of this area grow conifers—evergreen, cone-bearing trees with needles—the trees that point to a different direction for their origin.

As the glaciers advanced, native plants were wiped out, either bulldozed to destruction or forced to "emigrate" south, ahead of the formidable ice. In that emigration the zonation of plants was kept intact, maintaining pace with the southern advance of the glacier. Nearest the glacier, where the harshest conditions existed, only the small, hardy tundra plants could survive. Farther away, where the ice had not yet touched but the climate had become more severe, grew the cold-resistant coniferous trees (spruce and fir particularly) of the boreal forest. Even farther south, deciduous trees such as beech and sugar maple remained unaffected, though their relatives to the north had been obliterated.

This zonation is generally what we see today, but shifted back, so that the tundra is now 1,000 miles to the north of Vermont. Each zone, with its own identity and associated animal communities, is called a biome; those mentioned here—tundra, boreal forest, and deciduous forest—are only three among many worldwide.

After the glacier had reached its southern extreme and then retreated under a warming climate, the stripped land of the north became once again ice-free: living things could, after a long absence, begin to reclaim something of their former place. The tundra crept north, eventually to be replaced by the conifers, which in turn gave way to the broad-leaved trees. Yet it was not a total return to the way things were.

The deciduous forest could only go so high in the mountains; the climate, even with the glacier gone, still determined its upper limit. Where these trees had trouble surviving in the higher elevations they could no longer compete with conifers, so that the boreal forest remained intact. Similarly, higher to the peaks of many mountains only the tundra persisted in the harshest conditions, at sites with the shallowest and poorest of soils.

Today, with the glacier shrunk to only an Arctic ice cap, most of the tundra extends in a wide swath across northern Canada. The boreal forest is a broad belt below that, reaching down to southern Canada, and the realm of the deciduous forests extends below the boreal over much of the eastern United States.

But Vermont has reminders of a long-ago world before all these

White Mountain Section
Vermont–New Hampshire Upland Section
Green, Taconic, Berkshire Mountain Section
St. Lawrence & Champlain Valley Section
Lower New England Section
Hudson Valley Section

Vermont's Ecological Regions. A combination of geomorphology, bedrock, soils, potential natural vegetation, animals, climate, surface water, and disturbance regimes helps delineate distinctive ecological regions of the state. Very generally, the major forest types occur as follows:

Boreal Forest in the White Mountain Section, and at higher elevations in the Vermont-New Hampshire Upland Section and Green, Taconic, Berkshire Mountain Section.

Northern Hardwoods at intermediate elevations of the Green, Taconic, Berkshire Mountain Section and Vermont-New Hampshire Upland Section, and drier uplands of White Mountain Section.

Transitional Hardwoods in the St. Lawrence and Champlain Valley Section, Hudson Valley Section, Vermont-New Hampshire Upland Section near the Connecticut River, and the Lower New England Section.

Map by Tom Luther, from Ecological Units of the Eastern United States, USDA Forest Service.

changes took place. Tundra still lives on several peaks in the Northeast, in Vermont on two. These "islands" of only scant acres are hundreds of miles from the family that spawned them. Yet, because the climate in their locations mimics the Arctic, they are able to persist. Other rare plants of an Arctic heritage cling to steep, cold, inaccessible cliffs in a few places in the state, and the boreal forest of spruce and fir remains on many mountainsides above the hardwoods and in much of the Northeastern Highlands as the dominant forest type.

Bogs, too, are a memento of the Ice Age. In fact, bogs have kept a record of what happened after the glacier created them. In their partially preserved organic matter are pollen grains from species of plants that grew in the area at any given time in the past. Just from these pollen grains specialists can identify many ancient plants. In addition, using radiocarbon dating techniques, they can determine the approximate age of the peat level in which the grains are found. Changes in the forest over time are read from the layers of pollen: the deepest layers are from the most distant past since glaciation, the surface layers are from the present. Thus, which plants grew when can be fairly precisely ascertained. Bogs in Vermont usually show a sequence from bare lake clay bottom, to arctic-tundra species, to spruce and fir, to white pine, to northern hardwoods. In most general terms and brought to its ultimate expression, this has been the evolution of our forests

Vermont's Biological Diversity (1997). A snapshot of the state's biodiversity, based on known data and estimates of experts. T&E = on the state threatened and endangered list. S1 = very rare statewide. S2 = rare statewide. Chart courtesy of Vermont Agency of Natural Resources.

	Number of Native Species	How Certain?	Percent of Vermont Inventoried	Status
Vertebrates				
Birds	193 (breed) 254 (total)	95%	90–90%	11 T&E 24 rare (S1/S2) 1 extirpated
Mammals	54	99%	60%	5 T&E 4 rare (S1/S2) 3 extirpated
Fish	78 native 7 introduced 4 exotic	98%	50% cyprinids 100% others	5 T&E 10 rare (S1/S2) 1 extirpated
Amphibians	21	90%	40%	1 T&E 5 rare (S1/S2)
Reptiles	19	85%	40%	4 T&E 3 rare (S1/S2)

	Number of Native Species	How Certain?	Percent of Vermont Inventoried	Status
Invertebrates				
Insects (all kinds)	15–20,000 (est.)			
Butterflies and Moths (Lepidoptera)	1,750 (est.)	70%	5% 3 extirpated	2 rare (S1/S2)
Dragonflies/ Damselflies (Odonata)	97	65%	15–20%	21 rare (S1/S2)
Beetles (Coleoptera)	5,000 (est.)			
Ground Beetles (Carabidae)	450	5%	75-80%	3 T&E 51 rare (S1/S2)
Crickets/ Grasshoppers (Orthoptera)	100- 150	90%	20-30% (NW VT mostly)	
True Bugs (Hemiptera)	300 -400	90%	20-30% (NW VT mostly)	
Stoneflies (Plecoptera)	70 (est.)	?	5–10%	
Mayflies (Ephe-meroptera)	100 (est.)	?	5–10%	
Caddisflies (Trichoptera)	400 (est.)	?	5–10%	
Invertebrates other than insects	1,700 (est.)			
Centipedes/ Millipedes	15-20 30	95%	20–30% (NW VT mostly)	
Arachnids	650 (est.)	?	?	
Crustaceans (macro)	22 (7 crayfish, 1 shrimp, 4 isopods 6 amphipods)	95%	?	1 T&E 2 rare (S1/S2)
Zooplankton (copepods, ostracods)	200 (est.)	75%	25%	4 rare
Mollusks	180 (est.) (30 aquatic snails,	90-95%	20% aq. snails 5% ter. snails	4 T&E 5 rare (S1/S2)

Vermont's Biological Diversity (Continued)

	Number of Native Species	How Certain?	Percent of Vermont Inventoried	Status
Mollusks (continued)	100 terrestrial snails, 17 mussels, 25 clams)		75% mussels 5-10% clams	
Plants				
Flowering Plants (Angiosperms)	1,940 (est.)	95%	77%	134 T&E 167 rare (S1/S2) 78 historic (not seen since 1970) 6 extirpated
Conifers (Gymnosperms)	15	99%	75%	2 T&E 2 introduced
Ferns and Allies (Clubmosses, Horsetails, Quillworts Spike-mosses)	91	90%	75%	9 T&E 10 rare (S1/S2) 1 historic (not seen since 1970) 2 extirpated
Mosses and Liverworts (Bryophytes)	520 (est.)	75%	< 50%	2 T&E 10 rare (S1/S2)
Fungi—All	5–15,000 (est.)	?		< 1%
Fleshy Fungi (Mushrooms)	1,000 (est.)	?	< 1%	
Pathogenic	1,000 (est.)	?	?	
Aquatic	500 (est.)	?	< 1%	
Lichens	337	90%	< 50%	15 rare (S1/S2)
Algae—All	1–7,500 (est.)	?	?	
Charaphytes	12	75%	15%	
Diatoms	100–1,000(est.)	?	?	
Desmids	> 100 (est.)	?	?	
Planktonic	600–700	?	?	

since glaciation. Obviously, however, the evolution is not so simple as this; some forests have never achieved this bog "conclusion," and others have gone beyond it. Moreover, some bogs report on other things: they tell us, for example, that 4,000 to 6,000 years ago our climate must have been much milder than before or since, because trees and other plants of a more southern distribution shed their pollen here.

We know that Vermont's environment over the years since glacia-

Vermont's Natural Community Diversity

	Number of Natural Communities	Percent of Vermont Inventoried	Status	Percent Represented in Protected Areas
Community Type				
Terrestrial (Uplands)	42	50%	16 rare (S1/S2)	64–78%
Palustrine (Wetlands)	29	65%	16 rare (S1/S2)	62–69%
Aquatic— Lakes & Ponds	<10 ?	>90%	?	?
Aquatic— Rivers & Streams	<10 ?	>95%	?	?

tion has gone through many significant changes, but because of the substantial transformations wrought by humans over their tenure here—fires set by early Native Americans, intensive clearing of forests, and segmentation of landscape accompanying settlement (all discussed in the next chapter)—ecologists have found it difficult to reconstruct precisely what the "natural" pre-European contact environment of Vermont must have looked like. However, old historical accounts, original town surveys (where recorded witness trees give a rough percentage of species composition), and, most recently, classification and inventory of natural communities all help sew together the pieces of this quilt, revealing in the process what is a fascinating, interconnected assemblage of forests, wetlands, waters, and alpine areas.

The landscape of Vermont, then, reflect their different prehistoric origins: southern, northern, a mixing of the two. We are standing amidst them and looking at just one expression, the present one, of a landscape that is continuously changing, responding to whatever the climate—and geologic forces—dictate.

4

People on the Land

Tabiwadzoimalakwsak n'wlawongan waijiwi paamiaskaskwihlanna ta n'zidal mlondzapkatanal wji ahki. (Like the ash, may my heart remain green and growing, and my feet deeply rooted to the earth)
—Abenaki saying (no date)

With respect to the face of the country [Vermont] . . . I know of no country that abounds in a greater diversity of hill and dale, but I must add that those hills are in general capable of being converted into arable ground, and that the most craggy mountain, if cleared, would provide tolerable pasturage.
—Ira Allen (1798)

We have now felled forest enough everywhere, in many districts far too much. Let us restore this one element of material life to its normal proportions, and devise means for maintaining the permanence of its relations to the fields, the meadows, and the pastures, to the rain and the dews of have, to the springs and rivulets with which it waters the earth.
—George Perkins Marsh (1864)

These words tell of very different times from different viewpoints, the first as part of nature, the next looking ahead at a largely untouched territory, the last looking back at the damage white inhabitants had done in their brief residency in the state, the first stirring of a conscience about the land, the very beginning of a conservation ethic.

But, backing up, we should trace some of the history of Native Americans in Vermont, and how white Americans came to take over the land and waters, and how their values and struggles directed the course of the state.

Once it was generally thought that to the Native Americans Vermont was a no-man's-land, that they migrated through the area, hunted, fished, and warred here, but never chose to settle in these wild lands. However, relatively recent archaeological discoveries, although few, have shown otherwise. Indeed, Native Americans did live here for thousands of years before the arrival of white settlers, and their changing cultures reflected the changes in the environment from the Ice Age to modern times.

The first Vermonters were small bands of hunters and foodgatherers whom anthropologists call the Paleoindians. These original inhabitants lived during the dying stages of the last glacier and later—roughly between 12,000 and 9,500 years ago—in the Champlain Lowlands, and

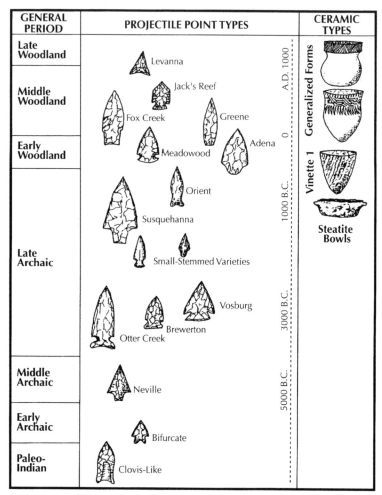

GENERAL PERIOD	PROJECTILE POINT TYPES	CERAMIC TYPES

Native American Artifacts. Different projectile point types and certamic types reflect environmental changes and cultural shifts in Vermont Native Americans since the last glaciation, a span of 12,000 years. Chart by Peter Thomas.

in all likelihood in the Connecticut River Valley, as well. This was the period when herds of caribou and mammoths ranged over the tundra plains, mastodons and other large plant-eating animals browsed in the scrubby spruce-fir forests, and seals, walruses, and whales swam in the newly formed Champlain Sea. The Paleoindians probably hunted these large mammals as their main food supply.

    We have little more than fragmentary evidence of the presence of the Paleoindians in Vermont, which comes from only fourteen sites.

Bands of probably twenty-five to thirty-five individuals apparently roved from place to place, following the movements of the animal herds and making use of available foods in season, but leaving little in the way of artifacts. At a single campsite on a hill above the Missisquoi River near Highgate and scattered elsewhere have been found the occasional fluted stone spearhead and knife, the only clues we have to these Native Americans' long-ago presence in Vermont.

Centuries passed, and the climate slowly warmed. The land changed under the different conditions and brought a new kind of vegetation to the state. The large animals of the cold northern regions disappeared, many of which became extinct. And the natives, too, under all these environmental changes developed new ways of living, more in tune with the landscape of this warmer period—the so-called hypsithermal interval, or climatic optimum. Some of the evidence that Native Americans shifted to new ways of life is in the different types of spearheads that have been found in conjunction with other artifacts that speak of a culture more than simply nomadic.

Gradually the environment evolved that characterizes Vermont today, with its complement of modern flora and fauna. This time of change for human beings here is called the Archaic Period; it lasted from about 9,500 to 3,000 years ago. The new name does not necessarily imply an influx of people into Vermont, but rather a change in the inhabitants' life-style that accompanied the changes in climate and vegetation. The Archaic Period natives were exceptionally fine hunters and food gatherers, but they seemed to do their foraging in rather well defined territories (even if those territories were large), as opposed to the earlier Native Americans, who roamed much further. In the Champlain Valley and elsewhere they fished, collected wild plant foods, and hunted deer, bear, and small game of the forests. Life revolved around the seasons, and the people accordingly shifted locations to where the food was: spring and summer lake fishing gave way to fall and winter hunting in the woodlands. But all the while, these people gathered wild foodstuffs—nuts, tubers, roots, eggs, berries, and the untold assortment of wild leaves—and it is with the Archaic Period natives that we have the first indications of the storing of food throughout the winter, thus implying the quasi settlement of people in an area.

The Archaic Period natives prospered in the Champlain Valley, and their population expanded. But other changes were in the making. To the south and west of Vermont dramatic discoveries were revolutionizing the lives of the people there. From the lower Mississippi Valley had spread a radical new idea: agriculture. With the shift from hunting and subsistence food gathering to farming, the former small seminomadic bands were supplanted in time by socially stratified villages and chiefdoms.

Because of Vermont's relatively harsh terrain and climate, agriculture among the Native Americans probably played a lesser role here than in some other areas of the country. Nevertheless, both the rise of social orders, including elaborate burial cults, in the Ohio Valley and the widespread exchange of ideas via trading networks influenced the Vermont Native Americans. Archaeologists recognize a shift in living patterns by the appearance of pottery, agricultural implements, cultivated grains, and exotic stone tools that were also used in ceremonial activities and indicate a more developed social order. This period is called the Woodland Period and lasted from 3,000 to three to four hundred years ago, or just prior to the whites' first view of Vermont.

The Woodland culture in its later stages apparently diverged into five language families, which were separated regionally. The two that figure importantly in Vermont prehistory were Algonquian, whose speakers lived in the Northeast and the Atlantic Coast territory, and Iroquoian, whose speakers inhabited the region around Lakes Erie and Ontario, and perhaps farther south. Many North American tribes spoke Algonquian dialects; the Abenaki tribe was the one that lived in western Vermont, furnishing many of its legends and place names, and it has numerous descendants today.

To date, very little is known about the late prehistoric period in Vermont, enough only to realize that the Champlain Lowlands region was a zone of great conflict among Native Americans of the Algonquian and Iroquoian language families. It is apparent that the Iroquois moved into the Champlain Valley from the west, attempted to settle in this Algonkian stronghold, and had brief, but serious, confrontations with the natives there. In fact, the immigration of Iroquois into Vermont may have had disastrous consequences for the Abenakis; facing this more warlike and highly organized group, the Abenakis probably abandoned their borders and moved to supposed safety north and east. But the battles went on, and the Abenakis may have continued moving back and forth in this region until well into the twentieth century.

About 650 prehistoric Native American sites are known in Vermont, covering the span of the Paleoindian to the late-Woodland stages. Although the major concentrations of Native Americans appear to have been in the Champlain Lowlands and Connecticut River Valley, further excavations will undoubtedly reveal sites in more upland areas.

By the time of European contact in the early 1700s, the descendants of late Woodland people in the region consisted of several independent groups—Passamaquoddies and Maliseets of eastern Maine and New Brunswick, Micmacs of Nova Scotia, and western Abenakis of Vermont—collectively called Wabanakis. (Southwestern Vermont was also occupied by another band, the Mahicans.)

The coming of white people into what is now Vermont, and

thereby into contact with the western Abenakis, was a momentous event in the history of this region, one whose tragedies and losses were mirrored sooner or later in every corner of the continent. As encapsulated in the introduction to Vermont's Historic Preservation Plan:

> The arrival of Samuel de Champlain on Lake Champlain in 1609 marked the beginning of the end of a way of life that had persisted for nearly 11,000 years. Although earlier fluctuations in climate, forests and food resources over this very long period of time had previously required slow but continual changes in ways of doing things, the intimate balance between Native Americans and their environments had allowed them to adapt to these changes successfully. No such balance was possible with the arrival and rapid territorial expansion of the European colonists, however. Natives suddenly found themselves competing for the same lands for crops, and European diseases to which they had no immunity decimated entire communities. War and dispersal dominated the Indian's world between 1600 and 1800 and, in the process, Vermont's native culture adapted and at the same time became nearly invisible to Euro-Americans.

Having suffered the loss of their land, persecution, ravages of introduced diseases (mortality rates of 80–90% in the epidemics of 1616 and 1633), and cultural undermining of their traditions and heritage, the Vermont Abenakis were brought to the edge of extinction. But they have survived. From an official estimate of only 229 Abenakis living in Vermont (1970 census), today (1997) they number perhaps 2,000 (with another 1,000 in Quebec), much of the "increase" likely attributable to the awakened sense of identity, pride, and desire for visibility brought on by the Native American rights movement of the 1970s and 1980s.

Bonded by the customs and culture of the ages, invigorated by new leadership and purpose, and guided by ancient wisdom, the Abenakis have held on to the slender threads woven through more than eleven centuries of their close, inimitable relationship to the land and each other. Those threads may someday be spun into another fabric, different than the original of course, but perhaps in its own way as rich, deep, and beautiful.

The French explorer Samuel de Champlain is credited as the first white man to see the land of Vermont, on July 4, 1609, as he sailed down the lake that now bears his name. He traveled with a group of sixty Algonkian natives on that trip, and when they reached the area of Crown Point, New York, they encountered the Iroquois enemy. In the ensuing battle the Iroquois were defeated—an event that was to set the stage for many years of bitter fighting between native and native, and native and white man, in what are collectively called the French and Indian Wars.

This was the time of colonization of the New World. The French had secured the northern and the English the southern New England regions. In the attempts of each to expand their territories, Vermont became a middle ground in the French-English conflicts. In these wars the French had more or less allied themselves with the Algonkian groups and the English with the Iroquoian: in their lust for land the Europeans put to use the animosities of these natives to achieve their own ends.

Vermont in the Late 1750s. Distortions, inaccuracies, and lack of detail reflect how little of the land west of the Connecticut River had been explored by Europeans at that time. Instead, the map of this region was created largely through second-hand, verbal reports. Vermont then was part of the "New Hampshire Grants," with only a few southern townships having been surveyed. Map courtesy University of Vermont Special Collections.

After about sixty-five years of fighting, the French were finally defeated, a victory by the British that some historians feel was due ultimately to the vengeful Iroquois. At this point—1763—the white settlement of Vermont began in earnest. For the English settlers the menace of enemies had been largely removed, land was available and cheap,

Changes in the New England Landscape. This series of dioramas at the Harvard Forest in Petersham, Massachusetts, depicts the change in New England's appearance from the time before white settlement through the 1930s. All the scenes are of the same spot.

(1) The original virgin forest of 1700: This mixed hardwood-softwood forest is what white trappers and explorers saw when they first came to the region.

(2) 1740: The white settlers began to carve their small subsistence farms out of the forests. These pioneers cut the trees to make way for crops and pastureland, using the wood for a variety of purposes.

(3) 1830: Land clearing at its most intense in New England. More than 75% of the region had been cleared of trees, and sheep and dairy farming predominated.

(4) 1850: Vermont farmers abandoned their homes and land to look for work elsewhere in the developing nation, especially the rich soils of the Midwest. White pines then began to grow in the untended open spaces.

and the potential of undeveloped territory beckoned migrants from southern New England. In the twenty-eight years from 1763 to 1791 Vermont went from a wilderness to statehood, from a population of 300 to 85,000. A phenomenal development indeed.

The white settlers lived far differently from the natives, and they brought great and quick changes to land and wildlife. Certainly the natives had modified the environment to suit their needs, including burning forests to enrich the soil, stimulate new plant growth for

(5) 1910: Reclamation of the land by trees. The white pines that had grown back were then ready to harvest. When these pines were clearcut, the understory hardwood saplings and seedlings were left to grow.

(6) 1915: The hardwoods take over. These trees, in the absence of competition from the pines, grew unabated and provided much food and low growth for many kinds of wildlife.

game, provide clearing for easier movement, and open areas for crops. But the natives were relatively few and their methods of plant and animal husbandry primitive, so that their impact on the land was considerably less than what was to follow.

Nevertheless, even before full-scale settlement by white people, severe inroads on Vermont's—and the whole country's—natural resources had begun. Buyers from the European fur companies had induced the natives to trap vast quantities of mammals to supply the

(7) 1930: The hardwoods have grown to merchantable size and Vermont is heavily forested again. This forest developed into the one in which we live, work, and recreate today. Photos courtesy Harvard Forest.

foreign markets with beaver, bear, marten, fisher, lynx, and other pelts for fashionable clothing. It was only much later, after Vermont's statehood, that the whites moved into the forests as trappers, and only after many of the valuable furbearers there had already been sorely depleted or virtually killed off.

The very heavy, unregulated year-round trapping, by both natives and whites, was only part of a longer process in which people doing different kinds of work had affected the land in various ways. With white settlers came yet another mode of life and a new kind of relationship with the earth. The settlers were farmers, bringing with them their own agricultural outlook on land use. They saw in Vermont great potential (once the land was cleared and worked, according to age-old custom), for frontier farming methods—planting the same crop in a field year after year, regardless of slope, without fertilization—had exhausted soils farther south. So the farmers in looking for fresh land came to Vermont, despite the hardships of climate and terrain.

The farms of the 1700s were small and self-sufficient. Wood, cleared to make way for fields, was a by-product of their existence, supplying the raw material for fences, houses, furniture, tools, utensils, and heating. Yet so great was the quantity of trees that most of the wood was burned simply to remove it. In addition, the woods posed a threat to the settlers, who were afraid of the attacking natives or wild animals that might be lurking there. As a result, the forests were opened up and pushed back, to allow room for farmland and to dispel real (or imagined) fears. The stately white pine were taken for ship masts.

By 1810 Vermont's population had grown to 218,000 and the land clearing continued up the mountains, down the valleys. The farming was mostly mixed grain and livestock, with the steeper, rocky slopes going into pastures and the richer lowlands into cultivated fields. The burning of felled trees also continued, and this too yielded products: potash, an excellent early fertilizer and raw material for soap, was among Vermont's earliest export items (used in Great Britain for cleaning raw wool), and the forests later furnished charcoal, fuel for the furnaces of the nation's new industrialization.

The felled trees were also the start of a vigorous logging industry that followed in the footsteps of settlement, concentrating on the white pines that grew abundantly in the Northeast. The early industry, though active, remained small, however, since most of Vermont's timber was inaccessible. Rivers and lakes were the sole means of transportation of softwoods (hardwoods did not float) to mills and markets, so only the forests near waterways were cut. The Connecticut River was a major funnel for logs cut in Vermont and New Hampshire and floated down to mills in the area and farther south.

Too soon it became clear to farmers who worked the Vermont hillsides that the land was more suited to merino sheep than to cattle or plow, so that sheep farming quickly replaced grain and beef farming as the dominant agriculture in the state. Also, by 1840 the national demand for wool was at a peak, and the Vermont sheep business boomed. Over 1.5 million sheep grazed Vermont's hillsides and valleys then, almost ten times the number of people here. Meanwhile, the cutting of the forests continued, greatly accelerated by the portable sawmill (invented and manufactured in Vermont) and the coming of the railroad, both helping to penetrate the remote timberlands.

Also, the canals provided new routes of transportation. With the opening of the Champlain Canal in 1823 (and Erie Canal two years later), Vermont and New York logs and lumber could be moved easily and in great volume to the south. But the canals also accelerated Vermont's deforestation. Timber was running out. As the Vermont Commissioners on Forestry stated in their 1884 report:

> From seventy to ninety percent of the native forests have been cleared off in the older settled and best agricultural portions of the state, embracing the district in the vicinity of Lake Champlain, all the principal river valleys of the state and the best upland farming towns, except in some small localities which are, or have been until quite recently, remote from railways.

As fate would have it, though, just as Vermont was exhausting its own timber supply, it gained access to Canadian logs via the Chambly Canal (opened in 1843), where loaded barges could go around the twelve miles of rapids of the Richlieu River and into Lake Champlain, thence to Burlington. There it would be piled on the wharfs until processed by numerous mills along the waterfront. Then the lumber

Burlington, 1877. Burlington was then the world's third largest lumber port, with many companies receiving and milling logs from Canada, New York, ad Vermont, then shipping them by barge and rail to Boston and New York City, for transportation elsewhere. Note the stacks of lumber on the waterfront docks, awaiting shipment from at least four different companies. Other wood-related enterprises shown include a furniture factory and door, sash, and frame factory. The town of Winooski is at the top left. Map courtesy Vermont Historical Society.

would go by rail to Boston or by Champlain Canal to New York, and thence to other parts of the country and world. Burlington grew dramatically as a lumber town: at its peak in 1873 it was the third largest port in the world (behind Chicago and Albany), with over 1,000 boats doing business there and the mills processing 170 million board feet. It was a boom time, but it was not to last.

Ralph Nading Hill, in his book *Lake Champlain, Key to Liberty*, summarizes the historical setting and what was to unfold:

> Lumbermen had reason to expect their bounty would pour indefinitely from the Canadian cornucopia, but such was not to be the case. For more than a century the forests had not been so much cut as mined; already a movement was afoot to conserve the last great stands on the Adirondacks' eastern slopes [to become in 1899 the 6-million acre Adirondack Park]. At the same time newly tapped forests in the American west were saturating the market. To fend off cheap foreign lumber Congress was induced, in 1893, to place a duty of $2.00 for every thousand board feet of lumber imported from Canada, with the result that within a few years the lake's third age of lumber was reduced to ashes.

Then beginning in the 1850s Vermont's economic growth met with a sudden reversal, most strikingly in the sheep farming, which fell as quickly as it had risen to prominence. All types of farming now dwindled, and families began to abandon their land and homes. It happened so fast that their leaving has often been referred to as an exodus.

A number of causes were responsible. The same agricultural methods that had impoverished soils in southern new England had not changed here. The expanding logging industry had moved deeper into the untouched forests and cut practically everything—but taking only what was marketable—then left when the trees were gone. Under the combined effects of farming and heavy logging, 70 to 75 percent of Vermont by the 1850s was open land, in the form of clear-cut areas, pastures, or croplands, and the hills and mountains, stripped of their protective trees, could no longer hold on to the soil—the streams and rivers became muddy with the runoff. The ill-farmed land became harder to work and less productive, or else simply washed away in the rivers. Hunting and trapping continued unabated, with few conservation laws and little or no enforcement of those that existed. Wildlife of the forests grew scarce, and fish that depended on clear, cold streams diminished or vanished completely.

The Green Mountains of Vermont, in short, had become a biological wasteland, offering little for people to live upon—a dramatic change from the bounty of a century earlier.

At the same time, new forms of transportation were giving access to unexploited lands elsewhere: the railroads and the Erie Canal provided cheap and easy ways out to the fresh and wonderfully fertile plains of the Midwest and West. There, the soils were boulderless, black, deep, and free for the settling. Sheep and cattle could graze by the thousands on what seemed like limitless acres of grass. There, new forests stood tall for the saw and ax. The flat lands could be easily worked with the newly developed agricultural machines, which were useless on the rocky slopes of Vermont (a new steel plow adapted to the thick sods of the prairie was invented in Illinois by a displaced Vermonter, John Deere—the founder of a now huge corporation).

Other social forces depleted the resources of the state. The growing industrialization of the nation offered new and lucrative jobs in the cities, and young people eagerly left the grind of farming for higher-paying work, work that appeared more glamorous. Then in 1861 the Civil War began, and nearly 35,000 men volunteered and left Vermont.

Thus, industrialism, new trades, westward expansion of a developing country, and a war drew people away from Vermont. New hardships awaited the emigrants, but even so, the lures of the outside world were bright. To the pioneer farmer and to the logger, especially, these opportunities must have seemed a blessing after the rocky, barren hills of Vermont.

Those people who stayed behind were left the legacy of impoverishment. The toll had been heavy: nonexistent or poor markets for their products, abandoned farms, plundered forests, rivers clouded with mud, many native species of fish and wildlife gone or on the verge of extinction.

In those days *conservation* had little of the meaning we give it today, and the act was rarely practiced. For the majority of people, there always seemed other places to go when the resources disappeared, better lands waiting and unending. But a few were troubled by what they saw and lived with. One of them, a Vermonter named George Perkins Marsh, became the spokesman for a rising land consciousness and expressed the new philosophy in his now famous book *Man and Nature*, published in 1864.

Marsh was a brand of Renaissance man, a philosopher, scientist, lawyer, naturalist, and linguist, with a knowledge of more than twenty languages. But he was also a product of rural Vermont, and carried with him all his life a deep love and special concern for his native state. As U.S. Secretary of the Interior Stewart Udall wrote of him in 1963:

> Science-minded and skeptical, the young New Englander rejected the easy idea that any resource could be exploited without concern for the future. Soil had a precarious purchase on the Green Mountain slopes. As a sheep raiser, lumber dealer and farmer, Marsh saw the damage done to the valleys of Vermont by land misuse. Overgrazing and overcutting were eroding hillsides; rivers overflowed; wood-growing waned; and as the woods were logged out, Burlington, once a lumber boom town, was forced to import timber from Canada to keep its mills and factories from closing down. Men were working against themselves, and by 1840 much of the Green Mountain country was already an exhibit of improvident land management. Not even in the cotton and tobacco belt were soils exhausted faster and forests mangled more thoroughly than on the hillsides of Vermont.

With his intellectual capabilities, George Perkins Marsh synthesized a conservation ethic that was to make a lasting impression on the country. He urged people to realize that our resources are not infinite and that nature works with countless interdependencies. He called for management of lands and wildlife with reason, prudence, and scientific knowledge. He knew that humankind must work with and within nature, not against it or outside of it.

Marsh was to give great impetus to the study and practice of forestry in the United States and to the wider arena of conversation as a whole. *Man and Nature* has become a landmark in the history of American conservation, being the first fully conceptualized expression of what we now call, variously, "the land ethic" or "conservation

Zadock Thompson. Quiet, gentle, well-liked Vermont schoolteacher, clergyman, magazine editor, historian, geographer, and self-taught naturalist. He was the author of the 1842 volume *Natural History of Vermont* (added to in 1853), the first compilation of the state's geology, plants, and wildlife. He was also Vermont's first State Naturalist. Photo courtesy University of Vermont Special Collections.

conscience." This monumental plea for resource management, growing out of scientific investigation, is what thousands of foresters and wildlife biologists today are working to satisfy: Marsh's book of 1864 is still the idea behind the act.

Out of the fields of the mid-1800s grew another forest, following the predictable sequence of plants from field to shrubby meadow to young forest—the stages of "secondary succession." White pine, one of the major pioneer species of tree in this part of the country, grew in profusion in the fields and logged-over areas. (In smaller quantities, paper birch, gray birch, and quaking aspen colonized other sites, often following the burning of the old forest.)

The pines grew densely, shielding the ground and excluding other trees. For many years they prevailed, until they were tall enough and had thinned themselves enough to offer growing space and light below for other trees. Since white pine is a pioneer species, intolerant of shade, it did not seed or sprout under itself. Instead, the more shade-tolerant hardwoods, such as sugar maple and beech, grew in the understory. The white pine had sealed its fate; hardwoods would be the future generation.

Fifty years or so went by. By the end of the century the pines were large enough to cut, and cut they were, in great numbers. Since clear-cutting was the accepted, easiest, and cheapest way to harvest the pines, the younger hardwoods previously sheltered were suddenly open to the sky and sun. But since they were not of marketable size they were, when not cleared away with the pines, left uncut.

These uncut young hardwoods now had a free rein to grow—and even those that were cut soon sprouted from the stump, as red maple and beech will do so readily, or, in more southerly locales, from the root, as chestnut, oak, and hickory do. By the 1930s many had grown to be suitable for lumber. But lumbering had come a long way in all the years it had taken these trees to reach this size: the relatively new applied science of forestry had begun to be practiced and, under the leadership of conservationist President Theodore Roosevelt and his strong, dynamic Chief Forester Gifford Pinchot, the concept of forest reserves (evolving later into the national and state forest systems) was born. With the lessons of indiscriminate logging still strong in memory, twentieth-century professionals approached the forest differently from their predecessors of the 1800s. They selected the trees they wanted and left the rest of the forest to grow and supply trees for the future. They began to manage the forest, to maintain its integrity and encourage its productivity. They knew that this resource could be treated like a golden-egg-laying goose that is kept alive.

As the second millennium of the present era draws to a close, the timber industry remains a big component of the state's economy, ranking first of all industries in the number of manufacturing jobs, with a combined work force (loggers, millers, wood manufacturers) of over 8,000 and estimated value (1993) of harvesting and manufacturing of $1.2 billion. (If forest-based tourism, maple syrup, Christmas trees, and horticulture are included, the total exceeds $2 billion.) It is certain that the demand for wood products, from paper to houses to furniture, will continue, even increase, in the future. But so will the demand for what the forests offer while still standing: fresh air, space, research and recreational opportunities, beauty, solitude, inspiration, and nontimber products such as medicinals, mushrooms, and maple syrup. Providing all these while ensuring the forest's integrity, non-human inhabitants, and productivity into an indefinite future will be one of the biggest challenges—for foresters, for ourselves—in years to come.

From the crops of Woodland Period Native Americans, through subsistence farming of early white settlers, through the years of sheep farming, to the dairy and diversified farming of today, agriculture re-

Modern Logging. Mechanized logging is quick and efficient. Here a skidder (top) drags trees out of the woods to a landing where a "slasher" (middle) picks them up, cuts them to length, and stacks them in the truck (bottom) for transport out. With increasing focus on environmental protection and worker safety, many new "low-impact" logging machines, systems, and practices are constantly being developed. Photos courtesy Hancock Timber Resources Group.

mains an important aspect of Vermont's social, environmental, and economic identity, despite declines over the recent decades. Over 6,000 farms still operate here (over 2,000 of them dairy), keeping about 130,000 acres in production and generating over $480 million in total sales of agricultural products ($330 million in dairy alone).

People tend to think of timbering and farming, past and present, as Vermont's primary industries, likely equating the activities with the forests and fields so prominently and attractively arrayed. One has but to see the official State Seal to acknowledge this with its big white pine in the center, standing in a meadow, flanked on one side by a cow and on the other by shocks of corn. Yet over the past two hundred years, often tucked away in the mountains, hills, and valleys here, other natural resource-based enterprises have been underway, yielding important products, some of world renown, and contributing mightily to the Vermont landscape and ways of life. Some have stayed, and are active and prosperous today. Others have disappeared as technologies evolved, tastes changed, supplies ran out, cheaper alternatives became available, or competition drew custom elsewhere.

Ironically, perhaps the earliest "industry" here grew out of the very forests that were so pervasively cleared in the late eighteenth and early nineteenth centuries: the processing of potash and its more refined derivative, pearl-ash, from the burning of huge quantities of wood, leaching the ashes, and boiling away the liquid to leave the gritty residue. Potash was used extensively as a fertilizer, for soap and glass making, in gunpowder, to dye fabric, and to cleanse raw wool (so-called *fulling* or *finishing*). This last provided to be a most important export commodity and source of income for settlers; in 1791 alone, over two million pounds of potash were shipped to Great Britain, as the islands by then were the world leader in wool production but had long since exhausted their own supplies of wood.

The sedimentary, metamorphic, and igneous rocks—and the rich variety of minerals deposited through the geologic processes and transformations described earlier—have been the bases of many interesting industries, some relatively short-lived, others long-lasting, even to this day. But regardless of their duration, all have been colorful.

From about 1775 until 1850, iron ore was mined as "bog iron" from swamps, marshes, and bogs, then smelted locally, especially in locales west of the Green Mountains and in the southern half of the state (e.g., Bennington, Tinmouth, Pittsford, and Rutland). With the opening of the Champlain Canal in 1823 and the easier transportation of product it allowed, the more local enterprises gave way to a fewer large-scale operations. (Charcoal, the fuel for the ravenous blast furnaces, had its own industry develop as a companion to that of iron; charcoal was first made on-site in earthen-mound kilns, but later was produced in larger quantities in giant stoves and brick kilns.) With the coming of the railroad in the 1850s, however, and opening access to iron-rich regions to the west, Vermont's once-prosperous iron industry died, and along with it the charcoal industry, their legacy only found in the rubbled remains of blast furnaces and kilns now concealed by the reclaiming forests.

The canals and railroads that ultimately led to the demise of the iron industry proved a boon to the "big three" of Vermont's stone industries—granite, marble, and slate, the first primarily associated with the great igneous deposits in the central part of the state and the latter two with metamorphism in the western. While these high-quality substances had all been discovered in the late 1700s and mined in modest ways, none had risen to prominence until the means for the efficient, long-distance movement of such heavy products became available. When it did, Vermont geared up to supply the hungry markets with some of the finest granite, marble, and slate in the world, a fame still earned—and exported—today.

Copper mining was also an important industry here, particularly in the late 1800s when the mines at Vershire and South Strafford, in particular, put Vermont second in the United States in production. The last of the active mines, the Elizabeth Mine at South Strafford, continued in operation until 1958, when it fell victim to stronger competition elsewhere and cheaper alternatives.

The unusual belt of dark (*ultramafic*) serpentine rock (former igneous ocean crust, or basalt, squeezed up into wedges and metamorphosed during the Taconic orogeny), extending along the central mountains from northern to central Vermont, has been the source for several valuable products. The 3,000-acre deposit of asbestos at Belvidere Mountain in Lowell and Eden, the largest in the United States, was mined from 1892 until 1993, when public concerns over health issues with asbestos led to its closing. Talc, soapstone (for stoves), and greenstone (or *verde antique*) have been mined since the late 1800s in other locations where this rock type surfaces.

There have been many other activities that have focused on Vermont rocks, minerals, and by-products of earth processes, at various times and for various periods: gold mining brought on by "gold rush fever" in the 1850s, most notably in the Plymouth area; in the southwestern part of the state, kaolin (clay) mining and processing from the early 1800s on, for pottery, china, and bricks; manganese mining in Wallingford in the mid-1800s; glass making from the sands of the Champlain Valley, from 1813 to the 1830s; flirtations with uranium prospecting in the Green Mountains the 1970s; explorations for natural gas in northwestern Vermont in the 1980s.

Even our water has been the basis of still other kinds of industry, directly or indirectly: innumerable hydroelectric generating facilities, lumber and paper mills, textile mills, and tanneries along rushing

Slate Quarrying, 1857. Extracting slate at the Allen Slate Quarry in Fair Haven. Alonson Allen was a successful and prosperous owner of several quarries in the rich slate belt south of Rutland, and employed skilled Welsh workers for the quarry work. He first produced writing tablet slates for school children, but later manufactured roofing tiles. Drawing courtesy University of Vermont Special Collections.

Vermont Marble. Blocks and slabs of marble rest in the yard of the Vermont Marble Company, ca. 1900. This famous white stone, derived from the shallow sea sediments over 500 million years ago, has been used in such well-known buildings as the old Senate building and Jefferson Memorial in Washington, D.C. Notice the hills behind, cleared of trees, a scene typical of Vermont at that time. Photo courtesy Vermont Historical Society.

Copper Mining, ca. 1880. The now gone village of Copperfield (population 1,500), near present-day Vershire, in the heart of Vermont's former copper mining district. The big structure is a 700-foot-long building with 24 blast furnaces for smelting. Company workers and families lived in the residences. Nearby was the active Ely Mine. This was at a time when Vermont was the leading producer of copper in the United States. The surrounding hills, stripped of trees to fuel the smelters, remained barren from the acidic (sulfur) fallout from the stacks. Photo courtesy Vermont Historical Society.

streams and rivers; shipyards, boat transportation, and, lately, marinas on the larger lakes such as Champlain and Memphremagog; spas and natural mineral springs at, for example, Dorset and Brunswick.

It might even be argued that the air here has attracted yet another set of industries—power generation from windmills and, perhaps, a goodly portion of recreation and tourism.

And certainly the people who have worked with these resources from centuries—Native Americans, Cornish copper miners, Scottish granite quarriers and Italian carvers, Welsh slate workers, Canadian loggers, and all others who have been here or come here—have helped shape the state's character, traditions, and history.

Earth, air, water, fire (the sun), and the forests and fields they make possible have all been treasured resources in their own right, gifts of a natural history that stretches so far back in time and connects us ahead to an unknown future.

Vermont today—a mixture of public and private lands; modest dairy and hay farms; villages, towns, small cities; industry, tourism, and roads to almost everywhere; and populated by more than half a million people—is 75 percent forest. This is a complete reversal from over a hundred years ago. The forest is, however, quite different from the one the white settlers encountered; and so long as we claim it for our needs and recreation, it will never be that kind again. But what the forest is now and what it represents are significant in other ways: it teaches us historical lessons in conservation, serving as a record of land use—and abuse—in our state. We have come a long way since 1850 and the first vision of George Perkins Marsh, but there is much need for even greater conservation efforts, much still to do to improve and maintain our beautiful landscape.

The human being is a latecomer in the evolution of the world, and the culture of modern Americans is but a flicker in that process. Nevertheless, in our brief dominion we have severely altered the landscape it took heaven and earth a near-eternity to form. In Vermont it is possible to study part of our history in the record of the land, and how it has responded to our actions. But we must remember that we are not yet done with weighing the balance. We can only hope that we will tip it gently in the right direction.

II Down a Mountain, Across the Forest

From a long time ago, when he dreamed as a boy, he remembered the sound. Beautiful creatures leaping under the sky, gone through brush, under trees, away, and only the soft echo their running left behind.

—Ray Bradbury, *Dandelion Wine* (1957)

Introduction

These ancient mountains surround us, frame our feelings, keep a steady watch over our presence here. They are large enough to draw wonder and admiration, yet small enough to invite intimacy. As we ascend their slopes on our hikes, their forests keep us company for most

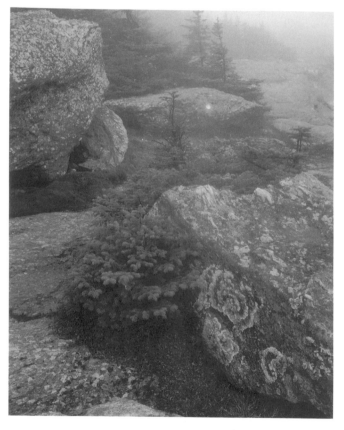

Alpine Regions: Stunted balsam fir, lichen-encrusted rocks, and the mist of clouds in the high elevations of Vermont's mountains. Photo by Louis Borie.

of our way up, until they shrink away and finally yield to the exposed rocks and wind. We have often honored them, at times feared them, and occasionally cursed them. That is to say, we love our mountains.

Some wag once remarked that if Vermont were flattened out, it would be the size of Texas. A whimsical notion, of course, but perhaps with a vein on truth in it. (How many miles of land and seafloor were crumpled into mountains over the millions of years?) Vermont is indeed a bumpy state, covered by hundreds, maybe thousands, of peaks of varying height, with five over 4,000 feet and a hundred over 3,000.

In kinds of plants and animals inhabiting the mountains—their biological diversity—it is generally true that, all other things being equal, diversity decreases from bottom to top, especially for the higher peaks. However, in terms of "unusualness" of species and allure for humans, often the reverse is true. And in the ironic reversals that so often happen in history, that which made the mountains so difficult for early settlers (and thus kept Vermont spare of development)—harsh terrain and harsh climate—is today not only tolerated, but desired for recreation, scenery, and space away from our own kind.

5

Alpine Communities

True alpine areas, where the conditions and vegetation are Arctic-like, are few and small in Vermont. They include two different kinds of places: small tundra areas on the summits of only two high peaks, and a few cliffs where the ecosystems differ from tundra. Both kinds of alpine areas in Vermont are clinging to a precarious existence.

The largest expanse of tundra in the state—close to 250 acres—occurs on the long ridge of Mount Mansfield. The summit of Camel's Hump, 15 miles south of Mount Mansfield along the main ridge of the Green Mountains, supports the only other tundra, of but 10 acres. Although true Arctic tundra is one of the largest vegetation zones on the North American continent, the Arctic-like areas of Vermont should be considered endangered communities, since they are so uncommon here and almost all the plants are either threatened with extinction or else extremely rare. Ironically, these regions are probably among the most appreciated places in the state, visited by thousands upon thousands of people, who come to look at the views or else hike across the areas. This very appreciation threatens the tundra plants.

The extremely harsh climate on the top of these mountains has been a condition the tundra vegetation has dealt with successfully for 10,000 years. But though they are biologically tough, the plants are extremely sensitive to physical disturbance. In addition, soils here are thin, and thus easily compacted by footsteps. Damage done is not quickly repaired, for alpine life processes are slow and painstaking. Many of the tens of thousands of visitors and hikers who come to the mountains are unaware of what the tundra really is and what it can suffer underfoot. They walk through what appears to them to be lawns of grass, but which are actually communities of tundra species. Quite unintentionally, they compact the thin "alpine turf" soils (a kind of peat) by their footsteps and crush the small, tender plants. Once the plants die, the bare soil quickly slides off the peak with the driving rains, opening the colony to erosion and permanent loss. To deal with these problems, special ranger-naturalists patrol Vermont's two alpine summits, protecting these special and irreplaceable communities by educating the visiting public.

Where the arctic plants live in these mountainous regions the climate is much like that of the true Arctic, far to the north. The frost-free growing season is only 90 days or shorter. The sun beats down directly, the winds whip across steadily. The year-round temperatures are

Tundra. The ridge of Mount Mansfield, looking north toward the "chin," more than 4,000 feet up. The 250 acres above tree line is the largest alpine tundra area in Vermont. Ranger-naturalists patrol the summit in summer, helping visitors and, by alerting them to the fragility of the environment, protecting the critical plant communities. Photo by Louis Borie.

colder than at lower elevations (the highest recorded temperature to date on Mount Mansfield is 85 degrees Fahrenheit). The soils are sparse, acidic, sterile, and prone to erosion on the steep slopes. Though water is plentiful from frequent rain, snow, and clouds, most of it the plants cannot make use of, since quick runoff and high soil acidity render it unavailable to them. Thus, these 4,000-foot peaks are in many ways near-deserts. Nevertheless, the plants that do exist above the tree line are well prepared to survive these arctic conditions.

In some regions of the state where magnesium-rich serpentine rock outcrops at higher elevations, an unusual alpine community exists, supporting its own special group of rare and endangered plants.

Plants

The alpine plants are low-lying and creeping, taking advantage of the more protected recesses where the winds cannot tear at them. Most are evergreen, perennial, and early bloomers, all adaptations that permit them to "get under way" as early in the spring as possible and not waste precious time or energy in such a short season. Most are able to retain water or restrict its loss much in the way desert plants do;

in fact, many superficially resemble desert succulents. Mountain cranberry, for example, has thick, fleshy leaves coated with wax, which effectively store water and reduce evaporation. Alpine bilberry, a close relative of the blueberries, has hard, leathery leaves that in another way resist water loss. Many of the plants—such as mountain sandwort, Bigelow's sedge, and black crowberry—grow in dense mats and have tiny, narrow leaves: these colonies soak up water like a sponge, at the same time offering little total leaf surface exposed to the sun and wind.

The complexion of the tundra changes with small variations in terrain and exposure. Moreover, the microclimate (the climate immediately surrounding the individual plant) may be strikingly different from that of the general region, contributing to the local differences in tundra vegetation.

On the gently sloping but windswept western exposures, heath plants predominate, with alpine bilberry and mountain cranberry especially abundant. Alpine sedges and grasses occupy the colder, northwestern localities, appearing like lawns or meadows: the dominant plant in such meadows is Bigelow's sedge. Scattered in rock crevices, gravelly soils, and other pockets are the three-toothed cinquefoil, the late-blooming mountain sandwort, and a nonflowering plant, mountain fir-moss, a type of clubmoss. A few tiny bogs fill in wet depressions on Mount Mansfield and contain many of the same plant species found in bogs at much lower elevations.

Diapensia. The small, rare arctic plant clings to existence at Mount Mansfield's summit, the only known location in Vermont for this species. To withstand the rigors of the alpine environment, it blooms early and quickly, has thick leaves to avoid desiccation and abrasion, and grows pressed into the protection of rock cracks and crevices. Photo by Robert A. Jervis.

Animals

Except for insects, which swarm in great variety over the alpine summits on summer days, animals are few. Even among insects, the vast majority are more common to fields lower down—rising wind currents apparently blow them up the mountains to these "meadows." A few, however, are true tundra inhabitants. One species of ground beetle, *Nebria suturalis*, is found only above 4,000 feet in mountains, and in Vermont is restricted to a few *yards* on Mount Mansfield.

The occasional tundra mammal is small and secretive, inhabiting tunnels through the vegetation. In a study of small mammals on Camel's Hump a researcher found only three species above the tree line: the hardy boreal red-backed vole, the deer mouse, and the meadow vole. The red-backed vole is a mouselike rodent that one would expect in the tundra, since all across the continent it lives in wet, northern environments and high elevations—it is even known to breed under snow. The deer mouse is a widespread, adaptable seed eater, and so is not a surprise in the mountains. The presence of the meadow vole is somewhat perplexing, however, because it is normally a field mammal of low elevations and not even found in the forests of Camel's Hump. It is likely that it reached the mountaintop following a fire that cleared a path through the forest to the summit.

No mammal is exclusive to these tundra regions. All live at lower elevations and some, such as the meadow vole, are more accustomed to grasslands than to tundra. An infrequent visitor such as the snowshoe hare wanders in to nibble on leaves and twigs, or to take the seeds and berries as they ripen. Even a moose has been seen, clomping across the ridge under the light of a full moon!

Birds

Even the more mobile birds are scarce on Vermont's alpine peaks.

Both Mount Mansfield and Camel's Hump have small flocks of nesting ravens, which remain through the winter. This large scavenging bird, native to the Arctic from Greenland to Alaska, is impressive in its size, shining coat of black, and graceful riding of the air above the mountains. It is heard often in flight around the mountain, with a sonorous, metallic "grawk-grawk." Most hikers to these regions have seen ravens, but few people have managed a glimpse of their nests, tucked in the ledges or in the crowns of the denser, trackless forest below.

The dark-eyed junco and white-throated sparrow are small seed-eating finches that nest directly among the tundra plants but migrate south before winter sets in. Hikers often see their young hopping about the rocks or attempting to fly from some low perch nearby.

In addition, the peaks are good places to watch for hawks, espe-

Smuggler's Notch. The east wall of spectacular Smuggler's Notch, showing the dominant feature called Elephant's Head. Rare arctic plants grow in the steep, moist cliffs, and peregrine falcons have returned to nest each year since 1988. Photo by Charles W. Johnson.

cially during the fall migration period, from late August to early November. Though these mountaintops do not rival other more famous places in New England and the East as vantage points for the hawk spectacle, they do let one observe these fascinating and graceful birds as they glide and fly south, flashing parallel to the ranges or spiraling up the thermal currents.

Alpine Cliffs

Tucked in the nooks and crannies of a few high-elevation cliffs in Vermont are plants of Arctic origin, but different from those found in the tundra. Though the climatic conditions on these cliffs are similar in some respects to those of the tundra, critical topographical differences help account for the two distinct biological communities. In summer, the rocky slopes, being often in shadow, are cool and moist. In winter, snow does not cover the vertical faces of the cliffs, so many of the plants are exposed to ice and extremely cold temperatures, even lower than those in the open but snow-blanketed tundra.

Such places are at Smuggler's Notch, near Mount Mansfield, and Mount Pisgah, beside Lake Willoughby. The cliff plants have evolved to cope with the stringent conditions imposed by these forbidding formations and climate. But unlike the tundra, the community here seems to be relatively safe from human interference, since only skilled rock climbers (and the most ardent naturalists!) come close to their sheltered homes.

Many of the rare and unusual cliff plants here are calciphiles (literally, calcium-loving), those that depend on calcium leached out of the metamorphic bedrock by water percolating through the cracks and crevices. Such exquisite and seldom-seen species as the mountain saxifrages (yellow, purple, and white), bird's-eye primrose, and the carnivorous butterwort cling to existence in these precipitous places.

The cliffs at Willoughby, specifically those of Mount Pisgah, are also where peregrine falcons first reappeared to nest successfully in the state after an absence of nearly 30 years. The peregrine (a hawk with the older name of duck hawk, acquired from its habit of hunting waterfowl) once bred in at least 27 cliff sites, or eyries, throughout Vermont. This magnificent bird, whose pointed wings extend almost four feet, is one of the fastest fliers, diving on its prey at speeds approaching 200 miles an hour, tumbling over as it hits the victim in full flight, circling back to claim the fallen prey.

Unfortunately, the collective effects of human disturbances over time drastically reduced its numbers by the mid-1940s. Falconers would take adults and immatures for their sport, while egg collectors gathered eggs at the eyries; hunters and farmers took their toll, believing the peregrines to be threats to wildlife or domestic animals; development intruded on some sites. But the main cause of their decline was pesticides, particularly the infamous DDT that was so widely broadcast in this country to combat a variety of insect problems. This chemical persists in the environment long after its use, accumulating in organisms progressively up the food chain. Though amounts in small animals may be minute, predators such as the peregrine and other hawks at the end of the food chain collected massive doses of DDT from the food they ate, often to levels a million times that of the environment. The lethal effects on the birds were many. Not only did the chemical kill them outright, but it also impaired their reproductive physiology, deformed embryos in the egg, and, most devastating of all, disrupted their calcium metabolism so that the weakened shells of their eggs were crushed by incubating parents. Thus, whole generations, not just individuals, were wiped out in a short span of time.

The U.S. prohibition of DDT in 1972, bolstered by a peregrine reintroduction program in Vermont in the late 1970s and early 1980s, were major steps in halting—indeed reversing—the downward slide of the peregrine (and others) toward extinction. Although the native subspecies of peregrine in the Northeast is believed extinct, and while still officially listed as "endangered" at both the state and federal level, peregrines have recovered markedly. In 1996 they occupied twelve eyries throughout Vermont (including Mount Pisgah and Smuggler's Notch) and raised seventeen young.

This martyred hawk, among others, has served as a gauge of our environmental health, and as a warning. We did respond in this case, through laws to moderate improvident actions and by banning DDT. So after doing so much harm to our wildlife, directly and indirectly, knowingly or otherwise, we should at least consider ourselves fortunate to have read the signs and even proud to have had the chance to right the wrongs. It is yet to be seen, however, if our response has been adequate or in time.

6

Coniferous Forests

Stretching across North America, Europe, and Russia is an immense forest of evergreens—coniferous trees, which are also called softwoods because their wood is generally not so hard as that of broadleaved trees. It is a forest primarily of spruce and fir, and is quite similar the world over. In North America this circumboreal forest occurs between the tundra to the north and the prairies and broad-leaved (deciduous) forest to the south. It comes into Vermont, but its distribution here is controlled by two factors: latitude and altitude.

As a forest of lower elevations, the coniferous forest occupies much of Vermont's Northeastern Highlands and the northern portions of the Piedmont, a good deal of which is swampy or boggy. These regions have much in common with New Hampshire and Maine—as well as the obvious affinity with Canada—even more in common than with other low-elevation areas of Vermont. Its isolation from the rest of the state is well expressed in "the Northeast Kingdom," a term coined by the revered late governor and senator George Aiken.

The coniferous forest reaches farther down the state, but at higher elevations in the mountains—this "Appalachian Extension" continues all the way south to the Great Smoky Mountains, though it climbs progressively higher in the warmer climates. The coniferous forest begins at about 3,000 feet in central Vermont but in North Carolina it starts at 5,500 feet; roughly 1,000 feet of altitude bring the same biological changes as 500 to 600 miles of latitude.

This forest has several pseudonyms: the Canadian zone, boreal forest, spruce-fir forest, north woods, and, in Russian, *taiga*. Except for less piercing winds (and it does provide winter shelter for many woodland animals), its climate is not noticeably milder than that of the tundra. The growing season is still short, precipitation as rain or snow is still great and spread throughout the year, and the temperatures are still low in winter (in summer, however, they can be higher than in the tundra). Upland soils are generally sandy-gravelly, acidic, and leached of minerals by the waters that continually gravitate down through the earth's porous spaces. It is truly a subarctic environment, and the kinds and numbers of plants here reflect this.

Bogs and swamps occupy many lowland and wet sites (such as embayments of lakes and ponds), with black spruce, tamarack, and heath shrubs predominating.

In the higher mountains in Vermont the boreal forest extends up to the tree line, or about 4,000 feet. As elevation increases, the spruces and firs become progressively smaller, more twisted, and stunted. At tree line they may be only a foot or two high, prostrate, and looking more like shrubs than trees. This stage, in which the branches are contorted and pruned by wind and ice, is known by the German word *Krummholz*, meaning crooked wood.

Below 3,000 feet, the spruce-fir forest begins to merge with the hemlock–northern-hardwoods association, with white pine as a common associate.

Red spruce and balsam fir are the climax species of the boreal forest in Vermont. They may grow together in near-pure stands, but often paper birch is present as a subordinate companion. This species of birch is a major pioneer in burned or cutover areas of the region,

The Northeast Kingdom. The glacially formed ponds and lakes are nestled in the wide valleys, while the spruce-fir forest cloaks the land. This is in Vermont's boreal forest realm. Halfway Pond is in the center, Cranberry Bog on the right, and Canada at the top of the photograph. Note the widely spaced trees in Cranberry Bog. Photo by Robert Candy.

and its proportions may indicate the extent of a former fire or logging operation.

The boreal forest in Vermont, Canada, and states to the south has marked differences. As opposed to the dominance in Vermont of the red spruce, in Canada the white is the common spruce. Very much south of Vermont, Fraser fir supplants the balsam fir of the northern latitudes. Vermont's alpine boreal forest also differs from the low-level boreal forest in the Northeastern Highlands: heart-leaved paper birch, a subspecies of paper birch, is the important birch in the mountains, whereas at lower elevations it is uncommon.

Owing to its high elevation and inhospitable terrain, the alpine boreal forest of Vermont has been little touched by human beings even to this day. But the extensive coniferous forests in the northern part of the state form the center of a pulp and paper industry that has a long history in New England. Because of the limited technology of the 1880s, spruce was at first the only tree used in papermaking, and not even much of this species was taken, as the market was relatively small. (In 1870, William Russell of Bellows Falls was one of the first to use wood pulp instead of rags to make paper in his factory.) But later balsam fir could also be used, and by 1912 even some hardwoods. With advent of the railroad in the mid to late 1800s and motorized vehicles in 1930 and the increasing demand for paper products, pulp production and transportation sharply increased, supplying Canadian and New England mills alike. This heavy use of the trees has continued up to the present, and a trip to the Northeast Kingdom can give the visitor an idea of the magnitude of the operations.

In the 1970s, forest ecologists first became alarmed at a rather startling die-off of high elevation spruce and fir on the higher peaks of the Green Mountains, particularly on the western sides, facing the prevailing winds. In some areas, as much as 40% of the trees was dead or dying. This pattern was also repeated in the Adirondacks and, to a lesser extent, in the White Mountains. Field and laboratory scientists undertook intensive and complex research to ferret out the causes of what appeared an abnormal situation.

From the earliest days of the debate over the cause of alpine spruce-fir decline, ecologists have identified and studied many possible causes that, individually or collectively, might answer the question: acid precipitation (pollutants entering the atmosphere and being deposited off-site through rain, snow, fog, and clouds), and/or its indirect effects, through physiological "poisoning" of the trees, leaching of certain essential soil minerals, release of other heretofore unavailable toxic minerals, additional environmental stress, and so forth; general global warming, with spruce and fir exhibiting a natural response to an environment that is becoming increasingly unsuited to them; periodic summer droughts and/or especially fluky winters; increasing

ozone pollution and ultraviolet radiation; even the natural phenomenon of trees reaching old age all at the same time (their origins dating
back to the extensive logging in the nineteenth century and forest fires
at the turn of the twentieth).

While the decline of alpine spruce and fir seems to have lessened
over the last decade, and thus the debate quieted some, it has spawned
important and far-reaching research on this and other aspects of forest
health in an increasingly crowded, industrialized world.

Vermont's boreal realm is part of the 26-million-acre largely unbroken "Northern Forest," sharing with its neighbors Maine, New
Hampshire, and New York a common biological heritage, forest-based
economy, and rural social tradition. For most of human history it
stayed well removed from public attention (except as a place to escape
the more feverish lifestyles beyond), due to the continuity of family or
corporate ownership, low human population, lack of development,
and relative stability of forest-based businesses dependent on them.
However, the economic boom of the late 1970s and early 1980s
changed all that forever, bringing much regional, even national, attention, and gave rise to one of the biggest and important environmental
issues of recent times.

It is a story of change, or more accurately fear of change, on a
grand scale. To summarize the situation in *Finding Common Ground*,
the report of the Northern Forest Lands Council (the group eventually
formed to make recommendations to Congress and the four states on
ways to deal with that change):

> Alarms sounded in the 1980s over possible historic shifts in land owner-
> ship and use . . . In 1988, about one million acres of forest land formerly
> owned by Diamond International Corporation went on the market . . . Ear-
> lier forest land sales chiefly occurred between timber companies, for value
> as timberland. Yet in the 1980s, the forest land was marketed, at least in
> part, for its development value . . . the impact of change on the important
> public values, on a scale never seen before, was perceived as an issue re-
> quiring attention.

And attention came fast. In the same year as the Diamond International sale, Congress, acting on the sense of urgency conveyed by Sen-
ators Patrick Leahy of Vermont and Warren Rudman of New Hampshire, financed the two-year Northern Forest Lands Study, seeking (in
their words) "reinforcement rather than replacement of the patterns of
ownership and use that have characterized these lands for decades."
The Forest Service, working with representatives of the four affected
states (Governors' Task Force), conducted the study, laying out an
array of possible strategies to conserve the region's large, productive,
and environmentally important forest lands.

Based on the results of the study and specific recommendations
of the Governors' Task Force, Congress authorized and funded the

Northern Forest Lands Council, a seventeen-member body composed of representatives of the four states' governments, private conservation organizations, forest landowners, and local interests, and the U.S. Forest Service, whose mission was to carry on the work of the study and make specific recommendations to Congress and the states. After four years of intense study, widespread and sometimes contentious public dialogue, and repeated drafts, the council made its landmark proposals in the report *Finding Common Ground.*

The council identified what it considered the main elements threatening the integrity of this vast forested landscape and the rural values, ways of life, and local economies associated with it. It recommended 37 ways that, if activated all together, would achieve long-lasting conservation of the Northern Forests. The recommendations fell into four categories: protecting outstanding resources, enhancing rural-based economies, providing education, and assisting landowners. Some noteworthy recommendations to the states were to establish benchmarks of forest sustainability, assess and conserve biodiversity (including ecological reserves), and provide property-tax equity to landowners. Of the federal government it asked for revision of inheritance and other taxes that adversely affect forest landowners, greater technical and financial assistance to the states, and institution of a national excise tax on outdoor specialty recreation equipment.

The council's multi-million-dollar effort has not been in vain. Since the report came out in 1994, the Northern Forest states and Congress have been busy on many of the conservation fronts it mapped out. Though the end is yet a long way from sight, and the public debate still continues over some of the issues (such as clear-cutting and ecological reserves) and methods proposed to deal with them, it seems possible that because of this expression of human will and desire, the Northern Forests can indeed hold on to much of their character and identity for the foreseeable future.

Plants

The deep shade under a dense evergreen canopy and the acidic soils derived from slow-rotting needles make the boreal forest a difficult place for most plants to grow. The understory flora, what there is of it, is scarce and poorly diversified, and only a few small trees and shrubs enter the spaces between the canopy and the ground. Most frequent are mountain maple, hobblebush, and mountain ash (not an ash at all but a member of the rose family that has been used as an ornamental for its attractive orange-red berries). On the ground, the few flowering plants are often evergreens, such as goldthread (so called for the color of its root), shinleaf, partridgeberry, and, under pines especially, trailing arbutus, with its delicate violet-on-white flowers showing through the late snows of April. Other herbaceous plants (plants

River Drives. The Connecticut River and its major tributaries were important routes in the nineteenth century for transporting pulpwood from northern Vermont and New Hampshire to mills in more southern New England. Only softwood (conifers) were transported this way, since hardwoods do not float. Crews would follow these drives down river, traveling in long, narrow "bateaux" that could handle the fast waters and ledgy areas. The crews would have to free log jams that formed at bends in the river and at falls. Horses were taken on the drives, on rafts, and were used to pull stranded logs off the shore and into the river. As a last resort, dynamite was employed to free an especially difficult jam. Here, bateaux crews work on the Deerfield River in southern Vermont (top), and spruce logs to be floated to the Connecticut River clog the White River in central Vermont (bottom). Photos courtesy William Gove.

without woody tissue) are sometimes found here that are more widely distributed throughout the mixed forests in the state. Starflower, bunchberry (a relative of the dogwood tree), clintonia, the circumboreal (appearing in the boreal forest worldwide) twinflower, intermediate woodfern, and bristly clubmoss are some of these more cosmopolitan species.

A difficult environment for plants that require light, the boreal forest is well endowed with saprophytes, those plants that lack chlorophyll and thus need no sunlight to survive; instead, they live entirely off the decaying remains of plants and animals in the organic matter in the soil. Fungi are the most widely recognized saprophytes, but in many cases are unseen for most of the year. Only when they put forth their spore-bearing structures called mushrooms do we recognize their presence. Otherwise, they remain hidden as fibrous networks underground or under the bark of trees. Indian pipe is also a saprophyte, but unlike the fungi it is a flowering plant, with arched

Chanterelle. Many kinds of fungi thrive in the boreal forest, where few flowering plants can grow in the acidic soils and scant light. Fungi are saprophytes, getting their food from decaying matter rather than manufacturing their own from the sun, as most flowering plants do. This is a species of chanterelle, a genus of wide-gilled, funnel-shaped mushrooms appearing in late summer, many of which are edible and sought after. Most chanterelles have a beautiful orange or yellow color. Drawing by Ann Pesiri Swanson.

blossoms that straighten up when turned to seed and with scale-like leaves of a translucent, waxy white. Curiously, though, the Indian pipe lives in conjunction with a root fungus—each requires the other living being in order to survive.

The pink lady's-slipper, without doubt the most familiar wild orchid to people in the Northeast, grows relatively abundantly in the boreal forest. Like the Indian pipe, it and other members of the orchid family grow in intimate partnership with their own specific root fungi. It is thought that the fungus supports the orchid by securing nutrients from an acid soil, which the orchid is unable to do by itself; indeed, it is the fungus rather than the lady's-slipper that seems to require the acid environment of the forest. Despite its name, the pink lady's-slipper in a coniferous habitat grows in two colors, the common pink and the somewhat rare white one, the reasons for which are not well understood. The white variety seems to be more common northward.

Mammals

As one passes on the earth from arctic, through temperate, to tropical regions, the number of species, whether plant or animal, grows, encouraged by the increasingly favorable conditions that last ever longer throughout the year.

The boreal forest in Vermont has a richer flora and fauna than the small tundra areas, but compared with the deciduous forest it is rather poor. On the other hand, the boreal forest, both alpine and lowland, is a refuge for some of the rarer and more intriguing wildlife of the state. This is owing in part to the special type of vegetation the forest possesses, but also in part to the large unpopulated and undeveloped stretches it encompasses, where the more secretive and elusive species can live without disturbance.

Two of the rarest mammals in Vermont are members of the group of boreal species, both of which were far more abundant everywhere before the white settlers entered the territory. Then they were trapped in considerable numbers all over the Northeast. The lynx and the marten (formerly "pine marten") are the phantom emblems of this forest and are now virtually restricted to the boreal habitat. The lynx is a wildcat, resembling the bobcat of the hardwood forests but with more grizzled fur and wide, furry snowshoe-type feet, good for traveling over deep snow. The marten is a fair-sized weasel that weighs 2 to 4 pounds and, though not particularly fast, is very agile and a proficient tree climber. It not only looks like a large squirrel but can act like one, as well.

Both species are highly efficient predators. The lynx, however, seems to rely in great measure on the snowshoe hare as its main prey—a habit that seems to lock the fate of these two populations inextricably:

Marten. Now a state endangered species, the marten was once a regular though never abundant inhabitant of Vermont's boreal and mixed forests. It has been the subject of a recent reintroduction effort. It is one of many of the weasel family in the Northeast, slightly larger than a mink. Photo by Susan C. Morse.

Lynx. Though there has been no tangible confirmation of the lynx's presence in Vermont for decades, occasional sightings keep alive the hope that it still lives here. There is reason for optimism: viable breeding populations do exist in nearby Maine and Canada, and suitable habitat is available in Vermont, New Hampshire, New York, especially in the boreal north woods. Photo by Susan C. Morse.

when hare numbers are low, so are the lynx's, and when the hares build their population back in the absence of heavy predation, the lynxes, in response, also increase. The marten apparently is less subject to such cycles, since it, like most weasels, has a more catholic diet. The marten eats mice, voles, red squirrels, hares, snakes, amphibians, and various birds and their eggs, depending on availability and the season.

Both the lynx and the marten require large tracts of undeveloped coniferous forest for the hunting and living—conditions certainly met in the extensive softwood swamps and uplands of the Northeastern Highlands. But neither mammal has been definitely sighted in Vermont for many years; the last documented sighting of a wild (not released) marten, for example, was in the 1940s. Though both species still live in isolated regions in New Hampshire, Maine, and Canada, some biologists believe them to have been extirpated in Vermont, saying these predators were never very many in the best of times and were the losers in the long aftermath of the excessive land clearing of the mid-1800s. Other biologists feel that, barring overdevelopment and drastic alterations in the composition of Vermont's boreal-forest region, it will be only a matter of time before both of these fascinating species reappear. Whether gone or not, the lynx and the marten are on the state's endangered-species list, and thus protected year round by law.

Over a two-year period (1989–1991) and in cooperation with the U.S. Fish and Wildlife Service and U.S. Forest Service, the Vermont Department of Fish and Wildlife released 115 Maine- and New York–trapped martens in the Green Mountain National Forest, in an attempt to reestablish natural breeding populations in Vermont. Plans were to perform additional releases in the northern part of the state. To date (1997), however, the results are uncertain, with surveys showing the original, transplanted martens surviving for some years, but with no evidence yet of successful reproduction or expansion of range, vis-à-vis the experience with their close relative, the fisher. With the program curtailed due to high costs in tough budget times and to the lack of demonstrable success, only modest surveys continue, with lingering hopes of uncovering new generations of marten. For now, however, the marten remains an endangered species in Vermont.

The word *predator* often strikes a resonating chord of apprehension, even fear, in some people. It can connote an aloofness, a wildness, a fierceness—even though such attributes are usually severely exaggerated to the point of becoming mythology. But nonpredatory wildlife in Vermont's boreal forest can also be awe-inspiring and fuel the imagination. One such is the state's largest mammal, and among the largest on the continent—the moose.

This ungainly-looking but magnificent animal was once a widespread resident of the vast evergreen wilderness across North America, but its numbers have shrunk considerably under the incursions of people into its native range. It existed in Vermont until land clearing in the 1800s pushed the mammal completely out of the state. But the moose has come back, appearing in low numbers in the late 1970s in its prime Northeast Kingdom range, then building its population and expanding its range through the 1980s and 1990s, especially along the flanks of the Green Mountains. In fact, they have been so successful that moose-car encounters—often with disastrous results—have become a matter of public concern (see map on page 88).

As the moose population built dramatically over the past two decades and spread to more mixed forest regions of Vermont, some biologists expressed concern that moose and deer might interact badly and have adverse consequences for one another. Moose, prodigious consumers that they are, might deplete food supplies for deer. On the other hand, deer, which carry but do not seem affected by a parasitic brainworm, might have lethal consequences for moose sharing the same range. However, these fears have been allayed. Vermont's land-use patterns, especially with reversion of farmland to forest, provide adequate food for both deer and moose; when competition would be most critical—in winter—moose tend not to concentrate in yards as deer do, but are able to move more easily through snow (due to different structural mechanics of the legs, shoulders, and hips) and shift to higher elevations where food is readily available. (Brainworm has proven to be a minor component of moose mortality as well, though it may have been more harmful in the 1970s when moose populations were very low.)

The result has been nothing less than amazing. The Vermont moose population as of 1997 is estimated at a hefty 1,500 to 2,000. In 1993 the state instituted its first, geographically limited, by-permit, four-day hunting season, which has grown modestly ever since. In the meantime, the thriving deer herd is perhaps around 140,000. These are old neighbors whose new balance is still in the making.

The lynx, marten, moose, and other larger mammals carry a romance and stature befitting the stereotyped picture of north-woods wilderness. But they are, of course, not the only mammals of these forests. Other smaller ones are an important part of the area, even if they take up less of our thoughts and dreams.

The snowshoe hare, also called varying hare for its characteristic change of summer to winter coat from brown to white, is the most widespread of Vermont lagomorphs (order encompassing rabbits and hares), occupying the high boreal reaches of mountains and the mixed forests below; it is absent only in the more agricultural areas of valleys. It is a hare, not a rabbit as it is sometimes called, distinguished by its larger ears and hind feet, lack of nest building, and young that are born fully furred, open eyed, and ready to run.

Moose. A bull in velvet. Moose spend a great deal of time in water in the summer, feeding on highly nutritious aquatic plants, staying cool, and avoiding biting flies. Rutting season is September to November, after which the antlers are shed. Though considered by some to be ungainly, the moose is fluid and graceful when running through woods and bogs. Photo by John Hall.

The red squirrel is the most often seen of these smaller mammals. It has a wide distribution and broad tolerance, being found wherever conifers grow, in urban or rural situations. South of Vermont, it shifts to deciduous trees, although only those of higher elevations. Less seen because of its nocturnal habits is the northern flying squirrel, not really a flier but a glider from tree to tree. This species nests and sleeps by day in tree holes left by woodpeckers or other natural cavities, and emerges at night to hunt for food. It is active all year and eats a greater variety of foods than other squirrels—the seeds from cones, which the red squirrel favors, but also insects, bird eggs, nuts, berries, and occasionally a small mammal. They will also pay surprise visits to home suet-feeders put out for woodpeckers!

Down out of the trees, other seldom seen mammals of the boreal forest are at work the entire year—in winter, under the snow. The widespread boreal red-backed vole, mentioned earlier, is common all over this region, including its mountainous portions, and, in the manner of all voles, feeds on a large variety of herbaceous material, such as leaves, buds, bark and roots. Searching the needles and furrowing into the humus layers of soil for ground insects, worms, insect larvae, and even other small mammals is the tiny masked shrew—one of several insectivores (the insect-eating family of mammals) that are residents of both softwoods and hardwoods, wherever moisture is plentiful.

Confirmed Moose Mortalities
Caused By Motor Vehicles
LEGEND

1990	40	Mortalities
1991	76	Mortalities
1992	52	Mortalities
1993	79	Mortalities
1994	84	Mortalities
1995	86	Mortalities
1996	96	Mortalities
1997	1	Mortality as of Feb. 11, 19

PREPARED BY THE
AGENCY OF TRANSPORTATION
SCALE

Taken as a group, the mammals of the boreal forest are a hardy lot, able to survive in a rigorous climate, in a region where the pickings are slim. The ecological relationships of animal-to-animal or animal-to-plant may seem simpler here than elsewhere, because here are fewer species than in more southern parts of the country. But each individual animal, to make it through a day or a year in this demanding environment, is involved in an incredibly complex and tenuous endeavor.

Birds

Birds of the spruce-fir forests are an interesting and changing group: the few and notable year-round residents, the unpredictable and sporadic winter visitors from farther north, the ephemeral summer nesters, and the seasonal migrants.

Though winter is a lean time for the bird—and therefore the bird-watcher—it can be a most rewarding period, for unexpected and unfamiliar species then come into Vermont. Many of the birds that visit the state's feeders, fields, and mixed forests in winter are true boreal species, breeding only in Canada. They move into the United States to spend the winter here, to proceed farther south in New England or beyond, or to wander from place to place. Their appearances are quite unpredictable, since their movements are not a true migration, but more a quest for food.

Most of such winter visitors are finches, a family of small to medium-sized birds with strong bills that can crack open the shells of seeds and nuts. In summer their diet is broad, from berries and seeds to insect larvae, spiders, beetles, and other "animal" matter. But in winter their choices are narrowed, to seeds that still cling to branches, buds, or the occasional hibernating insects they discover.

In this family two species of grosbeak (appropriately meaning "big beak") are numerous and common in Vermont, although over the years they do not consistently appear in the state: the evening and pine grosbeaks. Most years the evening grosbeak does arrive, often traveling in large flocks, stripping the trees of their seeds and buds, leaving the snow beneath littered with cone scales, twigs, seed husks, and bits of bark. Usually in late winter, when they are on their way back north to Canada for breeding, they will stop at bird feeders for sunflower seeds, having earlier picked clean the offering of the trees. Though now widely recognized in New England, before 1890 it was an unknown

Moose-Vehicle Collisions. (Facing page) The map demonstrates in a startling way how Vermont's moose population has been growing, through the increasing numbers of collisions with motor vehicles since 1990. Each moose symbol represents a collision where the moose died. Multiple collisions at the same site are given by the numbers. Moose mortalities from these encounters have risen steadily from none (up to 1981) to 96 (1996). Map courtesy Vermont Agency of Transportation and Vermont Fish and Wildlife Department.

species east of the Great Lakes. In the following decade it moved east rapidly. One researcher attributed this dispersal to the planting of box-elder as a shade tree in much of the East. When these trees matured to seed-bearing age, the evening grosbeak apparently leapfrogged to the East Coast, and once here was able to sustain itself on other foods. Still, one of the best places to observe evening grosbeaks is where box-elders grow—whether in towns or along rivers.

The pine grosbeak is more erratic than the evening grosbeak in its appearance, being abundant one year and totally absent the next. Furthermore, it may be present here in the worst of winters yet absent in the mildest. These unpredictable winter movements thus seem geared to food finding rather than severe weather. When the pine grosbeak is in Vermont it is conspicuous, especially the handsome male, with its burgundy-colored body and dark wings; in addition, this bird is somewhat the daredevil, picking up grit and salt on roads and waiting until the last second before flying from under an onrushing car.

Wandering far down the United States on occasion, but not often seen in Vermont, are two species of crossbill, finches whose name describes their outstanding physical feature. Their sharp-pointed bills do not meet as most birds' do, but cross at the ends, an awkward-looking but effective arrangement for the food they eat: the bills work like shears to cut cones from branches and rip off or pry apart cone scales to reveal the seeds inside. The white-winged crossbill is the more common of two species occurring here, but the rarer red crossbill is the more striking for its plumage of deep red.

Crossbills are among the earliest birds to begin nesting in the north country. Their nests, complete with eggs and sometimes even young, have been found in the boreal forests of Canada as early as January and February, in the full fury of winter! Whether or not most of the young from these early nestings grow to maturity, however, is open to question. Though we have no positive record of either species nesting in Vermont, it is suspected that they may do so in the forest of the Northeastern Highlands, if indeed not other places in the state where good boreal habitat is available.

The crossbills, grosbeaks, and other smaller finches, our occasional companions through late winter, begin to move north in preparation for breeding as winter yields to spring. Among these, the pine siskins and redpolls fade from rural areas in March and April as they depart for points north. Dark-eyed juncos and white-throated sparrows materialize in Vermont at about this time, on their way back to the higher elevations and coniferous mixed stands from their migrations south. Although for the most part the boreal-forest finches keep on moving through Vermont, to breed and nest in the woods of Canada, a few do stay, including most commonly the juncos and white-throated sparrows, which are apt to be found nesting in many mixed or coniferous stands throughout the state. The evening gros-beak, too, is now known to nest here.

With the dawning of May the boreal forest stirs with the daily ar-rival of small birds migrating north, keeping pace with the hatches or emergences of multitudes of insects. Most of these insect-eating birds in Vermont are the restless, jewellike wood warblers, whose winters are spent as far away as the southern United States, Central and South America, and the West Indies. As many as fourteen different species inhabit the coniferous forests in our state, some as breeders, others as transients on their way farther north—even as far as the Arctic tundra.

The nesting species fill in the slots and spaces in the forest, illus-trating well the concept of "niches"—the utilization of the complete environment by the members in it. The northern parula, a warbler, feeds in the upper reaches of the tree crowns and builds a nest of one particular species of lichen that grows there (old-man's beard). In the same area, the magnolia warbler keeps more to the understory vegeta-tion, while the Nashville warbler may be active high in the canopy, though placing its nest on the ground, under shrubs. Thus, although these birds occupy the same general area, there is no conflict: their ac-tivities are different and variously located, and since insect species change from place to place in the forest, their foods are also different. Living space is parceled out in discreet units that the warblers can use to best advantage.

But niches mean more than just spacing. They refer also to a faith-ful association of birds with certain tree species or forest types. The blackpoll warbler is a common nesting species in the higher elevations

Magnolia Warbler. This bird acquired its misleading name when observed in magnolia trees in the South, on its wintering grounds. It actually breeds in the coniferous forests of northern New England and Canada and is a fairly common warbler in Vermont, both as a breeder and as a visitor during migration. Drawing by Ann Pesiri Swanson.

of the spruce-fir forest on Vermont mountains, whereas the black-throated green warbler and yellow-rumped warbler prefer hemlock of the mixed forests. The rarer pine warbler is sometimes heard trilling in the crowns of pine trees, especially where they grow in pure stands. Rare, too, is the Wilson's warbler, a species found in openings in wet areas, such as alder swales. Stopping over in migration in the tall, open spruce stands are the Cape May warbler and the bay-breasted warbler—they will continue up the continent and few, if any, ever stay to make Vermont their summer home.

Many other insect-eating birds are found throughout this region in spring and summer. Tiny ruby-crowned kinglets, smaller and even more nervous and darting than the warblers, pick at twigs and needles for insects, insect eggs and larvae, and spiders. So small are they that their hanging nests are woven together with spider webs. The larger, warblerlike solitary vireo moves more slowly after insects and is heard singing high in the treetops. Olive-sided and yellow-bellied fly-catchers swoop out to catch meals on the wing, while the red-breasted nuthatch bobs up and around tree trunks looking for larvae or ants, then retires to its nest in a cavity of a tree.

A hike in the mountains may well reveal several species of thrush, a family whose more familiar members are the robin and blue-bird of towns and farms. Unlike these two, however, the forest thrushes are dull in coloration, their browns and grays protecting them in the dusky woodlands. Thrushes seem to sort themselves out according to elevation below tree line, with some overlapping. Highest up, least familiar, and rarely encountered is the gray-cheeked thrush, a North American boreal forest dweller heard here mostly in migration. Bicknell's thrush, once classified as subspecies of the gray-cheeked, is now regarded as a distinct species in its own right, the rarest of them all, with a range restricted to mountains in the Canadian maritime provinces, northern New England, and the Adirondacks of New York. In Vermont, it nests just below treeline on the higher peaks such as Mt. Mansfield, Camel's Hump, and Killington. Since the Bicknell's is so geographically and elevationally restricted, and so limited in numbers, recent proposals to construct new ski trails at peaks where the birds live have raised concern and prompted studies of their unique ecology and behavior.

Lower down, the Swainson's thrush is the common one seen and heard. As one proceeds down even farther, into the mixed woods, the Swainson's fades and is replaced by Vermont's state bird, the hermit thrush. This kind of replacement continues with other thrush species even down into the hardwoods.

The summer passes quickly and the young have grown to flight. By September most of the birds are noticeably anxious, in preparation for another migration. By the end of October almost all will have gone

Gray Jay. The "whiskey-jack" (a corruption of its Native American name) or "camprobber" to loggers of the north country, this is a bird of true boreal regions; it breeds in Vermont's Northeastern Highlands. It is a scavenger par excellence, sometimes approaching people closely and boldly to steal food or other items. Photo by John Hall.

from Vermont's rather solemn forests, having headed to milder southern regions, where winter food will be waiting.

Only a few birds choose to stay through the long, cold, snowy winter. Though these few may visit us only during some winters, they are unlike the wandering finches in that they remain in purely coniferous regions the entire year. In Vermont's northern boreal zone they may be considered permanent residents, since they have been found there throughout the breeding season, as well as at other times of the year. They have acquired the means to secure food in winter, when it is extremely hard to find (because of inactivity of insects, deep snow, and frozen surfaces). They are only a handful, and because of their relative rarity and isolated locations it is exciting to discover these birds.

Among these permanent residents is the boreal chickadee, almost identical to its ecological equivalent, the common black-capped chickadee familiar to most people, except for its cap color (brown versus black), slightly different song, and the habit of hunting for insects, insect larvae, spider eggs, and seeds closer to tree trunks than out in the branches. Seen less often and only in the larger bogs and swamps of extensive second-growth boreal regions is the black-backed woodpecker.

This medium-sized woodpecker, strictly a North American species, is suspected of breeding in the northeastern part of Vermont, where it flies from spruce to spruce, flicking off the bark with its large bill to uncover its insect food below. Though elusive, it is not particularly shy, and may give the viewer many minutes of observation. Even rarer is the three-toed woodpecker, commonly called the ladder-backed for the pattern that distinguishes it from the black-backed. This species is infrequently seen, and only in winter, but has shown up in Vermont in such varied places as the boreal forests of the mountains, the Lake Champlain islands, and, strangely, in the vicinity of Burlington.

Confined in Vermont to the boreal forests north and east of Island Pond is a species of grouse (chickenlike, nonmigratory ground-dwelling birds) that is rare both here and in the United States as a whole: the spruce grouse. Similar in many respects to the ruffed grouse of other areas in Vermont, it is hard to find, but when discovered it proves to be a most unbashful bird. Like many animals that have had limited contact with people, it has developed little fear of them, a habit earning the bird the slang name "fool hen"—it has even been caught by hand, without weapons or traps. Although it prefers to remain on the ground, it will take to the trees to roost or avoid danger, and in winter, when ground food is scarce or snow-covered, it will feed heavily on spruce and fir buds (which impart a resinous or turpentiny taste to the bird's flesh, according to those who have eaten it.).

One of the more flamboyant members of this select northern group of year-round inhabitants is the gray jay, formerly known as the Canada jay. It shows an unnerving boldness, and woodsmen have dubbed it "camprobber" for its habit of stealing their food and other items from camps, sometimes right out of their hands! "In its choice of food the Canada jay is even more omnivorous than the blue jay. It attacks almost anything that seems edible, and in winter is said at times to feed on the lichens. . . . There is no reasonable limit to its appetite. Any bird that will consume quantities of soap probably will take almost anything edible. Indians say that it will eat moccasins and fur caps, but its food habits have never been the subject of exhaustive investigation." (Forbush and May, 1925)

Birds of prey are busy in winter, trying to live off a catch that may come only infrequently. But unlike the species that have just been described, most are not confined to a boreal habitat. The goshawk has the reputation of being one of the fiercest, boldest, most ruthless of these hunters. It is indeed a powerful and aggressive predator, and is agile in the woodlands, but the reputation is overblown, probably owing to its large size (two feet tall), appearance (red eyes under frowning white "eyebrows"), hostility when its nest is approached in breeding season, and broad diet, which includes almost any living thing it can get its talons on, from small insects to large birds to mammals.

When passenger pigeons swarmed by the millions over forested areas of the northern United States, they supposedly were one of the favorite foods of the goshawk. As far as we can tell, the goshawk then roved well south into the broad-leaved forests, but with extinction of the passenger pigeon in the early 1900s and the reduction of forest-land all over New England, it steadily retreated to its boreal refuge, where it stayed until recent years. Within the past two decades, how-ever, goshawks have been returning to lower latitudes in increasing numbers. Nesting is not uncommon in Vermont now, even in the mixed woods, as several hikers have found out—much to their sur-prise and alarm—when dive-bombed by screaming defensive parent hawks.

Another group of predatory birds, the owls, are represented in the boreal forests. Though several species live there, the long-eared owl is the one most restricted to the habitat and is generally considered to be rare in Vermont. It is possible, however, that it is not so uncommon as we think, since it is a nocturnal bird, roosting quietly during the day, when it appears appressed to the trunks of trees, blending perfectly with its background.

In the course of almost every winter, rare Arctic birds of prey show up in Vermont. These are believed to be driven south in search of food, which has become scarce in their native hunting grounds. One, two, or sometimes several individuals of such foreign species stay the winter and set up territories in their adopted homes. Perhaps the most regular of these periodic invaders are snowy owls. They usu-ally select flat, open areas that may resemble their tundra landscapes (e.g., rooftops in Barre and on the breakwater of Burlington harbor), and there they feed on mice the way they do on lemmings in the far north. Another Arctic visitor is the very large rough-legged hawk, seen some years in substantial numbers, mostly as it hovers over flatlands, especially in the Champlain Valley. Among the once-in-a-lifetime sightings of Arctic birds in Vermont are hawk owls and the swift, pure-white gyrfalcons.

Amphibians and Reptiles

The homogeneity of the boreal forest, its paucity of plant species, its sterile soils, and its harsh environmental conditions severely limit the numbers of other animals able to live there.

The soil acidity and the lack of humus, caused by slowly rotting needles, on top of the glacial sands and gravels keep soil organisms—worms, insects, other arthropods, and the small mammals that feed on them—to a minimum. The long, hard winters apparently restrict cold-blooded vertebrates, too—the amphibians and reptiles.

The most common amphibian in this region is probably the hand-some black-masked, buff-bodied wood frog. Though it lives throughout Vermont, breeding in wet areas and moving to higher grounds later in the spring, it is found farther north than any other North American amphibian. It is known to breed not only in the boreal forest but even in the tundra, and has a habit that accommodates the extremely short frost-free season when it is active: it breeds very early in spring, often before the snow is gone, and after the female deposits her eggs in the water, she, unlike most other amphibians, abandons them, so that she can move on to other businesses of living. The eggs and young develop quickly, their time of maturation being compressed to keep in step with the short season.

Another boreal amphibian in the state, though with a less widespread distribution than in other regions, is the mink frog. So named because of the musky odor it emits when handled, the mink frog can be heard uttering its staccato mating call in a few areas of Vermont in spring. One can even hear it in certain high-elevation ponds and wetland spots in the mountains, as, for example, at Bear Pond and Lake of the Clouds in Mount Mansfield State Forest.

Reptiles are few and seldom seen in the boreal forest. The most frequently encountered is probably the semiaquatic painted turtle, either at the edge of a pond as it basks in the sun or in the woods as it makes its way in summer from the water to drier land for egg laying. Of snakes, the familiar garter snake, tolerant of many habitats, is the most common of a very few in boreal regions; it searches the forest floor for insects and small mammals to eat.

Insects

Anyone who visits the coniferous-forest regions in May or June knows that insects are abundant. Most notorious are the black flies, the small biting insects that begin hatching in early spring, in the rushing waters of brooks and streams. They rise out of the water in great numbers, the females (the males don't bite) quickly seeking blood meals from any source. They can be so many and so pesky that they drive animals into a frenzy and into the water or mud for relief. Many fishing and camping trips, planned in winter when thoughts of insects are faraway and dim, have been ruined—or at least made near unbearable—by this small, black monster. The black fly will be discussed again later, in another context.

People are not the only consumers of trees. In Vermont's northern regions periodic outbreaks of insect pests and diseases occur and often devastate thousands of acres of forest land. Many of the attacks seem to be a natural part of the ecosystem, however, since many animals—insects included—experience severe, sometimes violent, population cycles, from explosion of numbers to near-disappearance to explosion again. These cycles are most pronounced in the far north, where they are thought to be related, at least in part, to the lack of variety of plants and animals.

For instance, Vermont's coniferous forests have experienced a few infestations of spruce budworm, the caterpillar stage of which has a voracious appetite for needles of conifers. The latest outbreak began in 1974 and ended in 1985. More than 61,000 acres of trees were defoliated in the peak year, 1978. The caterpillar's strict diet of needles can come from various trees, but the animal concentrates on balsam fir. So the boreal forest, almost exclusively spruce and fir, suffers greatly. But what usually follows such an infestation is a sharp decline of the insect population—due to lack of food, increased predation by birds or parasitism by other organisms, disease, or a combination of these controls. The budworm numbers then drop to harmless proportions, the forest is able to regrow over time, and the cycle is complete. For economic reasons, we usually cannot wait for the natural cycle to run its course, which would mean losing many revenue-producing trees. So we must take measures to short-circuit the cycle, most often with the use of target chemicals that kill the budworm before it has a chance to reach destructive levels. This use of pesticides must be made with great discretion, however, lest they harm or kill other insects and wildlife.

Other Coniferous Forests

Though not referred to as "boreal" in the sense of the spruce-fir zone, other coniferous forests exist in Vermont, either as restricted, specialized types within a particular biophysical region or as stands mixed in with other, more extensive forest types. Since these forests usually darken the ground with perennial shade and live on dry, acidic, sterile soils, they often have some of the same understory plants as the true boreal forest, such as wintergreen, partridgeberry, and heaths of various kinds (blueberries, sheep laurel, etc.). Consequently, they may support some of the same kind of animals, notably birds, especially if the tracts are large.

White Pine Forests: These ancient pine forests stunned the new white settlers with their grandeur and the size of individual trees. It was not uncommon for them to grow over 150 feet tall and 8 feet in diameter (even reports of 200 footers, 10 feet through). Secure until the white settlers looked upon them as prized commodities, particularly for masts for sailing ships, and being resistant to fire, they may well have attained hundreds, perhaps even a thousand, years of age.

Few of the white pine forests survived the rapacious axe and saw of the late 1700s and early 1800s, and fewer still the repeated logging that followed. Their loss was not only an ecological and historic one,

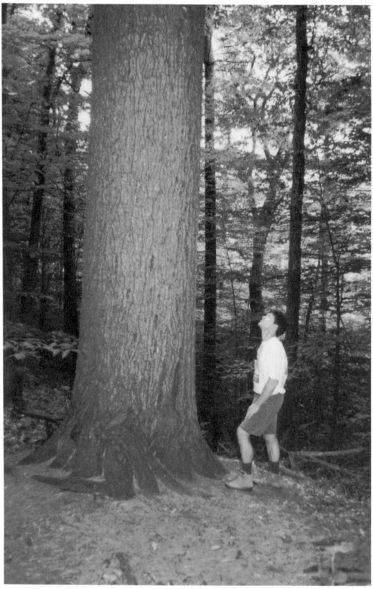

Old-Growth White Pines. Some of the largest native white pines in Vermont grow in Fisher-Scott Memorial Pines, southeast of Red Mountain, just north of Arlington. This is a 22-acre State Natural Area and National Natural Landmark, and the former writing retreat of well-known author Dorothy Canfield Fisher. The biggest trees here are probably Civil War era pines that grew up together following pasture abandonment. Photo by Charles W. Johnson.

but one of the spirit, as well. Robert Pike, in his book *Tall Trees, Tough Men*, describes this impression from his youth:

> A magnificent stand [of white pine] on the Connecticut River at Concord, Vermont, probably the last virgin pine in that state, was cut down in 1920, and a portable mill sawed it up. When I was a young fellow I used to wander through that grove of cathedral pine, many of which were from three to four feet in diameter, and to this day I remember the deep silence, broken only by a screeching bluejay, and always, in the tree-tops, a soft rustling, serious and solemn, a mysterious rhythm, like the breath of an eternal ruling power, and the hot, pungent odor rising from the thick brown layers of needles. And to this day I wonder that men could cut down such trees.

Red Pine Forests: In the Champlain and Connecticut River Valleys, and more southerly regions elsewhere (rarely in the north), red pine may occupy dry, sandy soils or, at the higher elevations, rocky slopes and

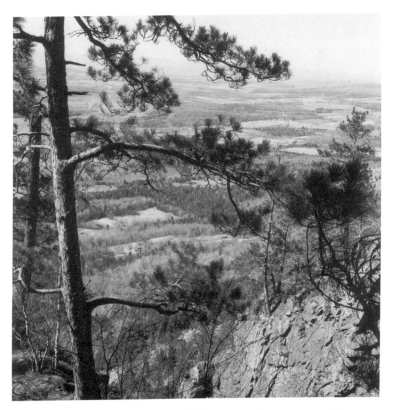

Red Pines. Atop the ledges of Bristol Cliffs, native red pines grow on the steep, thin-soiled slopes. The view here is west over the Champlain Lowlands. Photo by John Hall.

ridges. On the former, if allowed to they grow straight and tall, and on the latter their form is more usually short and gnarled. In either location, however, their presence is evidence of their ability to withstand fires that kill off would-be, less resistant, competitors. Red pine often grows mixed with white pine. Though a valuable timber tree (a "hard" pine), its scarcity relative to white pine afforded it a natural protection from the heavy logging of the latter. It was extensively planted by the Civilian Conservation Corps in the 1930s; those maturing plantations one can see in many areas of the state today.

Pitch Pine Forests: Before humans converted much of the vast sand plain region of Chittenden County to homes, yards, roads, and commercial buildings, it likely supported extensive pitch pine forests, accompanied by oaks and a unique assemblage of understory plants (some of which are now on the state's endangered species list). These sand plains, originating as postglacial lake or ocean deposits, have been systematically reduced to a handful of isolated sites, cut off from one another by the intervening developments. As pitch pine is not just a fire-resistant species but a fire-dependent one (to allow the cones to open and shed seeds, and to cut down encroaching vegetation), these forests require active management—periodic burning or removal of competing species—to perpetuate them, maintain their biological integrity, and retain their associated rare plant species. However, hand clearing is often prohibitively expensive, while burning is socially unacceptable where the forests are ringed with residences and other buildings.

While pitch pine is normally a dweller of dry, sandy areas, it does occur, unexpectedly and ironically perhaps, in a few bogs in the Champlain Valley. Indeed, it is a dominant part of the landscape of Vermont's largest peatland, Maquam Bog, in the Missisquoi National Wildlife Refuge, in the extreme northwestern corner of the state. Even in bogs, however, it grows on the drier hummocks, much as white pine occasionally does, keeping its roots up and away from the waterlogged hollows.

7

The Hardwoods

When the Europeans first took possession of North America, it was one continued forest, the greatest on earth. . . . Much of the largest part of Vermont is yet in the state in which nature placed it. Uncultivated by the hand of man, it presents to our view a vast tract of woods abounding with trees, plants, and flowers, almost infinite in number, and of the most various species and kind.

—Samuel Williams (1794)

Legend has it that the early American hardwood forest was so large, dense, and uninterrupted that a squirrel, if it wanted to, could travel from East Coat to the Mississippi River without touching the ground. An exaggeration, no doubt, but nevertheless it must have been a grand and imposing scene, even a forbidding one, that stood before those first white settlers.

But the wilderness meant something other than grandeur to the pioneers of those years, and their approach to it and way of life have left only fragments of the former virgin forest. In our state these areas are but small bridges from presettlement Vermont to today.

But though the virgin woodlands no longer dominate our landscape, and despite the changes in the forest that have been wrought, Vermont's woods have retained much of their original character. The hardwood trees that were cleared by our ancestors have returned, and although they exist in a different form from their predecessors, they are still a major component of the state, spatially, spiritually, and in terms of economics.

This is the forest of fall color, picture postcards, and maple syrup. It is a forest of great commercial uses and potential. A forest inspiring art, literature, and song. A place of recreation. It has been the area in Vermont most densely settled, and it harbors a wide variety of plants and animals.

The predominant association here—hemlock–northern hardwoods —is part of a large and fascinating forest system—the Eastern Deciduous Forest, encompassing most of eastern North America except the central and southern maritime regions. Though most people who live in it take its seasonal transformations for granted, on the world's scale it is a unique forest. Only China has a geographic region with a comparable climate and environment that results in a similar flora, but even there many of the species are different and the flavor of the land is not quite the same. In few other places on earth do the trees put on

101

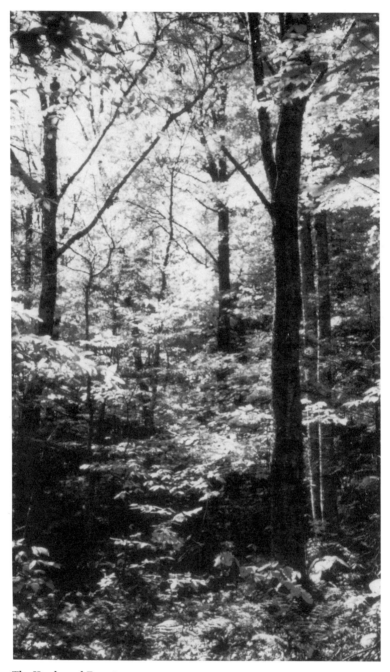

The Hardwood Forest. Photo by Robert A. Jervis.

delicate green leaves in spring (with wild flowers blooming on the ground), then continue through summer, and finally drop their leaves in a blaze of color in autumn. In few other places do the trees stand leafless through winter, storing their manufactured food in the protection of their roots.

In general, the hardwoods occupy most land in Vermont below 2,400 feet, except for that which is boreal forest or such special habitats as marshes and ponds—or space preempted by human beings for roads, buildings, and farms.

As mentioned earlier, Vermont's past and present agricultural, logging, settlement, and other land uses have left little in the way of "virgin" forest for us to see and experience (the term *old growth* is now preferred, for it conveys what can be observed and recorded rather than supposition about what may or may not have happened in the past). The manipulations were not all due to the white Europeans; in some areas, particular the lowlands where they concentrated most of their activity, Native Americans used fire for land-clearing, to make hunting easier, encourage berry- and nut-producing plants, and provide more open passage for travel. Even without these human-derived disturbances, it may well be that old growth forests here were never as prevalent as imagined, due to regular, periodic natural disturbances such as wildfires, hurricanes and other storms, winter damage, droughts, pest outbreaks, and beaver activity.

Old growth forests in Vermont do not fit the stereotypical image of "virgin" forests one often sees in films, reads in books, or hears in stories. Such fanciful depictions usually owe their origin to redwoods out West or rainforests of South America. Moreover, there is no one "old growth"; it varies with forest type, geographical area, and quality and history of the site. Some old growth here, say on ledge or outcropping, may not be tall and grand, but stunted, gnarly, and downright puny.

Nonetheless, and regardless of their former extent, as a general rule old-growth hardwood forests here have some defining characteristics:

- They are more than collections of trees. Rather, they are natural communities that have interacted and experienced continuity over long periods of time—continuity of generations, processes, and structure. In a sense, it is the land upon which the forest grows that is ecologically "old" (unmanipulated by humans).

- There are no detectable signs of influence by humans or domesticated animals, such as stumps, grazing, barbed wire, stone walls, fencing, tap holes for maple sugaring, etc.

- They have several species of trees, of many sizes and age classes (from big old trees, to large mature ones, to saplings, to seedlings); however, these trees may not be evenly distributed throughout nor occupy all levels equally.

- They may have some old trees with great diameter, but more importantly some have reached their maximum height, with crowns distinctively shaped ("cabbage-topped" for conifers, "ragged" for hardwoods).

• Dead trees are present: "high" snaps or snags (broken off in the branches), "low" snaps or snags (broken off lower on the trunk), and "tip-ups" (fallen).

• Gaps of different sizes and shapes occur in the forest canopy where trees have toppled.

• Decomposition and organic accumulation—in the leaf litter and elsewhere—have reached equilibrium. That is, losses to the system are balanced by gains.

• Where soils are deep and a disturbance such as a severe storm has caused a significant blowdown, "pit and mound" (or "pillow and cradle") topography may be noticeable—root masses of fallen trees are pulled up and exposed, leaving depressions in the ground (pits) and hummocks of soil and roots (mounds).

• Where soils are rich, they may support a diverse herbaceous flora.

Today, the precious handful or two of old-growth forests in Vermont occur as small, isolated tracts, ranging in size from a few acres to the largest at 125 acres (in the Green Mountain National Forest). As relicts and being rare, they have become "outdoor museums" for researchers, naturalists, and the just plain curious. However, with the focus now shifting to conservation of biological diversity, there is interest, purpose, and wisdom in allowing larger forest tracts, perhaps in the thousands or tens of thousands of acres, to turn into old growth, as active, dynamic, interconnected ecological reserves.

The term *hardwoods* is a broad grouping that in reality includes several different associations, depending on geographic location, topography, and conditions at a specific site. What is described below is, of course, only a generalization of a much more complicated picture, and only a way to organize the assemblages. Refer to the map on page 38.

Perhaps as much as 70% of Vermont's 4.5 million forested acres (more than half of the state's land base) is the classic hemlock—northern hardwoods. It dominates the landscape outside boreal regions, the Champlain and Connecticut River Valleys, and southern Vermont. Sugar maple, beech, and yellow birch are the most common members, with varying amounts of white ash, hemlock, black cherry, basswood, and others on what might be termed "typical" sites of intermediate elevations, modest topography, and moderately rich soils. Where soils are deeper and enriched by calcium from the bedrock (such as limestone and limy shales or schists)—and often at the base of slopes where downward-moving soils can collect and build—the percentages of white ash, basswood, butternut, and black cherry increase. At the higher elevations, usually between 2500 and 2800 feet, heart-leaved paper birch—sometimes growing almost as a monoculture—marks the transition to the boreal forest. In more poorly drained areas, hemlock, red maple, and American elm are more frequent (less so elm due to its

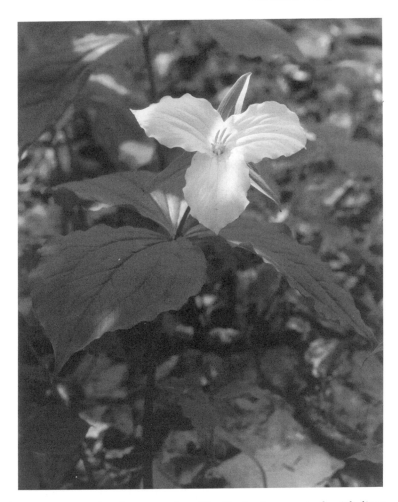

White Trillium. This showy member of the lily family grows in the rich, limy soils west of the Green Mountains, especially in the Champlain Valley. Its Latin species name, grandiflorum, refers to the size of its flower—the largest of our native trilliums. "Trillium" refers to its parts, each appearing in threes: leaves, petals, sepals, and seeds. Photo by Louis Borie.

decimation by Dutch elm disease; see below). On drier sites and especially in the southern half of the state, red oak is a more regular component, and white pine may persist for some time and grow to considerable size.

The northern hardwoods merge with the so-called *transition hardwoods* of southern New England in the relatively milder regions of Vermont—the Champlain Lowlands, Valley of Vermont, flanks of the Taconics, and the Connecticut River Valley—with oaks, hickories, black birch, and others becoming more common. Species composition changes markedly depending on bedrock, soils, and local climatic conditions. On drier, hilly slopes red oak, white oak, and shagbark hickory often mix with northern hardwood species. Where soils are thinnest and driest—steep slopes and ridgetops, particularly—grow chestnut oak (and rarely yellow, or chinkapin, oak), bitternut hickory, hophornbeam, and others. More restricted to the clay soils of Champlain Valley bottomlands are bur oak and, especially along riverbanks and wetlands, swamp white oak. Atop the scenic bluffs of limestone and dolostone overlooking many sections of Lake Champlain are northern white cedar, red pine, and white pine.

Species composition of the hardwood forests has changed over the thousands of years since deglaciation, with some changes due to slow climatic shifts, some to the manipulations or indirect influences of human beings. We know, for example, that Vermont's climate has at different times been much colder (peri- and postglacial periods) and warmer (hypsithermal interval) than today's, resulting in great shifts in the type of vegetation growing here. Rare relicts of these vastly different eras still persist, of the former in the disjunct tundra communities and the latter in individuals and small pockets of trees and shrubs of more southern U.S. distribution, such as tulip poplar, black gum, sycamore, black oak, redbud, flowering dogwood, sassafras, and great and mountain laurels.

From analysis of pollen in bogs and lake sediments, early town survey records, and other sources of information, we also are fairly certain that at the time of European contact with the New World, beech and American chestnut, in particular, were much larger components of the hardwoods: beech dropping from as high as 40 to 60 % to today's 10, chestnut from 15 to 20% to virtually zero. (In beech the change is attributable to a one-two punch of the timber industry favoring more valuable species such as ash and maple and the debilitating epidemic of nectria disease. Nectria is a European fungus that enters the tree via tiny holes made by the beech scale insect; the nectria/scale complex first appeared in Nova Scotia in the late 1800s and has slowly worked its way south ever since.)

The chestnut had been one of the most important trees in the eastern forests, for wildlife (its nuts provided bountiful food for wild turkey, deer, and many others), for human utility (durable, easily worked, handsome, and rot-resistant wood), and for its sheer beauty. But in 1904 an Asiatic fungus on nursery stock of Chinese chestnut was brought to New York and spread to the American chestnut. Within fifty years the American chestnut went from being one of the most common species of the hardwoods to virtual extinction, with certain but unknown ecological consequences. In Vermont, the chestnut survives only as occasional blight-resistant sprouts, a few venerable old individuals, and, most poignantly, as fallen trees that have not yet rotted away into history.

The human-induced threats to tree species, and therefore to forest composition, are a constant worry, especially in this age of quick, worldwide transportation of goods. Besides chestnut blight, Dutch elm disease (a fungus brought into the United States in 1909 with the European elm bark beetle) has wrought havoc among native American elms, and gypsy moth (escaped from a laboratory in Massachusetts in the 1860s where researchers were experimenting with the species as silk producers, and first noticed in Vermont in 1912) has had devastating impacts on hardwoods, particular oaks.

More recent threats loom, too.

White ash has been experiencing a decline of vigor, and later death, by what is generally referred to as "ash yellows." This was first noticed in the 1920s, but has most severely affected trees in the 1950s and 1960s; it continues as a severe problem up to the present (1997), particularly in southern Vermont. Current research indicates that this complicated condition is probably caused by a mycoplasma-like organism (a fungus or bacterium that affects the phloem) interacting with a virus and intensified by stress from pollutants, climate change, drought, and/or freezing.

The hemlock woolly adelgid, a moth accidentally introduced from Asia in the 1960s, has killed great numbers of hemlock in Pennsylvania and southern New England and could easily spread north, prompting Vermont and other states to institute quarantines on shipment of logs and nursery stock.

Butternut has been a valuable tree for as long as humans have lived on this continent. Native Americans and early white settlers used its nuts extensively, the meats for food and "butter" (oils skimmed off when boiled), the shells and bark for dyes; its wood now is used in furniture making. However, butternut is a species in trouble across its range. First discovered in 1967 but perhaps present in this country since the turn of the century, a canker of unknown origin has been attacking the trees, with devastating results. In fact, forest ecologists now have grave concerns over its future in the northeast.

Pear thrips, a tiny European insect that in its native habitat feeds mostly on leaves of fruit trees, was discovered in Vermont in 1985, attacking the buds and new leaves of hardwoods, peaking in 1988 with defoliation of nearly half a million acres, mostly in southern and south-central Vermont. As with gypsy moth, pear thrips populations now seem to be cycling from highs to lows, with impacts of high years still threatening to be severe.

Plants

So the picture of Vermont's plants is not simple, the state's being situated as it is, between several distinct forest types, the Northern and Southern, the Eastern and Western. When the great variety of landscapes, soils, bedrocks, and habitats is added as another component of the makeup of Vermont, we see the reason for Frank Seymour's statement, in *The Flora of Vermont*, that the flora here is *five* times as diverse as the rest of New England's.

Before the new leaves of the forest have unfurled completely, even before the snow has gone in many places, the wildflowers begin to blossom as the sun warms the sodden ground. The spring wildflowers ("spring ephemerals") of the Eastern United States are a special—in fact unique—flora. As in the case of the trees, China has a similar spring flora, since it has similar geographical and climate regions, yet even there the species do differ considerably from those of North America. The native herbaceous plants of Vermont are mostly perennials, taking many years to grow to flowering age, and each fall dying back to a rootstalk. They bloom very quickly during that brief time between the end of winter and the full leafing out of the trees, when the canopy closes out the sun. Broadly distributed in the more generalized northern hardwood habitat are such early-blooming wildflowers as violets, red trillium, Canada mayflower (false lily-of-the-valley), and spring beauties.

Where soils are thicker and richer, and especially where calcium has leached out of the parent rocks, the diversity of species increases dramatically. Very early in spring rises bloodroot, with its delicate, almost ethereal white flower. Like other members of the poppy family, bloodroot has an opaque, poisonous sap, but, as noted by its name, the sap is red rather than the usual white. In addition to bloodroot, blue cohosh, round and sharp-lobed hepaticas, spring beauty, Virginia waterleaf, and a number of others sometimes carpet this forest floor. Curiously, one common species of the rich woods, especially along river bottomlands, wild leek (or wild onion) puts up its leaves at this time; its flowers come later, after the leaves have died. This is the plant whose Abenaki name of "winooski" has been given to a major river and town in Vermont.

Trilliums seem to be everywhere. The most common, red trillium, grows throughout the region. The larger and less common white trillium is restricted to the limy soils near Lake Champlain and its islands; in fact, the best colonies of white trillium, nowhere common in New England, occur here—some places look as if they are covered with snow when it blossoms. Painted trillium grows in the intermediate elevations where conifers become more plentiful and the environments tend toward boreal in character.

Smaller flowers open daily under the increasing warmth of the spring sun. Depending on the site are the violets, in all their shades, the perfect spires of foamflower, the stars of starflower, the variable-colored round-lobed hepatica, and the nodding, yellow dog-tooth violet, or trout lily (so called for the markings on its leaves, which resemble a brook trout's). Above the tracery of blue-green leaves dangle wind-flowers and Dutchman's breeches. And on rare occasions the wood-land traveler comes across the purple-and-white flowers of the showy orchis, one of the state's few woodland orchids.

Flowers that come later in the spring are usually not so conspicu-ous. Jack-in-the-pulpit hides its cluster of fleshy flowers at the base of a leafy cup. The purple-brown flower of wild ginger often goes unno-ticed, since it is at or below the leaf litter on the ground, at the base of the plant's two heart-shaped leaves. Wild sarsaparilla, a widespread plant in Vermont that looks like a small, misshapen white-ash seedling, has a green spiked ball of nondescript flowers beneath a parasol of leaves.

Through the summer, colors continue to subside and even fewer flowers are to be seen in the deeper shade cast by the trees. A group of tiny woodland orchids, collectively called rattlesnake plantains, that bloom from midsummer to fall are often overlooked because they are so small. Their leaves are usually only 1 to 2 inches long and pressed against the ground; their greens blend perfectly with the surroundings.

Jack-in-the-pulpit. The so-called "Indian Turnip," whose root, though ex-tremely acrid when raw, is edible when dried or roasted. It was supposedly used by Native Americans as we use potatoes. The flowers are small and clumped inside the lower portion of the "pulpit," at the base of the "jack." The fruit when ripe in the fall looks like a small, red ear of corn. Drawing by Ann Pesiri Swanson.

The patterns of the veins on the leaves give the appearance of snake skins, hence the species' name.

Certain wild flowers signal autumn's approach. Bottle, or closed, gentian is such a flower, growing along many trails at the forest's edges. (This plant is so named because its flowers generally do not open, but remain shut like a bud, looking like a bottle. When the flowers open briefly for pollination by bees, the insects that linger too long inside get trapped.) The first frost may have taken place or not be far away, even in the guardianship of the woodlands, when two asters appear—whorled aster and white wood aster, both of which have white flowers. These two are members of a large worldwide "modern" family (*Asteraceae*, formerly *Compositae*), most of which are field species, such as dandelions, sunflowers, daisies, thistles, and goldenrods. In richer sites, zig-zag goldenrod blooms.

The wild flowers add an attractive dimension to the forests, but other kinds of plants also make an important aesthetic contribution to Vermont's woodland scenery. Most notable are the ferns and their allies the clubmosses and horsetails. Our state has more than 50 species of ferns and many more hybrids, perhaps half of which occur in the hardwood forest, its edges, and closely related but specialized habitats. The ferns, clubmosses, and horsetails we see here today are relatives of the tree-sized species that existed more than 200 million years ago in the huge, sprawling inland swamps of Pangaea. It was the incredible amounts of peat (partially decomposed organic matter) produced by the decomposition of these plants—their trunks, leaves, and even spores—that went into the making of the enormous coal deposits mined today in the United States and elsewhere.

There seems to be a fern for every situation. Many are tolerant of a wide variety of environmental conditions, and thus are widespread (e.g., intermediate woodfern and lady fern). Others, however, are more restricted to the rich, moist woodlands of broad-leaved trees. Still others prefer the younger open woods, where the light floods in. Even the wet bottomlands and riverbanks have their own species, such as crested shield fern, marsh fern, and ostrich fern, the last being the "fiddlehead" fern of spring foragers.

In limestone areas with cliffs, ravines, forest pockets, and other unusual landforms one may discover some of New England's rarer fern species. Many of these are probably disjuncts from both the north and south. The Vermont Valley, adjacent slopes of the Taconics and Green Mountains, and the eastern side of the Champlain Lowlands form a gallery of interesting, unusual ferns. The Brandon region at its center is sometimes called the "fern capital of the East" because of this diversity. Such exotic species as narrow-leaved spleenwort and male fern grow in the cold, moist ravines, while wall rue and slender cliffbrake hide in the ledges of cliffs and outcroppings.

Similarly, in northern Vermont are two rare species—both close relatives of the more common calciphilic maidenhair fern—that have evolved in close, indeed inextricable, association with serpentine. Green Mountain maidenhair, a state threatened species, is restricted to Vermont and Quebec, while serpentine maidenhair is more widely distributed in the United States, Canada, and Mexico, yet still dependent on the rock for which it is named.

Mammals

The mammals in Vermont's hardwood forests, especially the larger animals, have figured importantly in the state's economy through the years, both in the early days of white habitation, when trappers supplied fur to markets far beyond Vermont's borders, and now, when hunting and other recreations dealing directly or indirectly with wild animals are so popular.

In many ways, mammals have been the barometers of what has happened to the land. Numerous species were driven out by the initial cutting of the virgin forests; some left and never returned, but others—often with human help—have come back with vigor to the new forests of the twentieth century.

Before the white settler ever set foot in Vermont, far-ranging wilderness mammals lived over the region. The caribou, today found mostly in Canada and Alaska, was undoubtedly here, probably living in coniferous-forest swamps. So, too, was the elk, or wapiti, now an inhabitant of only our Western mountainous states, but which formerly was the most widely distributed of North American hoofed animals. It is certain the elk was in Vermont, because its antlers and bones have been found in a bog in the western part of the state. The scourge of the northland wilds, the wolverine, a large weasel of legendary ferocity, once lived at the northern limit of the state. And the bison, too, may have roamed into southern Vermont, where the burning of the forest by Native Americans produced an open range that would have been suitable for grazing. Although we have no evidence of the bisons' presence in Vermont, it is highly likely they lived here, as their bones have been found in Massachusetts, near Cape Cod.

These species disappeared early, being true wilderness sojourners and incompatible with the changes brought by the white settlers. They probably were gone prior to 1750. Others remained into times of denser settlement but eventually they gave way to land clearing and civilization. The timber wolf was one of the more famous of these animals.

Long the stereotyped villain of tooth-and-claw ferocity, the wolf was hated and persecuted by early sheep and cattle farmers, who saw it as the archenemy of their herds. An early Vermont historian, Samuel Williams, wrote in 1794:

> One of the most common and noxious of all animals is the WOLF. . . . His eyes generally appear sparkling; and there is a wildness, and a fierceness,

in his looks. . . . This animal is extremely fierce, sanguinary, and carnivorous. When a number of them associate, it is not for peace, but for war and destruction. the animal, at which they most of all aim, is the sheep. . . . They attack the deer, foxes, rabbits, and are enemies to all other animals; and their attacks are generally attended with the most horrid howlings. . . . There is nothing valuable in these animals but their skins. . . .

The wolf was bountied in 1779 and from that time until about 1820 it was a great sport to organize wolf hunts that served the purpose of ridding the countryside of what was seen as a severe danger. Concurrently, the breakup of the vast tracts of wilderness forest drastically reduced the territory the wolf required for its hunting. Together these factors served a death warrant to the timber wolf, and by 1900 it was gone from this region.

The history of the catamount in Vermont ("cat of the mountain," otherwise known as the mountain lion, puma, panther, or painter) is not unlike that of the timber wolf. This large feline—the largest ever recorded in Vermont weighed 182 pounds—was feared for its strength and allegedly wanton predation. It even had the reputation of hunting human beings. Evidently the stories were not completely fanciful, as authentic accounts relate how men and horses were chased. Even so, there is no record of deaths due to the mountain lion. Like the wolf, the catamount was bountied in the very early years of settlement, in 1779. Although questionable bounties were still being paid as late as 1894, it is believed that the last cat in Vermont was the one killed thirteen years earlier in the town of Barnard. This individual was mounted and is now on display at the Vermont Historical Society Museum in Montpelier.

Persistent rumors, many reported sightings, and even a few specimens (shot or found dead) in New York and Quebec over the years have kept alive the idea—the hope, for some—that the catamount has returned to Vermont, or perhaps has been here all along. The sighting of an adult and two young in Craftsbury in 1993, with subsequent recovery of scat containing catamount hair (confirmed by the U.S. Fish and Wildlife Laboratory), heightened the prospect even more, but did not dispel the doubts of many wildlife biologists familiar with mountain lions from other parts of the country.

The arguments against their permanent presence here are several. DNA analysis of all the cougars killed in the Northeast have shown that they are not the eastern cougar (*Puma concolor cougar*), but other (southern) races. Moreover, the hair in the scat of the Craftsbury animal was never DNA tested. The logical explanation is that animals seen are captives (legally obtained or not) that have escaped or been released into the wild.

Also, there is no evidence of a breeding population in Vermont, especially one big enough to support itself and avoid the perils of in-

Catamount (Mountain Lion, Puma). (Top) The last catamount shot in Vermont, posed with Alexander Crowell, who killed it in 1881 near the town of Barnard, in central Vermont. It was also the largest catamount on state record, weighing 182½ pounds and measuring 7 feet from nose to tip of tail. It now stands as a mounted specimen, beside the gun that shot it, in the Vermont Historical Society Museum in Montpelier. (Bottom) Emblem of wildness: a native returned, or still a fleeting uncertainty? Photos by Susan C. Morse (bottom) and courtesy Vermont Historical Society (top).

breeding. One authoritative biologist estimates a minimum of 250 adults would be needed for this.

If the cougars being seen are not escapees, might they not be at least transients, having dispersed from other areas of the country? If so, they would have to be coming from some place where they are known to live in the wild and, as far as we know, those places are only the southern tip of Florida and the Black Hills of South Dakota, either way over a thousand miles from here. As one expert cougar biologist has put it, "There is a whole lot of cougar-unfriendly habitat between here and there—cities, towns, roads, developments, and farmland."

So for now, as it has been for some time, the catamount remains an elusive, problematic member of our native fauna. It is a symbol, in a way, of a wildness we once had and of the potential for that possibility again.

These are the most vivid examples of animals that were too sensitive to endure the coming of the white settlers and the changes they brought. They fuel our imagination about the nature of that former Vermont. Most appear to have gone for good, their homes too much altered or their ways back too remote and full of obstacles for them to return. Despite this demise for many animals, however, there are others that, on the way to extinction, reversed their decline and have come back strongly. Often we have helped them return.

The white-tailed deer—a symbol of Vermont, in a way—is our most popular game animal, the embodiment of a rural, tempered wildness. It is a mammal of versatility and great adaptability. We all know it, but we almost lost it.

In the virgin forests of America the white-tailed deer apparently was present in substantial numbers, providing much food and clothing for Native Americans. But the arrival of white settlers and loggers soon changed that: deer were hunted the year round, supplying commercial meat markets; their forest habitat dwindled; no laws protected them. Their population dropped precipitously within a relatively short period of time.

Even before Vermont was a state, people were aware of the plight of the deer. The first laws to protect them here were established in 1741 by the New Hampshire Grants (the land of Vermont was at that time divided down the Green Mountains, belonging to the "New Hampshire Grants" to the east of them, and New York State to the west). As an independent territory, Vermont in 1779 set its first statute prohibiting the hunting of deer, from January 10 to June 10. This was the first closed season and it coincided with the institution of bounties on the deer's natural predators, the wolf and the catamount.

But despite this protection the deer had great trouble recovering from its earlier decline, and by 1800 it was nearly extinct in the East. In response, game laws became stiffer, the closed seasons longer, and ultimately it became illegal to hunt deer in Vermont (1865–1895).

White-Tailed Deer. A big buck in the fall. The species in Vermont was nearly extirpated in the mid-1800s, owing to the clearing of its wooded habitat, but it is now the most abundant large mammal in the state. Its population here probably exceeds 120,000 (1997). The deer's prime territory is the hills of the southern half of the state. Photo by John Hall.

But slowly the scene changed. To bolster the almost non-existent population, deer were brought to Vermont from out of state and released. All the while, the deer-preying wolves and catamounts continued to decline to insignificant proportions, and over time the forests made a comeback from the height of land clearing earlier in the century. With protective laws even tighter, freedom from predation, and shelter and food from the new forests, the whitetail's fortunes changed dramatically. By 1930 deer were once again secure in Vermont—as it turned out, too secure for their own good.

The white-tailed deer was supremely equipped to take advantage of the evolving Vermont. It throve on the interspersion of fields and forests, young timber and old, hardwoods and softwoods. It browsed on the vigorous low growth of the young forest, and fattened in the fall on the nuts of beech, oak, and hickory. It grazed on the sweet grasses of fields and the grains of standing crops. It retired to the haven of the softwoods for winters, where it found cover and food. In short, the way we shaped the land suited the deer's needs very well.

Our well-intentioned protectiveness, perhaps inherited from earlier years when deer were so few, allowed them to overpopulate their range. As a result, each year thousands faced starvation, especially during the lean times of winter, when twigs and buds within a small radius of the deer yards (wintering grounds) are the only available foods. Many of the animals that didn't starve were malnourished and weakened to the point that they were susceptible to disease and stress, from which they eventually died.

By the mid 1940s, their numbers had grown so much that biologists and foresters began to worry about the effects of too many animals for the habitat available: smaller, weaker deer; overbrowsing of winter "yarding" areas, which, when combined with especially hard winters, caused mass starvation; negative impact on hardwood forest regeneration because of their heavy consumption of seedlings; more encroachment on agricultural crops, to the ire of farmers; more collisions with automobiles. Through the 1970s, their population went through unhealthy boom-and-busts, from dangerous overabundance to precipitous lows.

State biologists wanted to rectify the situation by a long-term, two-prong approach: maintain high-quality habitat statewide, and have fewer but bigger and healthier individuals. This way, they felt, the state could achieve a sustainable population of deer, and thus sustainable hunting. However, attempts to reduce the high populations by allowing antlerless (female and young) hunting, successfully instituted in many other states for the same reasons, proved unpopular with Vermont hunters and the public, and failed in a storm of political controversy.

Undaunted, the Vermont Fish and Wildlife Department has pursued its goals through other means, bolstered greatly by its new efforts to involve the public deeply in management planning and decisions, but also by critical habitat protection and diversification of hunting opportunities (bow and arrow, black powder). With a relatively healthy population estimated now between 120,000 and 140,000, Vermont wildlife biologists are cautiously optimistic about the future of the whitetailed deer, and of the major sport that depends on them.

Although the white-tailed deer were a great and unexpected boon to the early white inhabitants of Vermont, as a source of both food and clothing, beavers drew the most intense interest, because their pelts were in high demand in Europe for fashionable fur hats. White traders from the fur companies accordingly hired the natives to supply them with beaver and other skins. The result was that within a short time after this trade was begun, many mammals in the East had been trapped to near-extermination. This relentless, single-minded plundering of the beaver, accompanied by the clearing of its prime habitat across the country, caused the animal to fall close to extinction in a broad region from the Atlantic seaboard to the Mississippi River. Zadock Thompson in 1849 remarked that this once common mammal in Vermont was probably gone from the state even before the middle part of that century.

Again, our immediate remedial action to cure this "sickness" was to institute protective laws. Beavers were first afforded year-round protection in Vermont in 1900. This measure brought little success, however, so that attempts were then made to restock the depleted population. In 1921 several animals were live-trapped out of state and brought to southern Vermont, and in 1932 some beavers imported from Maine were released in Vermont's northeast. All the while, the forests were rising anew, offering quantities of vigorously growing aspen, a favorite commodity of the beaver for its food and building materials.

Thanks to these efforts, today this largest North American native rodent is firmly reestablished in Vermont, as well as other New England states, and it is now highly successful on its own. Many people have seen the work of the beaver—felled trees, dams, lodges—if not the wary animal itself. It is now of sufficient numbers to allow trapping during a regulated season in winter, and in some areas it has actually become a serious pest, causing floods and gnawing into young timber stands.

Though beavers were the most plentiful and sought-after furbearers before white settlement, another mammal was the most valuable, per pelt, of any in the forest. The elusive and mystical fisher, often called "fisher-cat," sold for as much as $350 for a fine pelt, an enormous sum in the seventeenth century, not to say today.

Despite its name, the fisher neither primarily fishes for its food, nor is it a kind of cat. It is really a large weasel, with males weighing up to 12 pounds (the females much less), similar in shape to the marten, but sleeker, blacker, and bigger.

The fisher was never abundant in Vermont, because it requires a large home range: it is estimated that one animal's territory is 3 to 4 square miles, but within this area it may actually crisscross a total of 100 miles in its hunting. And since it was such a prize to trappers, and one of the easier mammals to trap, even the relatively few in Vermont were soon depleted, their extermination greatly accelerated by the clearing of the forest. Like the beaver, the fisher was to all intents extinct in our state by the mid-1800s.

Being a night hunter and an efficient predator, the fisher has been endowed with an aura of ferocity and evil comparable to that of the wolverine. It has been credited with carrying off dogs, cattle, and even children! The stories become ever more fanciful. But one of its real prey, an unlikely one at that, has played a decisive role in both its depletion and restoration: the porcupine. The fisher is one of the porcupine's few natural predators, being agile and quick enough to knock the porcupine out of a tree and attack its unprotected belly without getting quilled, although apparently it can withstand some quills without detrimental effects.

As the young forest matured in the last quarter of the nineteenth century and the first quarter of this one, porcupines became a serious

Forest Mustelids. Two members of the weasel family (Mustelidae) in Vermont's woodlands. The mink (top) prefers forested riparian areas (streamsides and riversides) and wetlands where it dens and hunts for mostly aquatic prey. Note distinctive white chin patch. The larger fisher (bottom) ranges widely and concentrates on terrestrial animals for its food. Note paired, zigzag tracks, typical of all weasels when running.   Photos by Susan C. Morse (top) and John Hall (bottom).

problem to the wood-based economy of Vermont, as they ate their way through the bark of many valuable timber trees. Porcupines grew rapidly in number, encouraged by the ideal habitat of the revived forest, the abundance of food, and an absence of enemies.

To combat this problem the Vermont Department of Forests and Parks, in cooperation with the Vermont Fish and Wildlife Department and the U.S. Fish and Wildlife Service, began a program in 1959 to restore fishers to the state, a recolonization the animals apparently were unable to do on their own. Theoretically, fishers could, in a natural way, control porcupines more effectively and cheaply than could human beings, with their artificial means of control. Between 1959 and 1967 124 fishers were live-trapped in Maine, brought to Vermont, and released in porcupine-problem areas. These imports were to supplement any native stock that might still remain and provide the nucleus for a renewed population.

The program has worked well: it appears that fishers have returned to their rightful place in Vermont. They have taken hold quickly, expanded their range perhaps even farther south than the original one, and have proved a significant control on the porcupines. They have built such a strong population here that they may now be trapped, as has been done under a highly monitored season since 1974. From trapping results wildlife biologists will gain insights into the population dynamics of this exciting "black ghost" of the forest.

The white-tailed deer, beaver, and fisher are some old acquaintances that have gone through hard times, at first hurt by our hand but later helped by us. There is at least one animal, however, that is almost brand new to the state, having made it here quite on its own, even in spite of us: the coyote.

No coyote had been seen in Vermont before 1948, but from the time of that first appearance until now it has found its way into nearly every section of the state—indeed, throughout the East. Many people have heard its ringing nighttime howls during the winter mating season or seen it loping along a field or through the forest.

The race here is the eastern coyote, distinct from its smaller counterpart, the western coyote. The eastern is believed to have acquired a larger size through generations of crossbreeding with the timber wolf of northern Michigan and Ontario. One author has named it "new wolf" for its characteristics intermediate between the wolf and the coyote. It is a pure breed and not a dog-coyote cross (the "coydog"; such crosses do take place but offspring after the first generation are a mixed litter, the individuals bearing the attributes of one or the other parent, or even earlier forebears; this means that coydogs do not breed true, and thus are not a distinct species).

The coyote's amazingly rapid immigration to Vermont, probably via Canada, is due to several factors: its ability in many ways to take

Coyote. One of the state's newer species, in the winter forest. This scavenger-predator has immigrated steadily eastward in the United States, arriving in Vermont in 1948. It now lives in every corner of the state. Photo by Susan C. Morse.

the place of the wolf, a high reproductive rate (the average litter is 6), the absence of natural predators, a renowned cunning, and an omnivorous, scavenging, opportunistic feeding habit. It is also a most hardy soul, having survived bullet holes, feet severed in traps, and, in one case, a missing lower jaw.

This wild canine has been criticized as a despoiler of deer populations, but the claim is unjust, for evidence shows that predation on deer is exception rather than the rule. A coyote occasionally may bring down a weak, injured, or sick deer, but does not have the means to cope with a strong, healthy one. More likely, it will eat the carcass of a deer previously killed by free-running domestic dogs or dead from other causes.

The coyote has been an important addition to our fauna—for most people a welcome one—providing a legitimate service as a scavenger, cleaning up remains within the natural community. It is one large mammal that can live alongside people and still remain wild, two traits our burgeoning civilization is increasingly requiring of wildlife.

But the mixed forests of Vermont continue to harbor its share of true wildlife, which can stir within us the romantic feelings only distance from humanity can bring. Perhaps none does this so well as the black bear.

Few people have seen this large animal (weighing up to 500 pounds), whose numbers in Vermont are estimated at around 2,500

L
P
S

Black Bear Habitat. The three types of areas used by bears in Vermont:

P = Bear production habitat. Regions frequently used by bears, including cub-producing females. Generally is contiguous and remote forest land. Contains habitat critical to bear survival and reproduction.

S = Seasonal habitat. Regional frequently used by bears, often containing critical seasonal feeding areas or vital travel corridors.

L = Low-use area. Regions infrequently used by bears.

Note where P and S zones become narrow (e.g., south-central and north-central parts of the state). These "bottlenecks" are especially critical and vulnerable to developments that might cut off north-south movement. Map courtesy Vermont Fish and Wildlife Department and Vermont Agency of Natural Resources.

(1997). It is reclusive, wary of human beings, most often seen by hunters in the fall, when it is preoccupied with gorging on nuts, berries, fruit, seeds, honey, and insect larvae in preparation for its dormancy in winter. The black bear does not truly hibernate, like a woodchuck and some bats, whose metabolic processes grind to a near-halt and body temperatures fall to within a few degrees of freezing. Rather, it semihibernates for long periods, occasionally stirring during winter's warmer spells. Its temperature remains close to normal and the female even brings forth her tiny young (weighing only a few ounces) every other year during this rest. Bears emerge from dormancy looking healthy, plump, and as if they had been active all winter, but soon become emaciated and ravenous, searching feverishly for food.

The black bear has experienced many ups and downs in its residency in Vermont. It was bountied as late as the 1940s, as a supposed threat to people, sheep, and crops. Its numbers are low enough now so that hunting results must be closely scrutinized, and biologists and wildlife managers must recommend timely management actions for its continued well-being. The great threat to the bear, as for so many wild animals, is the destruction of the habitat it needs to survive—the

Black Bear. Although this is the smallest species of bear in North America, individuals can reach weights over 500 pounds (Vermont's record to date is 525 pounds, a bear killed in Norton in 1965). The breeding season here is as early as June and July, but development of the fetuses is slow. The young, weighing only a few ounces, are born in winter to semihibernating sows, and then they remain with their mother for about 16 months. Sibling cubs stay together for another year, after which the family ties are broken and the bears become quite solitary. Photo by Susan C. Morse.

development of large currently unsettled forests will certainly have adverse effects on this grand and imposing creature.

The bobcat, too, has gone full circle in its relationship with humans, having been bountied until 1971 and now being protected by a restricted hunting season, which was initiated in 1976 and tightened in 1978. Contrary to its reputation, this predator feeds very little on deer, but rather mostly on rodents, small game, and, extensively, carrion. It is a mammal that intrigues us, but about which we know very little. Scant data are available about its life or population in Vermont, but perhaps a thousand live in the remote, rocky ledges or swamps of the state, undoubtedly many fewer than in presettlement times, yet more than at the probable low point of fifty years ago.

All these mammals have experienced one thing in common, change. Disappearing, reappearing, fluctuating, immigrating. And regardless of human influences and intentions, change will always be the way of nature. Such patterns are not restricted to these glorified members of the Vermont forest wildlands, either. Many of the "lower" mammals have also exhibited them.

The gray fox, for example, has worked its way into Vermont from Southern states and now lives in every forested region here. (Zadock Thompson in 1849 gave only brief mention of it, as it had not then extended is range far into Vermont.) This tree-climbing brother of the red fox is still a relatively unknown species, because its fur has not been desired for pelts as has the red fox's, and it stays deeper in the forest, rarely coming out in the open.

As could be expected in such a forested state, squirrels have done well in Vermont, although they, too, have experienced change. Red squirrels have always been abundant in the coniferous and mixed woods, as have the less noticed, nocturnal northern flying squirrels. The population of eastern gray squirrels, of deciduous areas, has fluctuated more, though they have never been scarce. (In the 1700s the black squirrel, now known to be identical to the gray squirrel except for its coat color, lived here in considerable numbers; in fact, it is estimated that they were as common as grays. However, for unknown reasons, the numbers dwindled in the following century and they are now completely gone from the forests, leaving us familiar with only the gray phase.) The gray squirrel undertakes periodic mass migrations, apparently triggered by poor nut years—following fast on the heels of years of abundance—which have allowed their numbers to build. One major migration took place in 1936, when hordes moved across Vermont from east to west, through the trees, over land, swimming the rivers and ponds.

Even the smallest of Vermont's mammals show pronounced high and lows in population from one year to the next. White-footed mice (of the woodlands) and deer mice (of fence rows, shrubs, and forest

Foxes. The gray fox (top) is less often encountered than its longer snouted cousin, the red fox (bottom), due to its more reclusive nature and deeper woods habitat. Coyotes apparently have supplanted both species to some degree, less so the gray fox, probably due to its ability to climb trees (aided by its claws, curved like a cat's) and thereby to avoid direct conflict. Photos by John Hall (top) and Susan C. Morse (bottom).

edges) are undoubtedly dependent upon the seed crop and its availability throughout the winter, the severity of winter, and other variables. Predation helps to control their numbers, but increased predation is usually a response to increased numbers of the prey and only later becomes instrumental as a damper on population size.

Vermont forests house one marsupial—a primitive mammal that suckles its young in a pouch called the marsupium—the opossum. A native of South America, it is one of the champion long-distance movers as far as mammals are concerned. It has progressed north through Central America and up the length of the United States, and first appeared in Vermont in 1920. Though primarily a resident of the transition hardwood regions, it has marched almost to the northern border, one showing up in Maidstone State Forest in 1977. With its naked tail, muzzle, and ears, it is seemingly ill prepared for the harsh winters here, but climate has not been a deterrent to its dispersal—it has gone from tropics to sub-Arctic zones despite a few frozen-off tail ends and tips of ears!

In many ways, the hardwood forests are more difficult places for mammals to pass the winter than the boreal forest. Without the protection of the leaves on the trees, the winds penetrate more bitterly and the snow accumulates in greater packs. Night can be brutal, as any heat gained during the day is quickly reradiated to the open sky. But the greatest threat to survival is the scarcity of food in these areas during the cold months.

To cope with the problems of the winter forest, animals have arrived at several solutions. A few hibernate in the true sense of the word. Others, such as black bears, chipmunks, squirrels, striped skunks, and raccoons, go into semihibernation, from which they can emerge during a January thaw or other warm spell to recharge themselves on food stored or found in nearby sources. White-tailed deer and moose move out of the hardwoods and into the softwoods, where they find food and shelter. They also grows a new coat of hollow, insulating hair for the winter. And some species keep up the search for food all winter within the hardwoods: the white-footed mouse and the insectivores, a group of insect-eating mammals that includes the mole and the shrew.

These small winter-active animals, with their extremely high metabolisms, demand a near-continual supply of food; they can starve within hours of eating. In winter they live beneath the snow. The odd-looking star-nosed mole works underground in the moist soil of lowlands and especially near lakes, deeper in the winter than in the summer as it moves down below the frost line in search of prey. It uses its fleshy tentacled nose to sense the movement of earthworms or grubs, then digs furiously with its spadelike front paws to reach them. A smaller relative, the short-tailed shrew, scours higher up either in the humus and leaf litter of the soil or in the low vegetation itself. This is the most widely distributed insectivore in Vermont, occurring across many types of habitats, at many elevations. Though small, it is a fearless hunter day or night and will attack mice and other prey larger than itself, as well as earthworms, insects, land snails, and other terrestrial organisms. The presence of this and other shrews is obvious in winter from the maze of tunnels that course through the snow.

Thus season by season, as well as century by century, the Vermont forest changes, and the animal inhabitants must follow its lead, either in the normal cycles of their lives or in response to what happens to their land. The mammals, whether the exciting wildlife of forest lore or the lowly creatures more in evidence, have been central to these intricate plays: the same stage, different scenes and actors.

Birds

After the piercing winds and cold-white silences of winter, the Vermont forests soften under the spring song of birds. But these sounds of rebirth actually begin much earlier, for those who tune an ear. The great horned owl signals the start of its courtship during warm spells in late January or early February. This largest of our common resident owls is the first bird of the season to mate and raise young in the hardwoods or mixed forests, and since the eggs are usually laid about March 1, the parents must incubate them continuously to protect them from freezing temperatures and heavy snow. Its feathers certainly help in energy conservation: the bird is well insulated from talon to beak, and even the toes and nostrils are covered. Among raptors, the great horned owl has the reputation of being fierce, the fiercest of all owls.

Breeding somewhat later, and slightly smaller and more a resident of moist woodlands and richer bottomlands than the great horned owl, is the barred owl. This species has no "ear" tufts, is steely gray- and brown-streaked, and has one of the most recognizable calls: a hollow, barking phrase that has been described as "who-cooks-for-you, who cooks-for-you-all." The screech owl and the saw-whet owl are the smallest year-round owls in Vermont. Both are cavity-nesters and often use the abandoned holes excavated by woodpeckers. The screech owl is a miniature version of the great horned owl, but has two color phases, red and gray, the reasons for which are not understood. The saw-whet owl is an elfish little thing, half a foot high, and preys on small rodents and insects of the night. It is bold and tame, often perching within arm's reach, at eye level, cocking its head as it looks at you.

March in Vermont is hardly considered full-blown spring if measured by human expectations, with snow still deep in many places and more snowstorms yet to come, but it ushers in the first bird migrants, those that arrive to scrape a living off the previous year's remains in the

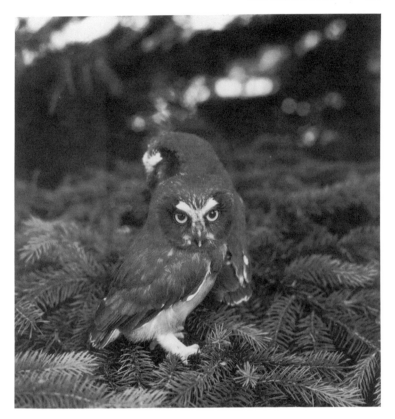

Saw-Whet Owl. A 6-inch-tall owl that lives in the mixed woods in summer, but prefers the protection of conifers in winter. Active mostly at night, it hunts insects and small rodents. Its name comes from one of its "songs"—a thin sound like a saw being filed. It is Vermont's smallest owl. Photo by John Hall.

trees or on the ground, or peck at the emerging signs of new life. Crows return from a winter in the milder lowlands nearby or south, out of state. Phoebes, earliest of all the flycatchers to appear, snag the few insects that have hatched or awakened from hibernation. Later in the month come flickers and yellow-bellied sapsuckers, two common species of woodpecker, in preparation for nesting; the males set up territories, marking the bounds by hammering on hollow trees, sap pails that hang on maple trees, or even tin roofs.

In March, too, comes the plump, peculiar-looking woodcock, a shorebird that for feeding and nesting prefers the upland habitat of forests and forest edges. The woodcock is restricted to the woodlands east of the Great Plains, and Vermont has one of the highest populations anywhere within this region. It has big eyes for night vision, a long, pliable bill for probing for earthworms, and short wings for rapid flight through the trees—attributes that have given this important game bird the colorful local names timber doodle and bog snipe. The male begins a strange but fascinating courtship ritual in early spring, a ceremony unlike any in the bird world. In the evening or early morning, sometimes even in night's darkness, he spirals into the air from his resting spot in a clearing. With a twittering of wings he rises, often to 300 feet or more. Then he drops, chirping, straight down to the spot he left, where he sits motionless, uttering an occasional buzzing "peent." After a while he repeats the performance. This elaborate activity is thought to be an effective way for the male to attract a mate and advertise its territory, as less ostentatious displays might not be noticed at night.

In May, new migrants arrive in the hardwoods daily, most pacing their progress north with the emergence of the myriad hopping, flying, crawling insects that crowd the summers in Vermont. The drab flycatchers return—the large great crested flycatcher to the tree crowns and the medium-sized wood-pewee and the little least flycatcher to branches lower down. They sit almost motionless on their chosen perches until insects fly by, then swoop out to capture them and return to perch again.

Warblers and vireos migrate at night in large flocks, and if grounded by a spring storm they may descend upon the hardwood forest in great variety and number. The two families are similar in size, habit, and appearance. Vireos, however, are slightly larger, slower, and heavier of bill than warblers. Further, male and female vireos look alike, whereas warbler males are the more strikingly marked and brightly colored of the sexes. The red-eyed vireo is considered the most common of all birds in the summer forests of New England; hardly a woodlot seems to be without one. Its repetitious song goes on when other birds are silent, through the day, through the season. Correspondingly, the redstart, a beautiful bird decked out in black and orange in the male, gray and yellow in the female, is likely the most common warbler in Vermont woodlands, favoring the second growth so prevalent here. Both species feed in the upper canopy for the most part, yet drop down to understory saplings for nest building. Each constructs the nest typical of its family—the redstart's is wedged in the vertical prongs of a forked tree branch, the red-eyed vireo's is suspended from horizontal forks of a sapling branch.

Songs reveal the birds. The ovenbird's "teacher-Teacher-TEACHER" is an unmistakable soft-to-loud phrase that swells up from the ground or near it, close to where this species builds its domed-over nest (this shape resembles an old-fashioned brick oven, hence the bird's name). The black-throated blue warbler buzzes up the scale, "trees, trees, trees," from the obscurity of the understory, while the black-and-white warbler courses the trunks of trees much like a nuthatch, issuing a thin, high buzz as it goes.

The thrushes, too, stake out vocal claims on their piece of this seasonal forest home. There is no mistaking their presence: the lucid flutes play from the shaded greens low in the forest and, in the evening especially, these songs impart a peace to the cathedrallike setting. In fact, the family of thrushes is considered to have some of the most beautiful songsters in the world, including the famous "lover's bird" of Europe, the nightingale. Like that species, the North American thrushes often sing at night, often in flight during migration. The three thrushes of Vermont's deciduous forests are the wood thrush, the hermit thrush, and the veery. All are a mellow brown above and white below, but differ in that the wood thrush has a heavily spotted breast and rusty-red head, the hermit a rusty-red tail, and the veery a faintly spotted breast. They are perhaps easiest to identify by song. Though their songs have a similar, beautiful flutelike quality, they are easy to tell apart.

The thrushes of the forest are well camouflaged in their subtle shade of brown, and they keep safely away in the understory and on or near the ground, where they feed and rest. But higher up, more brightly colored species (the males at least) weave in and out of the protective obscurity of the leaves. The male scarlet tanager, for example, the "black-winged red bird" of earlier days, blazons the canopy, and may be heard calling loudly—he is less often seen than heard—from a branch in a tree crown. (The silent and drab gray-green female is rarely seen, as she tends to business of the nest lower down within the branches.) The tanager is fond of oaks, or rather the insects parasitizing oak leaves and acorns.

Sharing the broad-leaved forest with the songbirds, and occasionally dining on them, are the winged predators—the owls mentioned earlier and, especially, the hawks. The accipiters (members of the genus *Accipiter*) are the most forest-oriented hawks, being able to maneuver easily and fly rapidly through tight spaces and the maze of branches. These hawks are equipped with narrow bodies, long tails that act like airplane flaps, and short, rounded wings for fast beats and quick changes of direction. Once the most common accipiter was the Cooper's hawk (the notorious "chicken hawk"), but it has declined sharply in the last ten to fifteen years, and has been considered for endangered status in Vermont. Its northern range seems to be filled more and more by the smaller sharp-shinned hawk and, to a lesser degree, the larger goshawk, both fellow accipiters.

Most of the buteos (the genus of large-bodied, large-winged, fantailed, soaring hawks) enter the forest only for nesting, since they are ill equipped for hunting in confined spaces. They are neither so swift nor so agile as the accipiters, and thus they capture few birds as prey,

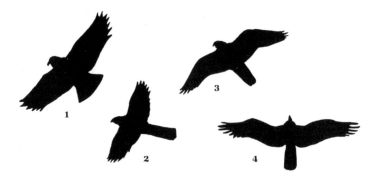

Hawk Silhouettes. Identification of the main groups of hawks is made easier by comparing differences in their silhouettes and flying habits. Size is not exactly proportion here. (1) Buteos: large bodies, broad wings, fan-shaped tails; they soar and circle high. (2) Accipters: smaller bodies, short, rounded wings, long tails; quick and darting fliers with a wingbeat sequence of flap-flap-flap-soar. (3) Falcons: long, pointed wings, long tail; the fastest fliers, with a rowing style of wingbeat. (4) Turkey vultures and harriers (marsh hawks): similar silhouettes, with long wings and tails, but vultures have larger bodies and smaller heads; both glide and soar, but vultures hold their wings in a more distinct V and tilt from side to side; harriers often fly very low over meadows or marshlands. Drawing by Charles W. Johnson.

concentrating instead on slower mammals and other land animals. The most common buteo statewide is the red-tailed hawk, usually seen circling high above a meadow or standing watch from a sentinel tree, looking for small rodents, rabbits, snakes, insects, or perhaps an unwary bird. The more streamlined red-shouldered hawk is most often met in its preferred habitat, the wet woods, rich bottomlands, and swampy areas. There it is regarded as the daytime counterpart of the barred owl—one writer mentions an instance of these two predators taking up communal residence, using the same nest, both raising young, but working separate shifts! The smallest of our nesting buteos is also the most complete woodsman: the broad-winged hawk is never far from the forest, staying concealed within its branches or flying close over the tops of trees. It is a rather quiet bird in the breeding season, only occasionally calling "pewee" in flight.

With all their appealing variety, color, song, and activity, the songbirds and raptors (hawks and owls) depart from the forest before we're ready to see them go. Fall migrations begin even before the summer has ended, with many flycatchers leaving in late August and the majority of warblers in September. With nesting done and the young grown to flight, a stillness settles over the forest. A new season is defined by the going of the birds.

The trip is only one peril for the long-distance travelers in an age of rapid development and land conversion. Many of these neotropical migratory birds (those that spend winters in Mexico, the Caribbean, South America, and Central America, and the breeding season in North America) in eastern North America have declined in the past twenty years, some significantly. After much research, most scientists feel the broad-based decline is primarily due to loss or fragmentation of habitat—both on their breeding grounds in the north and at wintering areas in the south. Migratory species are thus in double jeopardy, at risk on either end of their biannual treks.

As mostly forest-interior birds, the neotropical migrants here need fairly substantial blocks of uninterrupted forest for nesting and as protection from predation. As roads and developments punch into or chip away at formerly large blocks, they become divided (physically and ecologically) into smaller parcels. The nonforested parts often become the avenues of access for more urban, edge, or open-land species, such as cowbirds, which lay eggs in nests ("brood parasitism") of forest-interior species, or raccoons and cats that prey on them, their eggs, or their young. As the forest gets ever more divided, favorable habitat becomes continually reduced and predation increases, to where the birds either leave, become nonreproductive, or die.

Long-term studies indicate that as many as 71% of neotropical migrants have declined, some significantly. Among the species in this long list are the broad-winged hawk, black-billed cuckoo, chimney swift, ruby-throated hummingbird, least flycatcher, cliff swallow, house wren, wood thrush, red-eyed vireo, black-and-white warbler, scarlet tanager, indigo bunting, rose-breasted grosbeak, Lincoln's sparrow, and northern oriole.

As we move toward conserving the state's native biological diversity, or biodiversity for short—in all its complexity and for all its implications for how we conduct our lives—forest fragmentation certainly is one of the more critical considerations.

For these birds the migration in fall is less hurried and the period is less concentrated than in the spring. The birds seem to drift south, quietly, without the urgency of the migration that calls them to nest, done now with the defense of territory and the demands of rearing their young. To us, they pass less noticeably, not bunched in great flocks as in spring, and the males of many songbird species have changed their brilliant breeding plumages for less conspicuous fall feathers that they will wear through winter.

Earliest of the hawks to depart is the broad-winged hawk. This species forms large, spectacular flocks (some composed of thousands of birds) that begin to move out in early August, with a peak in mid-September. These flocks use rising thermal air currents to give them lift over the mountains: the birds enter low in the valleys, spiral up the updrafts, then peel off at the top and shoot down and south again. These are the famed "kettles" of broadwings that many people observe from mountain peaks here in Vermont and elsewhere in the East. Along these peaks, too, one may see other hawks passing in their time, the red-tailed and red-shouldered in late October and early November, the sharp-shinned in early October, and the goshawks in early November. (Appreciable numbers of the red-tailed do stay in Vermont, however, for they are able to hunt the open lands throughout the winter.)

Although most of Vermont's birds leave in the fall, a few other than the red-tailed hawks do remain behind. The birds and habitually stay through winter are not necessarily the same individuals year to year, but rather the same species as a whole. These birds have the wherewithal to survive given a source of food, as food, not climate, is the critical factor. This is as true for the seemingly fragile small birds as it is for the large—all can make it through the most frigid times if enough food is available.

Besides the solitary red-tailed hawks, other species of birds form nomadic feeding and roosting flocks for spending the winter in Vermont. Blue jays gang up in small numbers, aggressively searching for seeds, vegetable matter, or the remains of dead animals. Smaller birds, such as the black-capped chickadee and the goldfinch, congregate in larger flocks, scouring the areas for seeds still clinging to trees and shrubs or for hibernating insects and spider eggs tucked in bark crevices.

Sometimes these winter flocks attract individuals of more solitary species. White-breasted nuthatches, for example, are frequent winter companions of chickadees, although they keep to themselves within that loosely formed group. Indeed, the white-breasted nuthatch is one of the few species that shows territorial behavior in winter, as it guards feeding sites from others of its own kind. Moreover, it is unusual in that it maintains the male-female pair bond formed in the breeding season, whereas most small birds break the bond for winter and make a new one the following spring.

Whether or not woodpeckers stay for the winter depends on the diet of each species. The flicker, which feeds on ants, and the yellow-bellied sapsucker, which drinks tree sap, depart for obvious reasons. Some woodpeckers, however, are able in winter to chisel insects—hibernating adults or larvae—from bark or wood, using their long, barbed tongues to reach into the deeper tree recesses. The common hairy and downy woodpeckers remain with us, and are frequent visitors of suet-feeders in towns, as well as the trees of the forest. Pileated woodpeckers also stay, as our largest, nearly crow-sized woodpecker species. Once met it is not easily overlooked, with its great flaming crest, long bill, and resounding "ka-ka-ka-ka" call. Its work is obvious, too—it literally excavates dead trees in search of its favorite meal, the carpenter ant, making gaping holes a foot or so wide and several feet long; sometimes it almost reduces a tree to a pile of chips. It also carves out large cavities for its nest, and though it may nest in the same tree year after year, it never uses the same cavity twice. Perhaps this serves as a prevention against contaminating its young with lice or other parasites that have possibly infested a hole.

The pileated woodpecker has experienced a population resurgence, having fared badly during the years of clear-cutting and the subsequent young forest regrowth, as it requires large mature or old trees for feeding and nesting. Now that such trees are once again part of Vermont's scenery, the species has responded well and appears to be flourishing, much to the delight of winter bird-watchers.

One of the best-known birds of the winter woods is the ruffed grouse, or partridge, as it is known in the Northeast. Like the spruce grouse discussed earlier, it is a chickenlike bird with a big body and short, powerful wings suitable only for brief, fast flights. Owing to its relatively small home range, it eats many different types of food. One researcher found that it will feed on 120 kinds of items, including various insects, seeds, fruits, nuts, catkins, buds, twigs, leaves, needles, bark, and mushrooms.

In winter the ruffed grouse turns to buds as a staple of the diet, and aspen buds are sought most of all. This preference has been noted by wildlife managers, and in one state game-management area where grouse are being encouraged, sections of the forest are periodically clear-cut to allow quaking aspen to thrive (male trees of the species are favored, as their buds are larger and more nutritious than those of the female). To avoid enemies, endure cold spells, or simply spend the night, the ruffed grouse often plunges full-flight into a snowbank and buries itself. Many a cross-country skier or snowshoer has been startled by this bird blasting out from underfoot, in a shower of flakes and thunder of wings. Unfortunately, the grouse is sometimes entombed in this snow den by icy crusts that develop on the surface and prevent its exit.

The ruffed grouse has for a long time been widely distributed over Vermont, wherever mixed open woods exist. Conversely, its larger relative the wild turkey has had a checkered career in Vermont, and has only recently been moving north from the state's southwest corner.

In the time before white settlement the wild turkey lived in this section of Vermont, where ample nut-producing trees supplied its major source of food. The turkey was also plentiful south and west of the state, especially in the mountainous regions of New York, Pennsylvania, and Massachusetts, where beech, oaks, hickories, and American chestnuts provided bounty for this big bird. As these forests fell, however—the chestnut to virtually annihilation by the chestnut blight, a deadly fungal infection brought from overseas, and the others to the heavy cutting of the 1800s—the turkey became rarer and rarer. It is believed to have become extinct in Connecticut by 1813, in Vermont by 1842, and in Massachusetts by 1851; luckily, it always remained in the remote mountains of central Pennsylvania and New York.

With the redevelopment of the forests good turkey habitat returned to Vermont: where the chestnuts once grew, the oaks became even more dominant, offering their acorns as food. But the turkey is a nonmigratory bird and is restrained by geographical barriers such as lakes, rivers, and mountain ranges, so that it was unable to recolonize its former range in Vermont. Accordingly, in 1968–1970 the Vermont Fish and Game Department live-trapped 31 turkeys in New York, brought them to Vermont and released them in prime range in Rutland County. This was the beginning of what is now an unqualified success story. Turkeys have exploded into new areas, bolstered by an active in-state trap-and-transfer program. In a few short years they have reproduced so well and have swelled to such numbers that controlled spring hunting was instituted in 1973 and spring and fall seasons were opened in 1977. By that year turkeys had showed up as far north as Johnson, Stowe, and Chelsea. By 1997, it is estimated they occupy

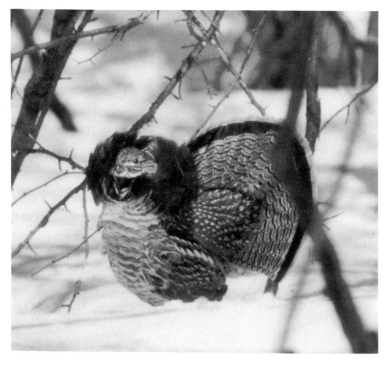

Ruffed Grouse (Partridge). A male puffing up his "ruff" (neck feathers) and fanning his tail during early spring courtship and territorial defense. The display also involves beating his wings rapidly, or drumming, at a clearing or on a special log. The drumming starts slowly then increases, sounding like the distant throb of a motor starting. In the north, grouse populations fluctuate from high to low to high again every 9 to 10 years. Photo by Edgar Strobridge.

Wild Turkey. A native of North America, the wild turkey was driven to extinction before 1900 in many parts of its range, including Vermont, by the disappearance of the forests it needed for food and cover. It was reintroduced to Vermont in 1969 and has since expanded its range rapidly and broadly. It now occurs in 70% of the state, far exceeding its former range, wherever hardwoods and foods on the ground are available year round. Photo by John Hall.

70% of the state, far exceeding their original range. Now, it is Vermont turkeys that are being exported to the wilds of New Jersey, Maine, and even West Germany for similar stocking programs.

Amphibians and Reptiles

Although they do not bask in the limelight in which birds and mammals seem to shine, other animals of the forest are plentiful, important, in fact integral to this community. They not only help give a complete expression to the diversified character of the hardwood forest, but they are also essential ties between the lower and higher forms of life. Significant among these animals are the amphibians and reptiles.

Many amphibians are members of the hardwood forests, and even though they spend some part of their lives in water, most are landlubbers as adults. So, implicit in their existence are seasonal movements, usually from water to land in the summer, after they hatch and pass through the early tadpole stages, then from land to water for the late-fall and winter hibernation.

Seen by most summer hikers are the eastern (formerly red-spotted) newts—in their more familiar land form called red efts—which hatch from eggs laid on plants rooted in a shallow pool or pond. They spend the first summer as gilled larvae totally in water. After three or four months, they crawl to land, having resorbed their gills and developed lungs for air breathing. They then become the beautiful orange creatures we see making their slow way over leaves and around rotting logs. After a few years on land, the efts go through another series of changes: they return to water, change base color to olive green, and grow a tail with a fin. Once in water, they stay there to mate, and the circle of their lives is drawn.

Since the adult has lungs and no gills, one may wonder how can it "breathe" underwater. Like frogs, these salamanders can respire in water through their skin and the lining of the mouth. Even on land, when hibernating, the red efts get some of their oxygen in this manner, as do another group of salamanders in our forests, the so-called lungless salamanders. These indeed have no lungs, and so would be expected to live in water. But this is not the case; most are land-bound as adults. Nevertheless, they must keep moist to allow gaseous exchange through their skin, which is why, when handling them, one must make sure they stay wet. Scientists believe the lungless salamanders evolved in mountain streams, later shifting to a woodland habitat— lungs in animals living in fast-moving water would be a distinct disadvantage, of course, so over time and the natural processes of evolution they lost their lungs. The change to life on land was permitted in part by the moisture in the rich forests, which allows respiration to continue through other organs in contact with the air and soil. Thus, lungs in these salamanders simply were never needed. Most of the lungless salamanders in Vermont show this old affinity with streams or pools, spending their larval stages there and later remaining near them always. The redback, dusky, and less common northern two-lined salamanders are the state's three lungless species.

Of the three, the redback is the land-dweller: it spends its entire life on land (the only Vermont salamander to do so), from egg to adult, under logs or rocks. Because of its secretive nature, the redback goes unnoticed by most people unless they actively search for it. However, it may be one of the most abundant forest animals here; research in a New Hampshire forest indicated that the total weight of redback salamanders was more than that of all mammals and birds combined.

The redback actually comes in three color phases, their occurrence likely linked to geographic and/or environmental differences. Most frequent at higher and intermediate elevations is the "red-backed," with its red (or sometimes orange or yellow) dorsal stripe running the length of the body. Sometimes mixed with the redback, but generally less common and usually at lower elevations, is the "lead-backed"—it actually appears a more uniform pewter gray all over, not just on the back. Rarest and in the most restricted locations is the "red" or "erythristic," with individuals of a screaming bright red or orange.

Woodland frogs and toads are everywhere here, also. The American toad, with its warty skin, plump body, and short hind legs, is the common species, with the Fowler's toad occasionally showing up in the extreme southern portion of the state. The American toad is familiar by appearance and its mating song, a continuous trill that can be heard throughout the spring and summer. The tiny spring peeper and somewhat larger gray treefrog—both treefrogs with sticky pads on their toes allowing them to hold on to twigs and branches—hatch in wetlands or ditches very early in spring, move to higher and drier ground later in summer, then move back to water in the fall in preparation for hibernation. When they awake in the spring we hear them clearly, especially the peeper, whose voice is surprisingly strong for such a little fellow, announcing its time of waking up and mating.

One of the most attractive frogs is the wood frog, mentioned earlier as a member of the boreal forest. Like the other frogs, it begins life in the waters of a swamp, pond, or pool, and moves as a young adult to land. This amphibian, with its remarkable tolerance for cold climates—found even well north of the Arctic Circle—is one of the earliest risers in spring, often quacking at the close of maple sugaring in late March or early April.

Vermont has relatively few reptiles and even fewer that might be called woodland. This apparently is owing to its hard winters of relatively long duration. Some people look on this as a blessing, since to them reptiles mean snakes and snakes mean danger. In actuality, there are some eleven species of snakes in Vermont, but only one is poisonous to human beings. That one, the timber rattlesnake, has a small population and a very limited range, is seldom encountered even there, and is most timid. It does not, therefore, pose much of a threat. But even early in Vermont's statehood, the timber rattler carried a bad name and was bountied (a practice that continued up to 1971). Later, snake hunters, developments, and roads reduced its small numbers even further.

The timber rattlesnake lives in very restricted areas in southwestern Vermont, where in the protection of rugged terrain of cliffs and steep rock outcroppings it dens up for hibernation through the colder months. Its most important denning site is now protected as part of a large preserve owned by The Nature Conservancy. In summer it moves out among the rocks or down to the more open areas to hunt, primarily for rodents. Though there is always the chance of meeting the rattler in the summer in these areas, the risk of snakebite is very small: the snake flees from people and strikes only if fearing for its life. Indeed, there have been no documented fatalities from snakebite in Vermont. In just recognition of the rattlesnake's precarious existence, the state has designated it an endangered species.

Vermont's only lizard and a New England rarity, the five-lined skink, was discovered for the first time in 1962 (reconfirmed in 1983) in extreme western Rutland County, in the same general vicinity as the timber rattlesnake: open transitional hardwoods with access to rocky outcroppings where it can warm in the sun in spring and fall. Justifiably, its extremely limited range and low numbers make it an endangered species in Vermont.

Of Vermont's other snake species, some, the garter snake, for example, are widespread throughout the state, including the boreal regions. Almost everyone recognizes the garter, with its black and yellow stripes running the length of its body (making the animal look like an elastic garter). Others, such as the rat snake of the southern part of Vermont, are more localized and sensitive to environmental change. The rat snake is nonpoisonous, but can leave the impression that it is dangerous because it may act aggressively and bite if bothered. It is a constrictor, suffocating its prey by squeezing before eating it. It also climbs trees with ease, and often eats bird eggs or fledglings. To identify this snake, one should note that it is all black except for the mottled underside, and is shaped in cross section like, to quote one author, "a loaf of bread." Small, secretive, and harmless species of snakes are found under stones or logs in the hardwoods and neighboring fields. Woodpiles are a favorite nesting place for two, the ringneck, with a yellow belly and ring around its neck, and the redbelly, with a red belly and three large yellow spots on the back of its head. Both feed on worms, slugs, insects, and some amphibians.

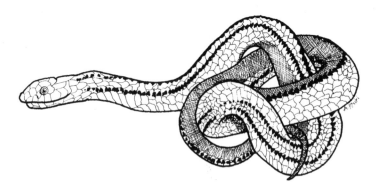

Redbelly Snake. One of several small, harmless-to-humans snakes in Vermont. This species with the beautiful crimson belly remains mostly in the woods, under fallen logs, and in woodpiles near houses. In winter it hibernates in underground dens. Like the garter snake, it gives birth to live young. Drawing by Ann Pesiri Swanson.

Terrestrial turtles are few indeed. The wood turtle spends some of its time in the water but is usually seen far away from it. This turtle's shell looks something like a small snapping turtle's—gray and composed of rows of conical plates that give it a sculptured appearance. Moving slowly over the land in summer, it eats a variety of foods, including berries, leaves, beetles, and slugs. But as winter approaches it heads toward a pond or lake, and by the time ice begins to form it has taken position on the bottom or buried itself in the mud, there to spend the cold months, well insulated by the water and ice above. During this period of dormancy, physiological processes in the turtle come to a near standstill, though at times it may move above on the bottom. Although totally submerged in water it is still able to breathe through highly vascularized anal sacs, much in the way that frogs and salamanders breathe through their skin.

In the repertoire of Vermont wildlife, the reptiles and amphibians are the least understood—their distribution, numbers, and activities throughout the year. Current research is under way to disclose more about these lesser known residents of our state, and it should add much to our understanding and appreciation of the north country.

Insects and Other Invertebrates

On warm days of winter, especially as the days lengthen with the coming spring, the woodland sojourner often sees black dots that appear on the snow, often in such numbers that the surface, especially in holes and depressions where they collect, looks as though pepper has been scattered liberally upon it. These dots are tiny, wriggling, jumping creatures called snow fleas.

Snow fleas are not fleas at all, but members of an order of primitive, wingless insects collectively called springtails. They are equipped with minute spring-like structures on the underside of their bodies that allow them to propel themselves through and over the snow. With the warming, brightening days, springtails emerge from the ground and migrate in masses through the snow to the top, possibly to eat pollen or other new foods that have drifted onto the surface, possibly to mate. At night or if it gets colder in the day, they return to the soil, where they stay within the organic matter in the leaf litter.

While we tend to think of snow fleas as black and appearing on the snowpack, there are actually many species of different sizes, shapes, colors, periods of activity, and habitats. Another form that one might notice is the larger, lavender-colored "snowmelt" snow flea that sometimes rafts in great numbers on the surface of clear pools of recently melted snow. Another, obviously not in Vermont, occurs in tidepools along the coast.

Soon, and to the surprise of many, some moths and butterflies begin to appear, flying about even on quite cold days and over the

snow in search of food and in preparation for mating. Species of noctuid moth—small and a rather nondescript brown—flutter about the
forest in the evenings and night, often drowning in sap buckets as they
drink the sweet nourishment. The mourning cloak, a large and attractive butterfly with brown wings edged in yellow, is often the first butterfly to appear as it emerges from hibernation under tree bark. It is
one of the "brush-footed" or "four-footed" butterflies, so called for the
shape of the front feet and greatly reduced front legs. It, too, flies about
the woodlands and borders in search of food, which it often finds ooz-
ing from broken twigs of maple and other trees.

Many other insects and invertebrates inhabit the various structural levels of these forests. In the moist, decaying matter in the soil or
rotting logs, millipedes scavenge and the predatory centipedes hunt.
Land snails and slugs scrape their meals from the leaf-litter ground
vegetation. Ground beetles scurry about over the surface. Bark beetles
and borers eat their way through the bark or trunks of trees, often leaving intricate patterns of "calligraphy" in their tunneling. In the
canopy, larvae (caterpillars) of moths, butterflies, and sawflies (types
of small wasps) dine on the leaves, often in such quantities that they
cause noticeable damage or defoliation.

Some of the most devastating are nonnative species that have
come by accident and been able to exploit their new homes before
predators (or humans) are able to control their numbers. However,
even native members can cause significant damage. Such damage,
however, is rarely lethal, due to predictable, periodic cycling of the insects from highs to lows, a system evolved over long periods of time
that protects both insect and host.

For example, the forest tent caterpillar (a confusing name, since it
does not build a silken "tent") cycles every six to sixteen years in Vermont. At the peaks the caterpillars (larvae) can cause significant early-
season defoliation of hardwoods, but at the lows they are scarcely
noticed.

The work of the maple leafcutter is quite familiar to most people:
neat, circular holes in sugar maple leaves as if made by a paper punch.
The small, steely-blue female moth emerges from pupation in the
spring and lays its eggs on leaves of maple (and sometimes other hardwoods). When the eggs hatch, the tiny larvae begin eating their way
through the thickness of the leaf (called *mining*). Later, when bigger
and no longer working the inside of the leaves, they remove the discs
and sew them flat together as protective cases. They continue to eat
and grow, adding ever larger discs as they do. In fall, the caterpillars
drop to the ground, spin cocoons, and pupate. Normally, the leafcutter
poses no great threat to the maples; however, in peak years the leaves
may appear to be shot full of holes and some trees actually defoliated.

Finally, one other part-time forest insect deserves mention if only for the considerable summer discomfort and annoyance it can cause to wildlife and humans alike. Deer flies (we have several species) hatch from eggs laid on plants in or near water and spend their larval stages in the muds and waters of swampy areas and ponds. The adults frequent the forest and its edges, the females in search of blood meals, the males of sap and nectar of plants. They are strong, swift flyers, apparently attracted—partly at least—by motion: one writer has observed deer flies chasing speeding cars and trains.

III Waters and Wetlands

A loon I thought it was
But it was
My love's
Splashing oar.

—Chippewa love song

Introduction

In traveling over the lands of Vermont, one cannot go very far without meeting water. The state gathers a lot of it as rain or snow in its passage through the year, channels it to rivers, and collects it in water bodies. Vermont is dotted with almost 600 lakes and ponds at least five acres in size, covering almost a quarter of a million acres. It is crisscrossed with waterways, nearly 8,000 miles of streams and rivers. It has more than 200,000 acres of wetlands, perhaps only half of what were here prior to European contact, representing less than 4% of the state's land base.

These waters are literal wellsprings and reservoirs of life—for myriad invertebrates that spend all or portions of their lives in water, for fish, for other animals that live on the food and drink it offers, and for us who depend on water for sustenance, recreation, and inspiration.

We have come a long way even within recent memory to regard waters and wetlands as more than just servants to us, more than a means to our ends. Water quality standards for the state are closely monitored and enforced. Research and management of lakes and ponds for their biological integrity and recreation use are ongoing. Vermont's first wetlands protection law went into effect in 1986.

> Gluskabe was given the job of preparing the world for his grandchildren, the human beings whom he would shape. His first action was to try to repair some of the damage he had done to the land, and so he filled the ravines he had created with water and shaped rivers and streams that would make the lives of his people good. These would be the center of their world, giving them not only water to drink and bathe in but also providing food and, of course, a way to travel through the mountainous land Gluskabe had shaped. These rivers slowed down and made ponds and lakes in the valleys below. In the spot where Gluskabe finally shaped his legs and stood, he left a great long hole in the earth, which, when filled with water, became Bitonbagok (At the Between, or Dividing Water) [Lake Champlain]. This name refers to the placement of the lake between the Adirondacks and Green Mountains. More recently it has also been used to refer to the division between the Iroquois and Abenaki.

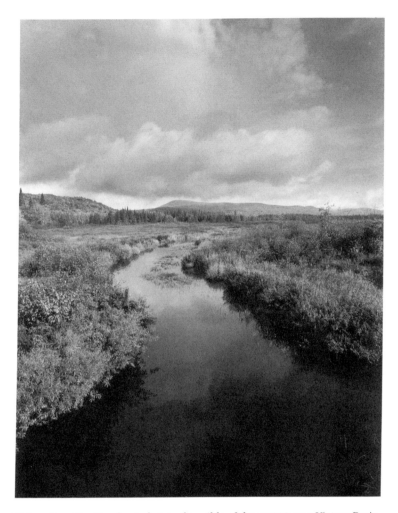

Victory Bog. Bog Brook winds into the wilds of the 12,000-acre Victory Basin. Though called a "bog," it is actually a vast complex of several types of wetlands (including a small bog), interspersed with uplands. It is an important area for many kinds of plants and wildlife. Photo by Robert Frechette.

Yet we have a long way to go still. Waters and wetlands are among our most vulnerable natural resources, as carriers and repositories of our pollution and wastes, as the unwitting incubators of introduced exotic plants and animals, and as desirable destinations for homes and vacations. Being so vulnerable and so important to life in the most embracing sense, it is all the more critical that we treat them with the respect they deserve and the care they need.

8

Brooks and Streams

The countless rushing streams that wind their narrow ways down
sides of mountains, cutting thin channels, are quite young. They are
the products of the Ice Age, when glacial rock debris laid new grounds
and dammed old drainages, and the melting water in all its volume and
force began to carve new channels. These boulder-strewn brooks are in
a hurry: geologists speak of them as being "immature" not so much because of their age as for their physical characteristics, yet for the most
part, by geological standards they are very young.

Many of our waterfalls are streams that are energetically cutting
through rock—these streams are "sawing" their way back into higher
elevations. They are shallow, clear, turbulent waters. Beginning cold
from the direct runoff of melting snow or newly exposed ground
water, they stay cold, for they are shaded by overhanging trees. In addition, the tumbling waters are well aerated, so the streams are saturated with oxygen. In this rush of water any soils and other eroded
material are carried quickly downstream, leaving only the heavier
rocks and gravel on the bottom, a composition we see in almost every
mountain streambed.

The pathways of streams and rivers, and the vegetated corridors
associated with them (collectively known as *riparian* areas), are acknowledged to be critical for birds and wildlife—not just those that
live there, but many that take advantage of the shelter and food in
their daily, seasonal, or annual movements.

Plants

The violence of the streams creates rigorous living conditions for
any organisms found there. The few plants growing in this environment are small and form mats closely adhering to the rocks, or else
they are free-floating. Green algae grow as slippery, tightly knit blan-
kets on rocks, close to the stream surface, in such a way that the rushing water will not strip them away. Several species of diatom—microscopic plants with intricately patterned glasslike shells—and other
unicellular algae float in considerable numbers in the waters, even
though many are borne away on the currents. Higher on the shaded
walls of waterfalls, moistened by spray, are mosses and liverworts.

Insects

A surprising number of insects, mostly as larvae, inhabit Vermont's streams; each species exhibits remarkable adaptation to the

147

Watersheds. The river drainage basins in Vermont, most of which empty into either Lake Champlain or the Connecticut River. Each major watershed is named for the dominant river within it. In planning for conservation of biological diversity, river basins are more appropriate than political divisions since they are more aligned with the biological characteristics and ecological functions of the landscape. Map by Peter Keibel.

Wetlands. At a glance, the array of Vermont's 200,000 acres of wetlands. Notice the concentration in the Champlain Lowlands and Northeastern Highlands: the former mostly marshes and hardwood/shrub swamps associated with Lake Champlain and its major tributaries, and the latter marshes, bogs, and softwood swamps of the boreal lowlands. Map courtesy Vermont Agency of Natural Resources.

A Woodland Stream. On their treks downhill from the heights of land, tumbling streams aerate the waters, transport organic matter, provide habitat for aquatic invertebrates, and become a source of drink and food for woodland creatures. Photo by John Hall.

swift waters. Some, such as the nymphs of certain mayflies (the most ancient of all existing winged insects, and the only one to molt as a winged adult), have slender bodies that glide in the currents. Stonefly nymphs are flattened and have filamentous gills located on their legs, these two traits allowing them to appress themselves to the undersides of rocks and thus minimize the effects of the current, while at the same time permitting them to get oxygen from the passing water. While one doesn't often see them doing so, certain species of water striders are able to fly considerable distrances to colonize new areas. As they search for small organisms to eat, water striders glide over the surface, some species in the quieter pools eddying behind logs or rocks, other in faster currents of the mainstream.

The infamous biting black flies are born in mountain streams. As larvae they look like black moss on the underwater rocks, holding on by means of small grappling hooks at the bases of their bodies. They have an ingenious way of gathering food while rooted to the spot: they make a net of salivary material and float it out into the stream, where it traps organisms and draws them back for eating.

Larvae of caddisfly species find other solutions to the problems of living in the stream environment. Some build protective cases of sand or small pebbles around themselves by cementing the particles to one another and to the bottoms of rocks. The cases are open at the head and face upstream. Food drifting by is captured in a net made of the same cementing material and the larvae pull it into the case to consume it. Almost any Vermont stream, at any elevation, will reveal these small cases fixed to the bottom of rocks. Other caddisfly larvae are free-floating but have hooks and claws on their legs for grabbing on to rocks and holding themselves in place.

Certain aquatic insects, sensitive species of mayflies or stoneflies, for example, are often important clues to stream health, with their presence, absence, or change in numbers being indicators of oxygen levels, amount of siltation, water chemistry, temperature regimes, and degree of pollution.

Born and grown in the streams but active as adults above and beside them are black-winged damselflies, a very noticeable species in the group of "broad-winged" damselflies (those that have wide wings throughout, unlike the "spread-winged" and "narrow-winged" whose wings are pinched down where they join the body). The black-winged damselflies are unmistakable with their large size, manner of flight (rather lazy floating and bouncing instead of the swift darting of most other species), and coloration—the males have shiny black wings and dark green bodies, the females gray wings with white spots on the tips.

Fish

The larvae of the stream, as well as the airborne adults, are vital food sources for the stream fish, including many of the less conspicuous minnows (species of sculpin, dace, shiner, sucker, darter, and others), as well as the more celebrated native cold-water dweller, the brook trout (or "squaretail"). This fish is a New England native that, with human assistance, has spread to almost all suitable waters of the northern United States. It is one of the smaller members of the salmon family, averaging a pound or less, although the state record to date is 5 pounds 12 ounces (1977). Even at 1 pound it seems large for many of the mountain streams, but it is well made for life in the swift waters, with a smooth, torpedo-shaped body. The species favors clear, cold, neutral-to-slightly-acidic fast-moving waters, and in October it moves upstream to spawn in the shallow gravel beds of headwater streams. There the rushing waters circulate oxygen through the nests (redds), and keep the eggs healthy. The brook trout can, however, also survive in ponds if conditions are right. For example, if beavers dam a mountain stream containing trout, the fish may continue to live in the impounded area if the water remains cool enough and free of silt. In addition to good water quality, brook trout require areas where they can take refuge from predators, as well as lie as in wait for catching their own prey: undercut stream banks, submerged logs, large rocks and boulders, and the like, places well known to trout anglers.

Rainbow trout share many streams and cold brooks with brook trout, but they also range into rivers and lakes if these waters are clear and well oxygenated. The rainbow is indigenous to the West Coast but has been transplanted all over the world, and in Vermont it seems to do best in streams that are more alkaline than acidic, as are its ancestral waters. In contrast to the brook trout, rainbows spawn in early spring, most heading upstream from the larger rivers into smaller tributaries with gravel beds and fast-moving waters. Interestingly, some forms of rainbow trout migrate to spawn and others do not. The migrating forms are physically different, with a flinty, plain coloration, from which they get the prename steelhead. A remarkable display of their movements takes place each spring at Orleans, a town in the northeastern part of Vermont. There, steelhead rainbows that have

A Waterfall. Many of Vermont's streams and rivers cascade into waterfalls of much variety and beauty. Over time and through the work of water, the rocks may become smooth sculptures. Photo by Louis Borie.

Rainbow Trout. The steelhead rainbows migrating. These are among the thousands of the species in Vermont that try to leap the falls near the town of Orleans, on their spring spawning run up the Willoughby River from Lake Memphremagog. This remarkable display can be seen from only a few feet away, drawing crowds of anglers and spectators each year. Photo by John Hall.

spent the year in Lake Memphremagog swim en masse up the Willoughby River and struggle up and over a long series of falls at the outskirts of town. Anglers and spectators alike line the banks, watching fish a few feet away as they rest in shallow pools between the rapids on this arduous annual ritual.

Birds

Only a few birds come to the mountain streams to feed. The belted kingfisher waits patiently on an overhanging tree branch, then bombs into the water after a small fish. If the attempt is successful, it will first stun the fish by beating it on a branch, before either eating it or taking it back to its young. The spotted sandpiper is a common sandpiper of exposed banks of streams and rivers, the only one of its family that nests regularly there. During breeding season it is easy to recognize by its spotted beast, teetering walk, and unusual flight, in which the wings are flapped tensely below the horizontal, creating the effect of a tightly strung bow twanging close to the water.

Flycatchers, such as the tiny least flycatcher or larger eastern wood-pewee of the broad-leaved woodlands, or yellow-bellied fly-catcher of boreal forests, might fly from their tree perches to catch insects over the open water.

During its migrations the little northern waterthrush—not a thrush at all, but a warbler with the color and markings of a thrush—is occasionally seen at streamside, walking over and among the rocks. It will not stay long here, however, as it begins its journey to South America before mid-September. The kingfisher often lingers as long as the water remains open. But finally, with the departure of these species, the streams will be without birds, and the sound of rushing water will be muffled by new-fallen leaves and then the snows and ice of winter.

Mammals

The stream is home to but a handful of mammals. Mink often live in dens adjacent to streams and readily enter the water for fish. Hikers sometimes see the northern water shrew—big for a shrew, being larger than a mouse—swimming in search of small fish or aquatic insects. This species is perfectly designed for its life in streams, rivers, ponds, and bogs of northern regions: its large hind feet serve as paddles, and its thick, water-repellent fur sheds water and insulates against the cold.

Tracks of deer, weasels, raccoons, skunks, and jumping mice indicate these animals' regular visits, for food or drink. During summer nights, also, come several species of bats, flying over in search of hovering insects. The tiny, yellowish eastern pipistrel, one of the country's smallest bats at less than a quarter of an ounce, is one of these nocturnal hunters.

Reptiles and Amphibians

Several species of salamanders, all in the "lungless" family (Plethodontidae), make their home in mountain streams, where among the rocks and stones at the edges they forage for food (mostly aquatic invertebrates) and hide, only occasionally venturing into the vegetated margins. Largest, sometimes growing to almost 6 inches long, is the spring salamander; its salmon-colored, seemingly translucent, body appears almost too fleshy and fragile for the environment. Smaller and more slender is the northern two-lined salamander, with its body usually a golden-yellow with a broad dark stripe on either side of the back. The two-lined often ventures on to land, and may be found well away from streams and rivers in moist woodland. Smallest and most tied to the stream is the northern dusky salamander. The northern dusky is fast and, with its large hind legs (compared to its relatively small front ones), is able to jump considerable distances, hence its more descriptive name of "jumping salamander."

The wood turtle is a rather uncommon inhabitant of riparian

areas, including streams with sandy or muddy bottoms where it can dig down to hibernate in winter. Occasionally it will move considerable distances from water into richer woodlands. Its numbers across its range have apparently been dropping over the last few decades, causing herpetologists worry about its future and the yet-unascertained causes of its decline.

.   .   .

So, the picturesque streams—vigorous and apparently hostile as they dash and plummet down the shaded slopes—are in reality full of special lives, molded to their special conditions.

9

Rivers

As the streams cut their way down the mountains they join and evolve into rivers—the wider, deeper, less turbulent waters of the lower elevations. Rivers collect the sand and soil brought down, and so are more turbid than the mountain waters. These bottom deposits accumulate and build a substrate upon which some special plants can root. The rivers have thus become habitats different from the streams above them.

Often it is hard to distinguish a river from a stream. Like any location of ecological transition, there are always zones of merging where the wildlife represents both contributors.

Rivers are generally much older than streams. Many have been cutting and eroding for not just thousands but millions of years. Most in Vermont are termed "mature," lying in the broad valleys they have helped to sculpt. Mature rivers have wide flood plains and a sinuous passage through the land.

Under natural conditions, rivers are subject to periodic flooding—especially in a place as wet as Vermont and particularly in the spring, when tons of melting ice and snow rush down the mountains. Late fall is also a prime time for flooding, when the ground begins to freeze and rainwater can no longer seep down, but rather travels over the surface to collect directly in rivers in quantities greater than the banks can hold.

The history of humankind in Vermont has been tied closely to the rivers. The rivers have provided animals and plants for food, good sites for settlement, and means of access into lands farther inland. Natives concentrated many of their seasonal activities near them and to this day much of Vermont's population is located along rivers. Times, however, have changed greatly in some respects, and our lives are no longer bound so intimately to the flowing waters. But for many people the rivers are no less important today than they ever were—if only for the spiritual gifts they carry.

Vermont's history contains records of a few severe floods, the most devastating of which occurred in November 1927. That flood, brought on by an Atlantic-coast storm that moved inland, caused 88 deaths and millions of dollars' damage statewide. The hardest-hit region was the Winooski River Valley from the Barre-Montpelier area to Burlington, where whole villages were swept away and 55 people lost their lives. To prevent a future calamity the newly created, soon famous Civilian Conservation Corps (CCC) began construction of three flood-

Connecticut River. The Connecticut River between Ascutney and Springfield, flanked by a series of step-like terraces. The farm (far left) sits on a high kame terrace formed when postglacial Lake Hitchcock occupied the valley; the house (center) is on the highest of several lower terraces cut by the Connecticut River over the last 10,000 years (the land has actually risen several hundred feet from postglacial rebound during the process). Photo by Charles W. Johnson.

control dams across tributaries of the Winooski River, one just north of Montpelier, one at East Barre, and one at Waterbury. Completed in the 1930s, they are still in use today. Several other flood-control dams were later built in other sectors of Vermont.

But most floods are not so bad or destructive as the one of 1927. Many riverside plants and trees are adapted to cope with seasonal flooding, and indeed many depend on it. Flood waters, if not too torrential, deposit a great deal of silt and fresh organic matter in lowland areas, thereby enriching the soils. In fact, flood plains, especially the broad ones of Vermont's major rivers, are sites of some of the most productive farmland in the state. In addition, as we shall see later, many fish and other wildlife rely on flooding for completion of their life cycles.

Most of the valleys we see today were cut by the rivers flowing within them. Some, however, were originally cut by ancient rivers and streams that flowed through the same general areas but which have long since disappeared and been replaced by the present rivers. The Connecticut River Valley was made in this way, where several smaller rivers were "captured" into one river and followed a glacially modified channel.

The oldest valleys have been continuously cut since the beginning of the Appalachian system by "subsequent" rivers: rivers that are parallel to mountain ranges. Most of Vermont's subsequent rivers therefore flow north-south. Some valleys, however, run predominantly east-west, having been cut by "superimposed" rivers running at right angles to the ranges—the Lamoille and Winooski rivers and part of the Batten Kill are good examples of superimposed rivers, flowing east to west right through the Green Mountains. Their valleys predate the rise of the mountains, following older rivers: as the new mountains rose, these existing rivers sawed through them. This explains why they originate east of the Green Mountains, where normally they would be in another drainage (going east into the Connecticut River), and flow west to Lake Champlain.

A few rivers, or portions of them, are classified as being in "old age." These meander through flat terrain, have numerous oxbows, and are laden with silt. The final repositories for materials brought down from above, they are almost at the end of their time of eroding. Dead Creek in Addison County, sections of Otter Creek, and the Winooski River as it approaches Lake Champlain are fine examples of rivers in old age.

Arrowhead Mountain Reservoir. This impoundment accentuates the sinuous curves of an old-age section of the Lamoille River, not far from Lake Champlain. The sands and silts deposited by the river collect on the inner curve, building large flats that are exposed when the reservoir is drawn down. Such exposed areas are good places to see migrating shorebirds in late summer and early fall. The "knobs" of mountains in the near background show the line of the Hinesburg Thrust Fault, running from near Bristol north into Canada. Photo by Warren Lavery.

River wildlife is rich. Most rivers have aquatic vegetation emerging from their edges, where the current is weak and bottom sediments have had a chance to build; old-age rivers have the most margin plants, because of their thick mud deposits. Aquatic insects, especially those that can propel themselves, appear in great numbers, as both larvae and adults. Freshwater clams, crayfish, and other bottom dwellers live in the fertile muds, and the sluggish currents help them secure their food. Such vegetation, insects, and other organisms in turn attract larger creatures in search of food, particularly fish, which, in their turn, bring human beings.

Archaeologists have good evidence of substantial Native American settlements along many of Vermont's rivers, especially the Connecticut River and larger ones as they approach Lake Champlain. The excellent fishing and hunting there provided year-round food, and, at least in the Champlain Valley, the climate was more tolerable than deeper inland. In addition, the rivers could carry them into new territory, and the openness of the water gave them views of approaching enemies.

The Connecticut River, one of New England's largest, most historic, and most biologically diverse rivers, has been the focus of a major, multistate/federal conservation effort. Passage of the Silvio O. Conte National Fish and Wildlife Act of 1991 authorized the U.S. Fish and Wildlife Service to study the entire Connecticut River watershed (7.2 million acres in Vermont, New Hampshire, Massachusetts, and Connecticut) and determine the possibility of establishing a new national fish and wildlife refuge there.

After years of information gathering and analysis, public meetings, correspondence, and a good dose of controversy, the U.S. Fish and Wildlife Service issued its report (including environmental impact statement and action plan) in October 1995, five years after the law went into effect.

The proposal is not in the traditional "national wildlife refuge" design, where the U.S. Fish and Wildlife Service buys, controls, and manages all the designated land. Rather, the proposed approach would be for the service to focus on use of voluntary efforts, partnerships, technical assistance, and cost sharing to help other conservation interests to carry out their land protection programs. In this manner, and working with willing landowners, state and local agencies would protect over 50,000 acres of identified important uplands and wetlands, while the service would protect over 26,000 (6,500 in outright purchase and 20,000 in conservation easements and cooperative management agreements). Education would also be important, carried out through many of the organizations in the watershed.

The future of the Conte Refuge—and the ultimate viability of this kind of approach to river conservation—now (1997) rests with Congress.

Fish

The brown trout, like the rainbow a nonnative trout species, lives in Vermont rivers of widely varying characteristics. Brought over from Europe in the last century it has become an important addition to the state's cold-water fisheries, particularly as it is more tolerant than are other trout of the increasingly silted, warm, and partially polluted rivers that are the results of agriculture and industrialization. As elsewhere south and west, the brown trout of Vermont has also become a major game species, reaching large sizes (the state record is 22 pounds 13 ounces, 1990) and possessing a cunning nature that entices the sport angler.

As one proceeds downstream from the mountains, the waters become deeper and more placid, the bottoms muckier with muds and silts; widening out from the shelter of trees, the rivers warm somewhat in the summer sun. In many places, in fact, the rivers come close to being ponds, where marginal vegetation increases, aquatic insects cruise the quiet pools in search of prey, and bottom inhabitants such as clams and crayfish become more numerous. The trout of the colder waters give way to smallmouth bass in many such rivers. Bass are better able to live in warmer waters, and with their laterally compressed bodies slide more easily through the weeds. Where the rivers flair out as tributaries of marshes, ponds, or lakes, northern pike may enter.

The pike is a long, large (commonly attaining 20 pounds or more in Vermont) warm-water fish closely related to the smaller, common chain pickerel. It is most noticeable in the spring, after the ice of the lakes has melted, as it enters the weedy, shallow riversides or adjacent flooded fields to spawn, thrashing the waters in a feverish activity. Its fighting nature makes it a fine sport fish, but it is also important to fisheries biologists, who use it to restore healthy proportions of gamefish populations to ponds and lakes that have become dominated by "pan" species—yellow perch, crappie, pumpkinseed, pickerel, and others. These species prey heavily on the eggs and fry of the game fish, particularly trout and bass, resulting in an overpopulation of pan fish and declining numbers of game. Moreover, the increased number of pan fish results in a decrease in the available food, and the game fish become stunted. The pike is a tough, highly effective predator—known at times to pull swimming ducks underwater or leap out of water at a cast lure in its flight—and when introduced into such bodies of water quickly reduces the pan fish to an acceptable level, thus helping the game fish rebuild their numbers.

The deeper water of some of the state's northern rivers—those connected to such large lakes as Champlain and Memphremagog—contain muskellunge, the famous trophy fish of the North Central states and Canada. In its prime range the muskellunge grows to great proportions, reaching 70 to 75 pounds, but Vermont is on the edge of its range and here it grows only to the size of the northern pike—for which it is often mistaken—reaching a record size in the Missisquoi River near the Canadian border of 29 pounds 8 ounces (1978).

The Atlantic salmon and American shad were two species that once came to Vermont rivers by the hundreds of thousands to spawn, running in from the sea to places far inland. Before 1800, salmon appeared each spring and summer in hundreds of rivers in New England, including the St. Lawrence, the Connecticut, their tributaries, and those of Lake Ontario and Lake Champlain. (The salmon of Lake Ontario's tributaries, however, apparently lived in the lake and did not migrate to the sea, as did the salmon of the other waters). In Vermont, the Connecticut River runs were among the most anticipated and celebrated rites of spring, testimony to the fecund cycles of Nature as she brought to reality this annual promise. But, once so plentiful, these two species both disappeared in the early 1800s, when dams supplying power to the emerging industries of Vermont, pollution from the by-products of the new white culture, and excessive commercial fishing by nets placed across the mouths of the rivers blocked their access to ancestral spawning grounds. It seems to be another of the tragedies of modern times, but this story has an epilogue, and maybe soon even a happy ending.

Salmon and shad are anadromous fish—they spend their adult lives in the ocean but move into rivers to spawn. The young fish hatched in the rivers remain in the place of birth for one or two years, until of age to travel downstream to the sea. At that stage they are called "smolts." They then stay in the ocean for a few years before achieving breeding age, at which point in spring they come back to spawn at the place of their birth. Unlike the Pacific salmon, the Atlantic species does not die upon spawning but makes its way back to salt water, and may breed for several years following.

Before white settlement of New England, the Connecticut River was the major way into the state for enormous numbers of salmon and shad. They entered from Long Island Sound and proceeded north through Connecticut and Massachusetts into Vermont and New Hampshire. The salmon continued upstream almost to the Canadian border, passing into smaller streams along the way, but the shad went only as far as Bellows Falls, prevented from further migration by the falls, and spawned only in the main channels of the Connecticut.

Salmon, in addition, evidently came up the St. Lawrence River, entered the Richelieu River, then moved down into Lake Champlain, though they stayed in the northern part of the lake, no farther south than Otter Creek. From Lake Champlain, the fish progressed up suitable rivers—including the Winooski—and streams to spawn. However, Lake Champlain was presumably a secondary point of entry as it was the Connecticut River that carried the reputation for the famous runs.

With the development of the white people's culture in New England, this annual passage of fish was disrupted. Improper commercial fishing took its toll. Siltation of the clear water that the salmon needed was the result of heavy deforestation and agricultural uses of the land. Small dams built on streams to provide energy for local communities blocked off the return routes for many salmon. Later, several major dams across the Connecticut River cut them off completely: the first was built at Turners Falls, Massachusetts, in 1798, and four others followed, none equipped with ladders to allow the fish to bypass the structures. Thus, as early as 1814 salmon and shad were gone from the Connecticut River. In the Lake Champlain region, the increasing siltation and pollution of the lake and the St. Lawrence River, along with the dams built across the spawning streams, had effectively eliminated salmon from there as well. So the fish no longer came to Vermont. In fact, they were practically extinct in New England—only to Maine did they continue to come, and then principally to one river, the Penobscot.

Concern for the welfare—the very existence—of both species led to attempts at their restoration as early as the mid-nineteenth century, futile though the attempts proved to be. Finally, in 1966 a program involving cooperation among Vermont, New Hampshire, Connecticut, Massachusetts, and the federal government was established to bring the salmon and shad back, once and for all. Under provisions of the agreement, all dams across the Connecticut River would have fish ladders, water quality would be improved to acceptable levels for the fish, and hatchery-reared young (fry) would be imprinted to streams and rivers throughout the original range, so that they would return as spawning adults.

Encouraging signs appeared within the decade following the program's inception. The first adult salmon showed up in the Connecticut River in 1974, albeit dead when found. By 1977 seven adults had swum their way to the Holyoke Dam, in Massachusetts, some 85 miles from the ocean. Then in 1978 a run of 99 salmon arrived at the Holyoke Dam and at the Rainbow Dam on Connecticut's Farmington River, the best run in 150 years. These were caught for spawning, although only two survived, owing to a deadly fungus infection that spread rapidly through the stock. In 1981, 529 salmon came back to the Connecticut, an all-time modern high. Since then numbers have leveled off, averaging just over 250 per year.

In 1981, a fish ladder constructed at the Vernon hydroelectric facility allowed passage of these migratory fish into Vermont/New Hampshire stretches of the Connecticut River (annual counts at the Vernon ladder have tallied lows of 0 (1982, 1983, 1989) to a high of 13 (1992) salmon). Fewer have reached more recently installed ladders at dams at Bellows Falls (built in 1984) and Wilder (1987). Now, the fish have access to the Connecticut River from its mouth to some 270 miles upstream; in fact, adult salmon have now been seen as far north in Vermont as the West and White Rivers.

Of the shad, in 1977 nearly 203,000—a record since observations were begun in 1954—were counted and lifted over the Holyoke Dam. These were part of the nearly 400,000 shad that now travel up the Connecticut.

With completion of the fishways at Turners Falls in 1980, as many as 300 shad moved into the lower portions of Vermont/New Hampshire Connecticut River waters. Since then they have appeared at the Vernon ladder each year, though their numbers over that time have fluctuated from less than a hundred (1981 and 1982) to just over 37,000 (1991).

The restoration program continues, with eventual success still a way off and only tentative. But with hope arising from past achievements and continued stocking from national hatcheries in Pittsford and Bethel, and state hatcheries in Vermont, Massachusetts, and Connecticut, the Atlantic salmon and American shad may once again come as messengers from the sea, time-honored riches from our treasured heritage.

Mammals

Down to and along the rivers come many mammals, to fish or hunt for waterside animals, to drink and wash, even to play. The ever-present raccoon, one of the country's most "successful" animals—despite an unbroken history of being hunted and the victim of the environmental pressures—pays its nightly visits to the river for amphibians, insects, and small fish that it is able to grab. White-tailed deer quietly edge in to drink, while mink run the banks or swim the open waters with equal ease. Beavers waddle inland from their riverbank dens to cut the trees that are destined to be their food.

The river otter, largest member of the weasel family in Vermont (weighing up to 25 pounds), was once much more prevalent than it is now. Otter Creek—a major river on the western side of the state, which was important to Native Americans for its fish and the transportation route it provided—was named by early settlers for the great numbers of otters living along its length. Despite their reduced population, owing to heavy early trapping and later development, otters are still with us, sparingly, along many of Vermont's rivers and lakes.

Otters dig dens in the sand of riverbanks or under logs not far from the water's edge, each den equipped with several underwater entrances. These mammals have a deserved reputation for playfulness, as apparently purely for fun they wrestle a good deal on land and in the water and "sled" down well-worn snow and mud slides near their homes. They are among the swiftest and most agile of mammalian

River Otters. The largest species of the weasel family in Vermont. Otters breed in winter and early spring, and the young are born 9 months later. Otter families travel repeated circuits in their search for aquatic foods, moving from place to place as the supply diminishes. In winter otters do not hibernate, but they may not be seen much, for during cold weather they remain underground and under the ice. The naturalist Ernest Thompson Seton in 1929 estimated that the population of otters in the United States was half of what it had been before white settlement. This drop in numbers was probably due to heavy trapping and increasing development along rivers and lakes. Photo by Susan C. Morse.

swimmers, able to catch trout in open water. Naturally, their main prey is fish, but they also hunt a variety of other animals—mice, muskrats, frogs, crayfish, and even the occasional duck.

The otter is supremely adapted for work in the water, even in winter. Its thick, well-oiled coat (oil from the large anal glands possessed by all members of the weasel family) both insulates the animal and repels water, the properties that made the fur so popular in earlier years. Webbed feet and a powerful muscular tail are used for propulsion and steering, and the otter can stay underwater for up to two minutes while fully active.

Birds

The rivers attract many birds, too, both those that fish for food and others. The great blue heron stands among the aquatic plants in quieter pools, ready to stab at a passing fish. A kingfisher will loop down the channel, rattling its call. A spotted sandpiper scurries around the sandbars in search of small organisms, and bank swallows sweep a few yards above the water surface, snaring insects. In the shrubs at the river's edge a male yellow warbler often sings "sweet-sweet-sweeter-than-sweet" as his territorial proclamation.

One might even be lucky enough to spot an osprey, especially during its peak migration periods in April and September, slowly flapping overhead or stationed in a tree with a good vantage point of the river. When on the move for food, this large fish-eating hawk hovers over its prey, then descends, wings folded back, hitting the water with an explosive clap and grabbing the fish in talons that are fitted with fine serrations for holding the slippery catch. Thereupon it bears the fish away to feed on it piecemeal in a tree, tearing it apart with its sharp, hooked beak.

The osprey apparently has always been rare as a breeding species in Vermont, with observers reporting only a few nests—even fewer successful—since the late 1800s and early 1900s. But it became ever rarer under the pall of DDT, with virtually no nesting or young here from the early 1960s to late 1980s. With the banning of DDT and an active state program to reestablish the species here, osprey have returned, beginning to breed here in 1988 and with the numbers growing steadily since. Now (1997) over twenty young are produced annually from six known nest sites, five of which are adjacent to Lake Champlain or its major tributaries. Despite this positive and encouraging sign, the bird remains an endangered species.

Great Blue Heron. Herons nest in colonies (rookeries or heronries), never very far from water. The largest Vermont rookeries occur in the Champlain Valley swamps. Herons are in the same family as bitterns and have many characteristics in common—including flying with crooked necks. Photo by John Hall.

Osprey. Also called the fish hawk, this bird has a large curved beak used for tearing fish apart—it eats only fish, which it catches in its talons when it plummets from the sky, hits the water, and seizes them. Owing to its diminished numbers all over the United States, it has been on the federal and state endangered species lists for many years. It probably was the victim of DDT (see text), but since the pesticide's banning in 1974, the osprey has appeared in Vermont in ever greater numbers and began nesting again in 1988. Drawing by Ann Pesiri Swanson.

Osprey Nest. Photo by Robert A. Jervis.

In earlier times we would have had a good chance of seeing another fish-eating hawk working the rivers and lakes, but today our chances are slim indeed: the bald eagle, which if ever sighted now is in the fall or winter. Whereas the osprey eats only live fish that it has caught, the bald eagle is not so fussy. In addition to what it can catch on its own—fish or otherwise—it will eat dead fish and other carrion, and will even steal from other predators, especially its near-rival, the osprey. There are no recent records of this raptor's breeding in Vermont, and those individuals seen here are the Southern race of bald eagle, breeding in January or February in the southern half of the United States and wandering as youths or nonbreeders to the North. If eagles follow the trajectory of ospreys and peregrine falcons, however, it may not be long before we see them nesting here along major rivers and other water bodies.

Invertebrates

In riverbottom muds of Vermont's rivers (and some ponds and lakes) live seventeen species of native freshwater mussels, historically an important food source for native peoples and later the basis of a small commercial button industry. As a group, and since they cannot move about, mussels are especially vulnerable to degradations of both the substrates in which they live and the waters they depend upon for food (microscopic plants and animals) and reproduction (certain fish are hosts to their larvae and provide for dispersal). They have faced, and continue to face, a gauntlet of threats from dams, pollution, regulation of river flows, channelization, gravel mining, and siltation due to excessive erosion and dams.

Consequently, they no longer are abundant and, indeed, few are even common. Seven species are restricted to the Lake Champlain drainage, and three to the Connecticut River drainage. One species, the dwarf wedgemussel, has been found only (worldwide) in one 18-mile stretch of the Connecticut River (it is listed both federally and in the state as endangered), while three others are listed as state threatened.

The recent explosive invasion of the zebra mussel in Lake Champlain (a nonnative species first appearing in North America in the Great Lakes in 1988 and in Lake Champlain in 1993) and its rapid population expansion present a new, enormous threat to native mussels in the region. Having already seen great masses of the small zebra mussels cloaking the larger natives (zebra mussels attach to hard surfaces, unlike the native mussels), thereby suffocating them, starving them, or inhibiting reproduction, scientists feel the threat is so real, palpable, and immanent that one species has been proposed to be moved (1997) from threatened to endangered status, with six more added to the threatened list.

Invertebrates, like most organisms, are particular to the kinds of

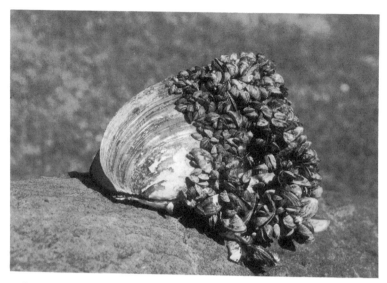

Zebra Mussels. Since their initial discovery in Lake Champlain in 1993, zebra mussels are confirming the fears of aquatic biologists: ever-greater numbers cluster on solid objects—clogging water intakes, coating pilings and boat bottoms, and, in the example shown, massing on native mussels, often to the point of literally suffocating them. Photo by Brian MacDonald.

habitats in which to live. Mussels, as described, inhabit the muds of river bottoms, while along the banks crayfish may dig their burrows. On the drier, flatter shore sands, stones, or cobbles, insects of various kinds live, hunt, or forage. Notable of these are the tiger beetles, many species of which are associated with rivers and streams. Tiger beetles, both as larvae and adults, are highly predaceous on other insects. The adult is a quick, agile runner over sand and rock, yet able to fly short distances when necessary to capture prey or avoid danger. The odd-looking larva—the original "doodlebug"—resides in a burrow it has dug in sand or pebbles, with its outsized head plugging the entrance hole, and waits. When an insect steps unwarily on the head, the larva clamps down with its huge jaws, anchors itself in the burrow with hooks on the lower part of its body, and drags the helpless victim to its doom.

Three species of tiger beetles currently (1997) are listed as threatened in Vermont, due to their very limited range and the uncertainty of long-term habitat security.

10

Marshes

Leveling out, a river of Vermont glides into a pond or lake, and we notice changes. The river has become sluggish. The water is shallow and shows the rich, muddy bottom. The plants reach out into the channel and begin to dominate the scene. One has entered the special world of the marsh.

Marshes are the first general type of wetland we have encountered in this study; the two other types in Vermont are bogs and swamps. All wetlands are alike in that they are water-saturated—although they are not necessarily underwater—most of the time, long enough, at least, to allow formation of wetland (hydric) soils and growth of wetland plants. Their differences are most obvious in the vegetation. Marshes have herbaceous, grassy-type plants; swamps have trees and/or shrubs; and bogs develop a floating mat of sedges, heaths, and sphagnum moss. Additionally, marshes and swamps have some water flowing through them, whereas bogs are near-stagnant, with water slowly passing through only under certain conditions and at certain times of the year.

In most cases marshes are a specialized zone of a lake or slow-moving river. This zone, called the littoral or shore zone, may be well on its way to becoming land. The marsh is one of the biologically richest ecosystems in the world, and therefore one of the most fascinating. It has flora and fauna of wide diversity, and produces, purely in pounds of vegetation, much more than forests or grasslands. It is a breeding place for many birds and a spawning ground and nursery for crustaceans, mollusks, worms, insects, amphibians, reptiles, and fish. It is a hunting ground for mammals of several species and a vast feeding and resting area for migrating birds, both waterfowl and others. In short, for many of Vermont's residents it is home, and for the large numbers of birds we share with other states and even countries, it is an irreplaceable oasis.

Although marshes may be the littoral zone of lakes, not all lakes have them. The physical structure of a lake basin, its location, and the kind of bottom sediments (or lack of them) may prevent the formation of a marsh. Lakes or lake sections that have steep sides cannot support plants of the shallows. Similarly, lakes with rocky bottoms, lacking the necessary clays and silts for soil, do not have the organic base upon which a marsh must sit in order for plants to grow. And where plants can't grow, a marsh can't exist.

A Marsh. The thick herbaceous vegetation of a marsh provides homes and hiding places for many invertebrates, fish, amphibians, reptiles, birds, and mammals. This is a small bay of Lake Champlain, near Charlotte. Photo by Louis Borie.

Many areas along the eastern shore of Lake Champlain and its tributaries have excellent marshes. There the littoral zones is wide and declines slowly, is filled with clays and silts brought down from the uplands to the east, and is practically without currents, which would remove the soil buildup. Other areas of Lake Champlain on the Vermont side and most of the New York side are unsuitable for marshes. Steep walls and deep bays along the thrust fault line in Burlington Bay and Shelburne Bay, for example, prohibit this kind of development.

Marshes are sensitive environments, constantly changing under the seasonal fluctuations in water level, always in the middle of the battle between land and water. They are dynamic communities, whose inhabitants and visitors depend on these very tensions for their propagation. For instance, most marsh plants are very choosy about conditions. Some, such as the smartweeds, require sites that are alternately wet and dry. Others, such as wild rice, grow on deep, rich soils that are covered with 1 to 3 feet of slowly circulating, nonfluctuating water. Some species of fish (the northern pike and bullhead) spawn in newly flooded fields nearby, while many ducks time their egg laying to the high-water period in spring, instinctively counting on the level to drop gradually, so as not to threaten the nests of their newborn.

But, vital as marshes are to wildlife, people have not always recognized their value or treated them with the respect they deserve. Since they occupy flat, low-lying areas and are usually in scenic surround-ings, they have been filled for building developments. Those who view them as wastelands dump in them the refuse and by-products of human consumption. They have been drained for mosquito control or conversion to farmland. Because marshes are a great purifying filter for the waters entering them, they have become sewers of pollution from rivers upstream of them. Even altered drainages in areas outside their bounds affect marshes adversely: stabilized water levels kill the marsh, because they discourage the propagation of many marsh plants and thus accelerate the shift to dry land.

Vermont is fortunate in possessing some of the finest marshes in New England, thanks to the fact that it has so far escaped the massive developments undergone farther south. Nevertheless, even here much has been lost, and the future is as questionable in Vermont as it is else-where. Public conscience must lead us to preserve what we have left. In 1986, Vermont instituted its first wetland protection program.

One of the major controversies in New England within modern memory was the proposal to construct a large flood-control dam across the Richelieu River in Canada, which would have affected the water levels of Lake Champlain and thus its associated wetlands. The proposed dam would have had a movable up-and-down plate within it, to work in concert with a widened and deepened river basin. To-gether these features would have allowed a greater volume of water to flow out of Lake Champlain during flood times, especially in the spring, thereby preventing inundation of the farms and houses built on the Richelieu floodplain.

Although operators of the dam would attempt as much as possi-ble to mimic the natural cycles of the water level of the lake, the peaks that cause flooding would have been eliminated. And flooding is es-sential to the vitality and ultimate existence of the wetlands. Exten-sive research indicated that as much as 28 percent of the total wetland acreage would have dried out, and the spawning, nesting, nursery, and feeding areas of countless species of fish, birds, mammals, and other animals destroyed.

Due to changing social and economic times, and to public pressure stemming from an increasing sensitivity toward wetlands, the dam was never built—a fortunate thing, say those who consider natural wet-lands impossible for all our money or best engineering to replace.

Plants

In the thick, fertile underwater soil the marsh plants take root. Further enriching the mud, the plants that die add nutrients to what is brought downstream. The water circulates slowly, replenishing the oxygen and distributing dissolved minerals. The foundation of the marsh is laid.

Marsh Profile. The inhabitants of a marsh. Nearest the edge are the emergent plants (e.g., loosestrife, burreed, and arrowhead, left; iris, right) with most of their leaves and stems above water. Farther out are the floating-leaved plants, with long, flexible stems and flat, floating leaves (e.g., a pondweed, left, and water lily, right). Deepest are the submerged plants, totally below water, from which they get their nutrients, rather than from the soil (here watermilfoil). Birds (here black-crowned night-heron), fish, and other animals are active in all zones of the marsh. Drawing by Ann Pesiri Swanson.

The plants grow aligned in fairly distinct zones, determined by water depth, exposure, and other factors. Farthest out, in the deepest water, is the zone of submersed plants. There such species as watermilfoil, elodea (the "algae" of aquariums), and pondweeds spend all their lives at or near the bottom, never even breaking the surface. They generally have finely divided leaves and lack the firm outer layer of tissue (cuticle) found on land plants. Since the water buoys them up, the plants also do not need reinforcing tissue. Instead, they have air cells throughout their stems and leaves that provide flotation and act as oxygen reservoirs. These specializations allow the plants to absorb nutrients and oxygen directly from the water, which is necessary because their root systems are little developed, if at all, and the soils in which they grow are oxygen-poor, owing to the concentrated decomposition of dead plants. This ability is one important reason the submersed plants flourish in waters that have become polluted by sewage and the runoff of artificial crop fertilizers. They thrive, to the point of excess, on these abnormally high amounts of what to them are nutrients, and can in fact choke out shallow bays and ponds, as has happened in many places in Vermont and elsewhere.

The next zone toward land from the middle of the marsh is that of the floating-leaved plants. In this area the marsh bottom and surface have been brought closer together by the buildup of organic matter from submersed plants and the accumulation of sediments. The tough, wax-coated horizontal leaves of the water lilies float and ride the waves at the surface, while their long, leathery stems bridge the gap to soil, where they are more firmly rooted than the submersed plants.

The next zone, that of the emergent plants, is usually the most extensive. Plants here have thick, flexible air-filled stems and bladelike leaves that rise out of water and bend and sway with the winds. Roots are well developed and supporting, and the large underground tubers persist for years. Within this zone there are further subdivisions: in deeper portions wild rice, pickerelweed, and arrowheads may grow; in shallower areas are burreed and cattails. In places more like soggy fields than water-covered marshes, many species of sedges and rushes are conspicuous.

The expanses of marsh vegetation harbor innumerable insects, fish, birds, and other organisms. The tubers of burreed and arrowhead are a favorite food of muskrats and ducks, and the nutlets of the former abundantly nourish migrating waterfowl in the fall. The tall, golden "meadows" of wild rice, too, yield their crop of seeds to thousands of ducks, geese, and songbirds fattening in autumn. But more than food, the plants are also a maze within which the nests, young, and adults of many species of birds are protected throughout the year.

Birds

The black duck, mallard, and blue-winged teal are the only common ducks that nest in great numbers within the marsh vegetation in Vermont. These are in the group variously known as "puddle," "dabbling," "pond," or "marsh" ducks. They ride high in the water, tip (not dive) into the water for food, and can fly directly into the air from either a standing or a floating position—this ability is a definite advantage in the tight, narrow spaces of a marsh. The mallard has been a highly successful species that originally came from the prairie states but moved steadily east, its immigration assisted by people who raised it as a domestic bird and then released it into the wild. Mallards and black ducks are closely related and have similar habitat and food requirements; occasionally, mallard–black duck hybrids occur. Since the mallards' arrival in Vermont, many authorities believe that they have been competing with, and supplanting, the blacks. But though mallards now outnumber blacks west of the Green Mountains, east of the range, and statewide over winter, the black ducks still are the more abundant.

Another common dabbler is the wood duck, the variegated male of which is without question one of the most beautiful birds in North America. Though frequent in marshes, it has a wider distribution in swamps and wooded pond areas, where it nests in the cavities of trees and feeds upon nuts, tree seeds, and the smaller grains and vegetation at waterside. We shall take another look at this species later.

The other group of ducks are the diving ("bay") ducks, which ride lower in the water, dive underwater for their food (vegetable and animal), and must skitter over open water before they can become

Mallards. Now the most common ducks in western Vermont, mallards also closely rival black ducks east of the Green Mountains. They may hybridize with the blacks, as well as with domestic ducks. Here ducks and drakes feed together in shallow, open water in the spring. The females are the quackers; males (here distinguishable by their dark heads) have a quiet nasal "peent."
Photo by John Hall.

airborne. Consequently, they mostly work the deepest water, near or beyond the zone of submersed plants. The one diving duck that regularly nests in Vermont marshes is the ring-necked duck, but it is generally found only in the boglike sedge and heath marshes of South Bay of Lake Memphremagog (Coventry Marsh, see Appendix I), where it finds suitable nesting material. The other diving ducks nest in Canada or in other habitats where mature woodlands are within flying distance of water. These species will be discussed in more detail in chapter thirteen, "Ponds and Lakes."

All Vermont ducks breed early in the spring, and soon after mating lie low throughout the incubation, brooding, and raising of their young. The females stay on or close to the nest, while the drakes, once done with mating, move off to be by themselves. Both sexes molt all their flight feathers soon after breeding, which renders them incapable of flying. Being so vulnerable, they remain in seclusion until new flight feathers grow in, and during this time they are silent and very hard to find. Both sexes molt all their body feathers as well, but the drakes change "clothes," donning a drab plumage like their mates'. In the fall, the drakes molt back into breeding feathers and will keep them through the winter until the next "eclipse" molt the following spring. This unique molting pattern appears to be related to the particular reproductive physiology of the family: ducks form pair bonds on their wintering grounds—which is why the drakes acquire their breeding finery in winter—and move north together in early spring. This allows them to set up nesting very quickly, without the time-consuming courtship and breeding rituals that most other birds perform. Moreover, ducks can "afford" to molt only in summer, since even though flightless they can still obtain food then, and a molt at other times of the year would leave them either exposed in the cold months or unable to migrate.

The dawn of a spring day is the time to hear and see others of the extraordinary birds of the marsh as they cackle, babble, chuckle, croak, whinny, laugh, or sing their strange mating and territorial messages. The Virginia rail trots over and around the roots, stems, and leaves of the aquatic vegetation, its way through this mini-forest made easier by a laterally compressed body and wide, splayed feet. This is the most common rail in Vermont, nesting in drier patches within the marsh, usually on mats made of cattails. The closely related, darker common moorhen (gallinule) is more visible than the Virginia rail as it swims out from cover, bobbing its head and paddling around by means of partially lobed feet. Its weird henlike cackle is a sure clue to its presence. The little "hell-diver," the pied-billed grebe, looking much like a small duck, with its long neck, small bill, and stubby tail, has the ability to adjust its position in water by expelling air from or taking it into air sacs within its body. When in danger it lowers itself like a submarine, with only its eyes and nostrils above water, but when swimming freely it rides high, with a good view. This grebe is a regular nester in Vermont, and in summer is sometimes seen swimming around with its tiny young on its back, in the manner of all grebes. It moves quickly around the marginal vegetation, in and out of the marsh, then sinks below the surface after a fish, or circles closer to land for insects and crayfish.

Standing on firmer ground or in the shallower stretches of the marsh, an American bittern may be seen, a secretive but relatively common bird of this habitat. The bittern is much like a heron in appearance and in its habits of dainty wading and snatching fish with its long bill. But unlike herons, it nests in pairs or loosely formed colonies with the marsh, rather than in well-knit but often large colonies in trees. It has a variety of colorful nicknames, such as "stakedriver," "thunder-pumper," "stump-knocker," "butterbump," and "bog bull," most of which are attempts to describe its strange call. Listen to the marsh. You can often hear this liquid, pulsating throb, which seems made more by machine than bird.

American Bittern. When alerted to danger this bird will stand straight up among marsh plants, bill pointing to the sky, and stay motionless except for a slight swaying to mimic the movement of vegetation. This vertical stance, combined with protective coloration, causes the bird's stripes to blend with the marsh plants, making the bittern practically invisible. Drawing by Ann Pesiri Swanson.

Terns are usually thought of as fliers of ocean coasts or large lakes, circling and plopping into the water after fish they have spotted. But the black tern seen over larger Vermont marshes is an exception. It looks much like an oversized swallow as it twists after insects it captures in flight. Furthermore, it builds its nests on floating rafts of vegetation within the protection of the marsh, rather than in large colonies in open, rocky prominences, as do other terns. Small colonies of black terns return to Vermont each year to nest in a few marshes along Lakes Champlain and Memphremagog; one of their best breeding populations is in the Little Otter Creek Marsh west of Ferrisburgh.

Smaller, nonaquatic birds reside in the upper levels of emergent marsh plants. The ubiquitous red-winged blackbird slings its cup-shaped nest between stalks of cattails and the little marsh wren and swamp sparrow often keep each other company, mixing their bubbling, chattering songs. The rarer sedge wren is found farther up in drier areas, nesting in sedges and other wet-meadow plants adjacent to the marsh proper.

As one might suspect, hawks and owls are not common sights around marshes, since theirs is not the world of dense, low vegetation or pervasive water. A peregrine falcon might come rocketing over to snatch a duck or other bird in flight. But the harrier ("marsh hawk") is the hawk most frequently seen, as it tilts, tips to change direction, hovers low, then drops straight down to catch a snake, frog, rodent, or bird within the vegetation. The short-eared owl seems more hawk than owl, and indeed in many ways it resembles the harrier. It hunts a great deal by day, especially in the evening and early morning, flies with the gliding, twisting, hovering motion of the hawk, and is one of the very few owls that scrape together a nest in the openness of field or marsh edge—most other owls retire to tree holes left by woodpeckers, which they modify. And like the harrier it hunts in a variety of nonforest habitats: fields, marshes, croplands. With all these traits in common it is not surprising that these two birds may be found together, though usually only in the spring or fall, as the short-eared owl rarely spends the summer here, moving north for breeding.

For migrating birds, the waterways of Lake Champlain and its marginal marshlands (most of which are on the Vermont side of the lake) make up a major branch of the Atlantic Flyway, one of the routes between breeding grounds in the Canadian prairies and tundra and wintering grounds in the South or along the Atlantic coast. The Connecticut River is another branch of that flyway, but with smaller concentrations and varieties of birds. In these areas there is a magic about October and November, in the restless southbound waterfowl passing over, dropping down to feed and rest, congregating by the score for the evening to rise again by morning. The puddle ducks filter into pools and shallow-water areas: blacks, mallards, blue-winged teal, wigeons, pintails, shovelers, wood ducks, gadwalls, and the later-arriving green-winged teal. At the fringes of the submersed-plant zone and out into the clear open water flock the divers, including common goldeneyes, buffleheads, ring-necked ducks, and the greater and lesser scaups.

The bittersweet stirring of autumn drifts down in the honking of Canada geese and in the flash of the white-and-black wingbeat of snow geese. Flying high, they are almost part of the sky, until they wheel in for evening feeding. Before 1954 the Canadas had been only migrants through Vermont to their breeding grounds far north around Hudson Bay, James Bay, and the Northwest Territories. But in that year 44 wild geese were pinioned and released at Dead Creek Waterfowl Area in Addison, and a small flock has bred there ever since, and even attracted free-flying wild individuals. Now over 75 pair breed here, producing 200 goslings each year, and upward of 4,000 geese stop down in fall migration.

For people who love the outdoors the autumn marsh has a special feel, an ineffable nostalgia that comes of the smell of dying leaves, the golden-brown trim of cattails, and the sharp blue sky. Through an early fog the sounds bring us closer to winter, remind us of the sadness of losing summer. Unseen wings beat on the water, the wind glances over the jacket. The marsh has meaning like no other place on earth.

Mammals

For hunters, bird-watchers, and other observers of nature, the birds of the marsh are the most relished discoveries, receiving the greatest attention. But one can scarcely be unaware of the other lives that are part of this rich reservoir.

One of the most evident of these other beings is the muskrat, known mostly from its cattail lodges. This rodent actually builds two types of lodges, a smaller one for feeding only, and a larger, thicker, well-insulated one for year-round living and the raising of young. In winter when the surface is frozen over the 'rats swim beneath the ice to cut and gather plants for food, and return to the lodges via one of several subsurface entrances. Muskrats that live by rivers or ponds usually do not build lodges but rather dig their homes into soil banks, much as beavers do.

The muskrat was one of those fortunate mammals in the early years of our country's settlement whose fur was scorned when that of so many others was in huge demand for coats and other fashionable items. It apparently has always been abundant in Vermont and elsewhere in the East, and even today, when muskrat fur has become more prized, its population remains high and steady, owing to proper management and closely regulated trapping.

The mink, also a former undesired species but now a valuable furbearer, often dens up in unused muskrat lodges or digs burrows at the land-water interface, from which it can move out quickly to capture fish, frogs, insects, snails, birds, and small mammals, including the muskrat. Minks are the year-round archenemies of muskrats, often plundering the muskrat population in an area. This usually occurs in low-water years, when the muskrats' lodges are left high and dry or their bank dens are separated from water, so that the animals are forced to travel overland. Being exposed and ungainly on land, they fall extremely susceptible to predation by minks, which are as comfortable and quick on land as in the water.

Reptiles and Amphibians

Species of reptiles and amphibians in marshes may be many or few, depending on the size, location, and nature of the marsh, and whether or not it is isolated or with access to more open water of rivers, ponds, or lakes.

Where plant species and vegetative structure are diverse, one might see (or more likely hear) one, several, or all of the following, at various times of the day or night during the breeding season: spring peepers, gray treefrogs, American toads, green frogs, bullfrogs, northern leopard frogs, and pickerel frogs. Most, however, disperse to other habitats later in spring and summer—for example, peepers, treefrogs, and toads to the woods, leopard and pickerel frogs to wet meadows. Of salamanders, the aquatic adult eastern (red-spotted) newts often swim in the marsh waters in search of insects and other invertebrates to eat; they may also bury themselves in mucky bottom to hide, or hibernate through winter.

Especially in big marshes and with access to rivers, ponds, or lakes, a few species of turtle may occur, though they are certainly not restricted to this type of landscape. Most common are the painted turtle and snapping turtle, both of which might spend a good portion of the spring and summer (except for egg-laying, which occurs on dry land) in the marsh and the winter buried in the marsh muds.

More topographically isolated, vegetatively uniform marshes, such as a slough dominated by cattails, are apt to have few, if any, breeding amphibians and reptiles. However, there are often surprises. In one such marsh in 1975 on Grand Isle in western Vermont, herpetologists discovered the only known state site for striped (western) chorus frog, a species at the extreme eastern limit of its range (it was rediscovered in the same place in 1985, but has not been heard or seen since 1986, up through 1997). Similarly, the spotted turtle, a common species in more southern states but very rare here, has been found in only one location in extreme southeastern Vermont, in association with a rather typical marsh/shallow pond complex.

There are countless more stories of the marsh, and many must go untold here: the multitude of insects that swim through the underwater spaces or fly out from hatching to other areas, small crustaceans that are invisible to us as they cartwheel in the water or settle in the bottom ooze, fish that zigzag in search of smaller prey, tadpoles that become toads, frogs, or salamanders. But the stories are there if we listen closely enough, or read them thoroughly. They tell us of one of the most splendid mysteries in the natural world.

11

Bogs

Many people regard bogs as places to be avoided, as soggy wastelands unsuitable for agriculture, forestry, recreation, or other worthwhile activity. But as a special kind of wetland, bogs are significant and intriguing ecosystems, unlike any other. On the world scale, they occupy enormous portions of Canada, Russia, and Scandinavia, where they are used for many commercial purposes, including mining for fuel substances, building material, and peat moss. Though most in Vermont are tiny by comparison with the bogs of those countries, the state boasts some fine, unspoiled ones.

The occurrence of bogs in Vermont depends on several key environmental factors, abundance of water being one of the most influential. North in Canada, the boglike landscapes spread for thousands of unending miles as "muskeg." There water is almost always available, since evaporation is reduced by the short ice-free season and in many areas the permanently frozen ground (permafrost) just below the surface acts as a barrier to the downward-percolating water. But in Vermont, where summers can be somewhat dry and permafrost does not exist, bogs have developed only in depressions where drainage is slowed or stopped and water collects in the low areas. With impeded water flow and little or no oxygen supplied from the outside, decaying plant and animal remains rapidly consume what oxygen is available in the basins. Eventually, the waters become deficient in oxygen and stagnate. At that point, dead matter cannot be well decomposed, as the agents of decay (primarily bacteria and fungi) cannot live without oxygen. This is also the reason that bogs, contrary to their popular impression, do not have a "marshy" or "swampy" smell. The relatively rapid decaying of organic matter in swamps and marshes (due to the presence of oxygen that allows decomposers to function) releases great quantities of methane and other gases, which build in the mucks until they bubble out, especially when the sediments are disturbed. In bogs, however, this process is greatly slowed and reduced, so odors cannot be detected. Whatever dies here is "pickled" in this acidic, watery environment. In this way, the organic matter accumulates as peat builds into mats in which plants and animals are often preserved intact. In fact, in some European bogs human bodies (probably those of executed prisoners) have been almost perfectly preserved for thousands of years.

The process of peat formation has been taking place for millions of years. Indeed, peat is the precursor of coal—given enough time,

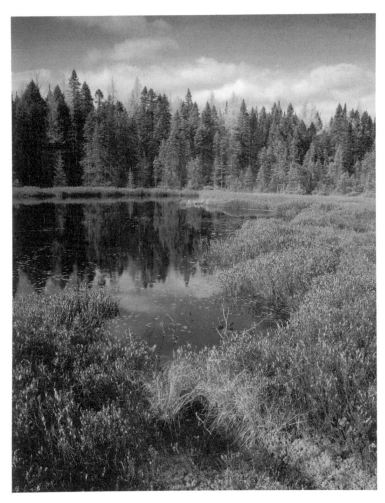

A Kettle Bog. A small bog in central Vermont exhibits the classic kettle (or closed basin) bog appearance. The open water is surrounded by a quaking mat of heath shrubs (here predominantly leatherleaf), below which are sedges and sphagnum mosses (both in center foreground). Ringing the outer perimeter of the mat are trees, mostly tamarack and black spruce. Photo by Louis Borie.

material, and compaction, peat is transformed into lignite, then soft coal (bituminous), and finally hard coal (anthracite). A small deposit of lignite in Brandon, once mined for fuel, has yielded some fine fossilized plant remains. Elsewhere, the vast coal beds in this country and elsewhere around the world were made in just that way, in enormous boglike swamps that existed long before the Ice Age, more than

200 million years ago. When we burn coal today (or peat, as is still done in several countries) we are merely completing the decomposition begun so long ago, but in a greatly accelerated way.

Technically, a bog is only one type of peatland. The formation of different types of peatlands is due to different combinations of basin topography, seasonal water level and flow, minerals present, climate, and the vegetation itself. In peatlands with deep basins and almost totally blocked drainages sphagnum mosses and heath shrubs predominate. These are the true *bogs*, whose peat builds to a point where the surface of the mat, the only area of growth, rises above the water table, and the living mosses and other plants on the mat become isolated from the water and nutrients below; rain and snow are then the only suppliers of these essential ingredients. They become moderately to strongly acidic.

In peatlands that retain some contact with groundwater and thus have some water flowing through them, sedges and grasses are the dominant plants, with sphagnum mosses being scarce, restricted to more oxygen-poor areas, or lacking entirely. These are called *fens*, and their vegetation remains in contact with the groundwater throughout the year. Whereas bog water is often highly acidic, fens may be mildly so or even basic, owing to the flushing away of acids, replenishment of minerals, and introduction of some oxygen by the moving water. Under certain circumstances both bogs and fens support trees; bogs generally have black spruce, fens tamarack and, if sufficient calcium is present in the substrate, white cedar.

Many older bogs in Vermont began as kettles—ponds or small lakes created at the end of the Ice Age when huge blocks of ice became separated from the retreating glacier and were lodged in steep-sided depressions in the land. These blocks were then buried in glacial till and the depressions were sealed. As the ice slowly melted, the depressions eventually transformed into ponds. Conditions were right for boglike plants to invade, and the process of bog formation began.

In these kettles, peats accumulate on the bottom of the basin, while the buildup and expansion of the mat and its peat over the water create "false land" at the surface. Mats may be very thick (some are more than 40 feet deep) yet may still be floating in the water. But the mats are not like floating pieces of wood; rather, they resemble saturated sponges, forever sinking with the added weight of live and dead plants, yet remaining in suspension. In certain circumstances, a mat can become thick enough to support a person—anyone who has walked on a "quaking bog" must agree that it is appropriately named, as it sways and bobs with every step!

Besides those that have arisen in kettles or small basins, some bogs here have other origins and/or followed other paths of development. Several, such as Colchester Bog and Lake Carmi Bog, formed in bays of big lakes, cut off from the circulating water of the larger bodies by gravel bars; thus, the bays became, functionally, isolated ponds. A few began as shallow lakes, filled in with peat, then, because of the nature of the local climate (cool, wet, and short summers, particularly), were able to extend beyond the original boundaries of the lake and onto the surrounding upland (a process called "swamping" or *paludification*). One of these, Peacham Bog in Groton State Forest, not only has extended its boundaries laterally, but also has accumulated peat in the center, so that the bog appears slightly domed or "raised" (higher in the center than at the margins), as occurs often in more maritime or arctic regions of the north, where moisture is plentiful year-round in the form of rain, snow, and fog, or the long cold and prevalent overcast reduce moisture loss.

Another type of peatland, strangely, is to be found not in the lowest depressions in the land, but on some of the highest peaks. The alpine turf soils of the tundra regions of Mt. Mansfield and Camel's Hump, among others, are actually thin peats—"blanket" bogs of sorts, built of centuries of fallen twigs, leaves, and other organic matter derived of tundra plants and animals. The montane climate that allowed these soils to form is similar in many respects to that of the maritimes where raised and blanket bogs form: cool temperatures year-round and abundant moisture, both directly from ample precipitation and effectively because of the overcast (they are in the clouds a great deal) and long winters.

Development of peatlands is unimaginably slow. Though they may be initiated in the relatively short span of 100 to 200 years, many present-day bogs were formed early after the waning of the last glacier, about 10,000 years ago. Less well developed bogs are much younger, of course, some in Vermont being only two to three thousand years old. All biological activity in the bog is drastically slowed down, owing to the environment's cold temperatures, acidity, and lack of oxygen: for example, an 80-year-old tamarack in a bog might be only 3 inches thick, with annual growth rings so narrow they can hardly be seen, whereas a tamarack of the same age on land a few feet away might be 12 inches in diameter.

Plants

The bog plants growing in the mat are among the most exotic and beautiful of North American flora. Many are found only in bogs, partners to the rigorous features of these places. And, no bog exactly resembling another in physical, chemical, and biological characteristics, the bog's vegetation may include many species or few; a plant may blanket the mat in one bog and be absent in the next.

Plants of the bog have to contend with a gamut of adverse conditions: a sterile "soil," where nutrients are hard to come by, since organic

Cotton Grass. The white puffs of hare's-tail cotton grass seem to float over a bog in spring. Cotton grass is not a grass, but a sedge that grows in the wet peat soils of bogs and alpine areas. Photo by Robert A. Jervis.

matter is little decomposed; acidic water within the mat; scant oxygen for respiration and growth; direct exposure to the elements, especially in treeless bogs; unsteady footing for roots; and, always, the wetness. In many ways, as said earlier, these conditions are similar to those in the tundra on the mountaintops, and though individual species may differ in these two places, the manner in which their plants handle the problems is much the same. Indeed, two families—sedges and heaths—are among the most prevalent plants in both areas.

Ironically, though water is pervasive in bogs and is essential to their formation and development, it is largely unavailable to bog plants, mostly because of the acidity of the peat waters. The plants have acquired several adaptations that allow them to conserve what water they manage to collect. Sedges have thick, solid stems and narrow-bladed leaves, both of which reduce potential evaporating surfaces. Sphagnum mosses have two types of cells, live ones at the mat surface that manufacture food and absorb water from the rain and air, and dead subsurface ones that act as water-storage vessels. Common heaths—leatherleaf, Labrador tea, bog laurel, bog rosemary, blueberries, cranberries, and others—have tough, woody stems and firm, leathery leaves, both attributes helping to restrict the amount of water passing through the plants to the outside.

The problem of obtaining nutrients, especially nitrogen and phosphorus, in such a sterile environment is solved ingeniously by three bizarre plants that actually trap and consume insects and other small organisms. Botanists believe that these carnivorous plants supplement nitrogen directly from their victims, and while it is not essential to their survival, it does allow them to grow more robustly and reproduce better. Strangely, the carnivorous plants are of southern origin, not from the North, as are most of the bog members. Evidently, they grew in comparable wetland areas in the South and were pushed north during he climatic optimum, found a satisfactory home in our bogs, and stayed even after the climate cooled.

The pitcher plant is the largest and most conspicuous of the carnivorous species. Its big, hollow vase-shaped leaves are equipped with little downward-pointing spines on the lips surrounding the opening. Insects attracted to nectar in the veins crawl through the opening, follow a "path" of red veins downward, slide down the smooth interior walls of the leaf, and fall into the liquid at the bottom; their escape is prevented by the smooth leaf surface and the spines. There they drown. The liquid in the leaf contains digestive enzymes that immediately begin to dissolve the insect, and one can often find at the bottom of the leaf the chitinous remains of insects, the indigestible leftovers.

Pitcher Plant. The leaves of pitcher plant growing from the sphagnum moss mat of a bog. This carnivorous plant's structure and special mechanisms for capturing insects are described in the text. Photo by Louis Borie.

Sundews are tiny carnivorous plants, almost hidden in sphagnum, and though there are several species, each captures insects in the same manner. Sticky spines radiate out like a star-burst from the flat, quarter-inch leaves. When an insect alights on the leaf, it is instantly stuck as if on flypaper. The leaf responds to the presence of the insect by folding around it, and remains that way until the insect is digested, whereupon the leaf slowly opens to set the trap for the next meal. Of the five species of sundew in eastern North America, Vermont has two: the more common round-leaved (which may be found outside bogs, in roadcuts, ditches, or other exposed areas), and the spatulate-leaved, more restricted to the margins of floating bog mats.

Within the mat or floating in pools in the bog are species of carnivorous aquatic plants, bladderworts. Found also in other habitats, such as marshes and shallow ponds, they are closely related to the butterwort, the carnivorous species in the high alpine area of Smuggler's Notch. The bladderwort has tiny ($\frac{1}{16}$-inch-long) sacs on its finely cut leaves, and each sac has an opening with a minute "trapdoor." When a microscopic aquatic organism swims by the sac and touches the opening or a hair sticking out by the opening, a stimulus triggers the inflation of the sac. This inflation creates a current that sucks the organism into the chamber. The victim cannot swim out the opening, because it is blocked by the trapdoor. As the organism is "eaten" the water is pumped out, the sac deflates, the trapdoor relaxes, and the plant is ready to repeat the process. The most common species in Vermont bogs is the horned bladderwort, although it lives unseen by most bog visitors until it puts up a beautiful yellow flower in midsummer.

Of all bog plants perhaps the greatest visual treasures are the wild orchids. Though unexpectedly small, their blossoms are exquisite in design and color, and even in bogs most orchids are uncommon. These qualities have made them rewarding finds for botanists, naturalists, and photographers, but also, unfortunately, for those few people who desire the plants for selfish personal possession. Many bogs have suffered through loss of their orchids by such unscrupulous collectors. Not only does the collector deprive us of something in its natural setting, but by taking the plant that person is disrupting the botanical environment. Scientists now know that most orchids grow in close, inextricable association with underground fungi: there is one specific fungus for one specific orchid. Without this symbiotic relationship neither survives. Thus, removing one partner destroys both this relationship and, therefore, the two plants.

Fens, not bogs, actually have the greatest diversity of orchids; in fact, many bogs are totally lacking orchids, whereas some rich fens have many species.

Orchid flowers are of all colors, from the purest white of white bog orchis, to the sulphur of the yellow lady's-slipper, to the variable pinks, lavenders, and blues of calopogon, rose pogonia, and arethusa. They may be single flowers, such as the several species of lady's-slipper, or multiples on a stem, such as the lady's-tresses. The plants are as small as the inch-high twayblades and as tall as the two-foot showy lady's-slipper. All orchids here are insect-pollinated, their flowers often intricately designed to appeal to, deceive, accommodate, and sometimes trap specific kinds of insects. In all, close to 30 species of orchids grow in Vermont bogs or in swampy woods nearby. Though they are a relatively minor component of these landscapes, they certainly have gathered a big share of the attention.

Wildlife

The strange lure of bogs does not rest with plants and wild flowers alone. A good variety of insects in the bog attracts some food-seeking vertebrates, such as the four-toed salamander, which works its slow way over and through the moist sphagnum mosses. In bogs with open water, painted turtles are not uncommon, being seen with their heads poking above the water surface or swimming along the edge of the mat. The small bog turtle one would expect to be found in Vermont bogs, as it is in neighboring New York State, but so far it has not been sighted here. The turtle is rare even in its main Western and Southern range, where it seems to be almost exclusive to bogs and boglike habitats.

Mammalian inhabitants are mostly small rodents that feed on the vegetation and stay within its protection. Of particular interest is the southern bog lemming (lemmings are vole-like natives of the North, especially boreal and tundra regions.) This tiny lemming uses runways and tunnels in the bog mat for traveling from place to place, and for nesting and raising its young.

Birds

The bird life of the bog is not exceptionally rich, but a few fairly rare species may appear, some even nesting. Breeding here has been ascertained, though infrequently, for the Lincoln's sparrow, a northern species that builds its nest well hidden in the sphagnum mat. The red-capped palm warbler, another rare but possibly Vermont-nesting bird, uses two habitats: bogs in breeding season, open grasslands and fields in migration. One might see a yellow-bellied flycatcher higher up in the trees of a bog, waiting for a flying insect to come near, or hear the mighty call of the tiny ruby-crowned kinglet from the thick maze of spruce branches. One might also see a small flock of rusty blackbirds flying over to the swamp trees outside the bog.

Insects

Of all animals in bogs, insects undoubtedly are the most abundant and diverse. Some are more or less bog-dependent, such as the butterflies bog copper and jutta arctic, whose larvae eat the leaves of only certain bog plants (large cranberry for the bog copper, cotton grass for the jutta arctic), or the species of small mosquito that spends its larval stage only in the waters of pitcher plants, thriving in the liquid that consumes other insects. Several species of dragonflies also are endemic to bogs.

.   .   .

Bogs intrigue and attract a variety of people. Whatever their purpose, most visitors pause upon entering, feeling the strange, special qualities inherent to these places, the aura of unearthliness that human beings of all times past have surely sensed.

12

Swamps

The word *swamp* conjures up impenetrable jungles of vines, Spanish moss, underbrush, and fallen trees with snakes dripping off branches and the waters dark with sinister, unseen dangers. This may be the picture of tropical swamps, but Vermont swamps are nothing of the sort. Rather, they are a wetland and a type of forest all their own. Southern swamps are generally deep-water and can be explored well only by boat. Northern swamps as we have here, however, are shallow-water, usually more suited to foot-slogging than boating.

Swamps are considered wetlands because they are saturated most of the year. They differ from marshes in that they contain woody vegetation—shrubs, trees, or both. In many cases, swamps are the final stages of the filling in of a pond. Although technically swamps are the penultimate product of changes in the landscape proceeding from open water to marsh to shrubs and trees and finally to dry land, because of water saturation the final stage may never be reached—or at least it may be extremely slow in evolving—so for all intents and purposes the swamp is in fact the end product of this evolution.

Swamps exist in either boreal- or deciduous-forest regions. Some of the best-developed and most extensive swamp systems in Vermont occur in the spruce-fir regions of the Northeastern Highlands, where they are composed largely of tamarack, black spruce, balsam fir, and a smattering of white cedar, all trees typical of certain types of bogs. Deciduous areas with floodplains, riverbanks, deltas at the mouths of rivers, and edges of marshes support swamp white oak, silver maple, cottonwood, red maple, black ash, and elm, their proportions in the forest depending on locale. Pure hemlock swamps are also frequent, especially in cool, shaded ravines. Some of the finest deciduous swamps are in the Champlain Valley, tied closely to the large marsh and river systems there. Green ash is an important component.

Cedar swamps (of northern white cedar) occupy lowland areas in regions where the bedrock is calcareous, such as limestones of the Champlain Valley or limy schists in eastern Vermont. Such swamps have a distinctiveness about them, imparting to visitors an unusual sense of seclusion and secrecy, with shade dappled by sunlight coming through the thick tangle of branches, richly dark soils, mounds of roots and tipped-over trees, and lush ground vegetation. Although cedar is known to be able to attain great age (perhaps as old as 800 years), there are few old-growth cedar swamps left in Vermont; many

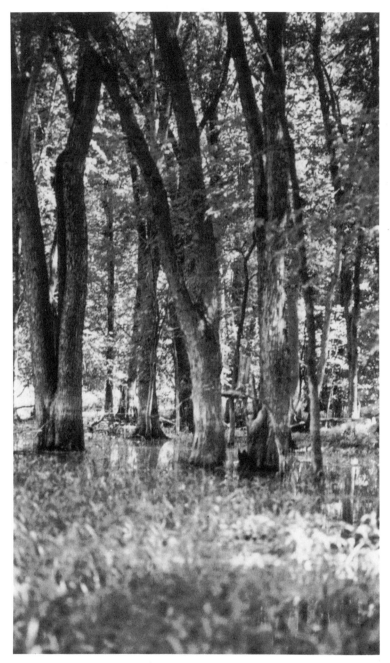

A Swamp. A silver maple–swamp white oak forest near Lake Champlain. The plants and animals here are adapted to the seasonal flooding. Note the high-water mark on the trunks of the trees. Photo by Thomas R. Meyers.

swamps have been cut over for their lumber value (shingles, posts, fencing), inundated by water backed up behind dams (human or beaver), or filled for development.

One truly Southern swamp tree grows in a few isolated pockets in the state, a reminder to us of the existence of the climatic optimum of more than 4,000 years ago. Individual trees of black gum, or tupelo, occur in part of the Champlain Lowlands or as small, aged relict stands in the most southeastern corner of Vermont, in the Connecticut River Valley. The black gum grows to be one of the oldest trees in New England: one researcher determined it to reach more than 400 years in age in an old-growth stand in Maine. The trunks and branches of these ancient trees are often contorted and the bark is deeply furrowed—one can almost feel the weight of their years bearing down on them.

The trees living in a swamp must be able to get oxygen to their roots and support themselves in a tenuous footing in soggy soils. In deep-water swamps, the trees may therefore develop "knees" (pneumatophores), which buttress the trunk and raise part of the root system completely out of the water. But the trees in Vermont's swamps, which are shallow-water, rarely have such structures; rather, they have shallow, spreading root systems, which create a broad base and put the roots in closer contact with the air, although not completely out of the water.

Plants

Bushes and shrubs are strangely lacking in many treed deciduous swamps of Vermont, but herbaceous vegetation is usually lush. It grows atop the hummocks of fallen trees, where it can get a foothold, as well as relief from saturation. Sphagnum mosses, true mosses, and ferns—tall cinnamon and royal ferns—are particularly luxuriant. Jewelweeds, nettles, the early-blooming marsh marigold and late-blooming turtlehead are common rooted flowering plants. Tiny duckweeds, whose flowers are almost microscopic, float like a dense algal mat in the many pools, dangling their free roots into the water.

In shrub swamps, the vegetation may be thick and difficult to get through. Viburnums are well represented, with witherod, nannyberry, and arrow-wood all to be found. Speckled alder, winterberry, whose berries stay bright orange red through the snow season, and many species of willow may also be present. The fragrant sweet gale (one of the bayberry family), leatherleaf, and mountain holly are common to many shrub or boglike coniferous swamps in central and northern parts of Vermont.

Cedar swamps can be some of the most floristically rich areas in the state, distinguished by such unusual species as pink pyrola, one-flowered wintergreen, naked miterwort, and orchids (yellow lady's-slipper, twayblades, calypso, and others).

Black Gum. One of several old, big trees in the swamps near Vernon that are rare vestiges of the hypsithermal interval (4,000–6,000 years ago), when Vermont's climate was considerably warmer. The main range of black gum is now southern United States. Photo by Charles W. Johnson.

Mammals

Wildlife in a Vermont swamp has not the distinction of a Dismal or an Okefenoke. For the most part, animals in our state's swamps either are typical of a wet woods or are passing through the area while foraging or hunting. When the swamp is located next to a lake, however, many water-based birds and mammals may take refuge or come to nest in the swamp. This is a perfect habitat for minks (sometimes called water weasels) and raccoons. Both make their meals of fish, frogs, or other aquatic animals, as well as land prey. Raccoons, in addition, take advantage of the fruitful offering of trees and shrubs.

Swamps house many mammal species that live in other habitats as well. The woodland jumping mouse, with its long tail and kangaroolike feet, is not uncommon in many wet-woods situations and may be quickly identified by its very long jumps—almost leaps—over fallen trees and plants. The smallest mammal in the world, weighing ⅑ ounce, the pygmy shrew is busy hunting its food day and night, summer or winter, in swamps and other forest areas here and across northern North America: this little insectivore must keep up a feverish search for prey in order to fuel a body that consumes more than its weight per day. Red squirrels, snowshoe hares, otters, fishers, bobcats, black bears, and white-tailed deer are present in varying numbers in the larger, more remote, and especially coniferous swamps, either residing there or traversing the area in their forays for food.

Raccoon. A mammal of great versatility, the raccoon is at home in swamps as well as towns. In swamps it will usually den up in tree cavities and eat a variety of foods, including bird eggs, various plants, invertebrates, amphibians, fish, and carrion. Photo by Thomas R. Meyers.

Birds

The barred owl and red-shouldered hawk nest in many swamps, along with a multitude of songbirds. Where conifers are abundant, the yellow-bellied, olive-sided, and alder flycatchers are three of that family to be seen or heard. Also, without much trouble, one may view sizable flocks of rusty blackbirds and hear the vociferous winter wren and northern waterthrush. The last is a warbler that is more "swampish" than most others in its family, walking around the fallen logs and hummocks, building its nest on the ground, and issuing a strident song that rings through the swamp.

Perhaps the most notable birds of the larger swamps near Lake Champlain are the herons. There they congregate for nesting. The large great blue heron we often see stab-fishing in river shallows, marshes, or the edges of ponds, but the smaller green heron, more oriented to the swamp or marsh, stays away from the eyes of the average visitor.

Heron nesting colonies (called rookeries) are often large. Those of the great blue may contain hundreds of birds, the green heron's rookeries being smaller and not so tightly knit. The nests themselves appear to be a loosely thrown-together mass of sticks and twigs and, in the case of the great blue, often are placed high in the canopy. Despite the protection afforded by height, the young great blue herons are made nervous by intrusions, especially by human beings, and will regurgitate a recently devoured meal of fish if approached too suddenly. It is strange to hear the plopping of dead fish as they rain down from the high nests to the ground!

Swamps are also choice nesting sites for some of the state's cavity-nesting ducks, when they are within striking distance of suitable bodies of water. The wood duck is, by far, the most abundant, but not so long ago it was almost a thing of the past in Vermont and elsewhere in New England. Extensive logging of the mature trees needed for nesting, drainage of wetlands for crops and urbanization, heavy predation on its eggs and young by the ever-present raccoon, and the relative ease with which hunters could shoot it all helped to bring wood-duck populations to a precarious low by the turn of the twentieth century. It was threatened to such a degree that in 1918 both Canada and the United States declared a moratorium on its hunting. Thanks to this protection by law, the maturation of America's forests, and the willingness of adult wood ducks to adopt nesting boxes (which were placed in the marshes and on the edges of ponds, away from raccoons and other predators), this beautiful bird was able to build back its numbers. In Vermont the wood duck is now at its best in regions containing nut-bearing trees—the oaks, hickories, and beeches—since nuts make up a major portion of its diet.

Although several duck species nest in tree cavities, there is always a touch of incongruity about such water-oriented birds standing or sitting in trees. But one soon realizes their rightful place there, as expressed by the wildlife biologist Reuben Trippensee (1953):

> The nest of wood ducks is made in cavities in trees made by pileated woodpeckers or gray squirrels, or just cavities where decay has removed the heartwood. Such sites may be near the water or at considerable distance from it. . . . The entrance hole can be unbelievably small and still be large enough for the female to enter. She flies directly into the opening and by some unknown mechanism stops with little injury to herself. . . . After the eggs are hatched, the female coaxes the young from the nest by calling to them and leading them to the nearest water. The young birds are able to swim as soon as they are dry and look like yellow bumblebees on the water.

A widely distributed diving duck of ocean bays and large inland lakes, the common goldeneye (known to hunters as the "whistler," for the sound its wings make as it flies) also builds its nest in tree cavities in swamps, but heads to the open water for clams, crustaceans, and submersed aquatic vegetation. The breeding population center of this medium-sized duck is in Canada, with Vermont as its southern limit.

The other cavity-nesting ducks of the swamp are the mergansers ("sawbills"), which use their narrow, tooth-edged bills for catching fish. Two species of these divers frequently nest in Vermont: the common merganser and the smaller hooded merganser. Their habitats and food preferences keep them from competing with each other, even

Wood Duck Box. Wood ducks readily use such human-made boxes for nesting, substituting them for the tree cavities that are their normal homes. The boxes have helped wood duck populations build back from serious lows earlier in the century, when large trees suitable for nesting were severely depleted by intense logging. Now the species is one of the most common ducks in the Eastern wetlands. The conical predator shield below the box keeps out raccoons, water snakes, and other predators of nests. Notice the large spider web constructed in the birds' absence, a quick way to see if the box is inhabited or not. Other cavity-nesting animals sometimes use the boxes, among them common mergansers, hooded mergansers, owls, and flying squirrels. Drawing by Ann Pesiri Swanson.

though they may nest in the same area. The common merganser pursues small or medium-sized fish such as perch and pickerel in the waters of lakes and large rivers, whereas the hooded feeds mostly on small fish, tadpoles, insects, and even some vegetation in ponds, sloughs, and slower rivers, never far from the forest.

On several occasions, two or even three cavity-nesting ducks have used the same site at the same time: eggs of wood ducks, hooded mergansers, and goldeneyes have all been found together in one nest box at several wildlife refuges in Vermont. But these nests, called "dump nests," are usually formed very early in the breeding season and are unsuccessful, as they are abandoned.

Reptiles and Amphibians

The swamp is a fertile breeding area for reptiles and amphibians. Frogs are the most noticeable, especially in the early spring, when they arise from hibernation and fill the days and nights with their territorial and mating songs. Spring peepers, wood frogs, and gray treefrogs are especially active then, as is the larger, terrestrial pickerel

Gray Treefrog. Somewhat warty like a toad and able to change color from brown to gray to green depending on surroundings, this is the larger of Vermont's two species of treefrogs, but still is only 1¼ to 2 inches in length. With its long legs and toes—the latter equipped with sticky pads—it readily climbs plants, particularly shrubs and small trees. When giving his sustained trill at spring mating time, the male inflates his chin sac like a tiny balloon. People may hear an individual calling from a tree in summer and think it is a bird.
Drawing by Ann Pesiri Swanson.

frog, identified by a call that is described as "a finger on a balloon." Several species of salamanders live in Vermont swamps, least conspicuous of which are the so-called "mole" salamanders—the spotted, Jefferson, and blue-spotted are those occurring here—which spend most of their lives underground, in this case in the rich damp soils or under logs, emerging only in spring to migrate overland to traditional breeding locations, usually temporary woodland ponds (also called vernal pools).

One mole salamander, the Jefferson, is rather plain and slender. The other, the spotted, has big yellow spots on a black background and is one of our larger and more handsome species. It often takes up winter residence in house foundations, after having moved over considerable distances from the waters of its hatching, and is found crawling over the floor when the basement has been partially flooded by rain or melting snow. After winter this strong migrant will travel steadily until it reaches water by mating time.

Studies indicate that Vermont's mole salamanders have declined drastically in the past few years, and the suspected reasons are habitat

Spotted Salamander. One of the largest and most handsome salamanders in Vermont, measuring 6 to 7 inches from nose to tip of tail and with yellow spots on a deep back background. A so-called mole salamander, this species spends much of its life in the soil or under logs; for winter it often moves to hibernating areas, such as between the stones of house foundations. At night in the rains of early spring, it migrates en masse to traditional breeding places, usually vernal pools. Drawing by Ann Pesiri Swanson.

destruction and, more insidious, environmental degradation from industrial air pollution in the East and Midwest, which are brought here by the prevailing winds and "dumped" in the rain and snow.

The northern water snake lives in the swamp, as well as other watery areas—it is equally likely to swim in marshes, rivers, and ponds, or slide over the land nearby, for this reptile is semiaquatic, able to hunt on land as much as in the water. Though it has a distinct skin pattern of irregular dark-and-light-brown bands and patches, in water this snake seems to be completely dark, and has led many people to believe that the poisonous cottonmouth (water moccasin) has somehow found its way into Vermont. In reality, the cottonmouth comes no closer to us than southern Virginia, but this unfortunate misidentification has caused the water snake much persecution. Though it is defensive to the point of biting if handled, the water snake is nonpoisonous. It feeds mostly on small nongame fish, amphibians, and other aquatic animals, in addition to several land species, and it may actually do a service to the fisheries by helping to weed out the less desirable pan fish, leaving more space for the game species.

Other Forested Wetlands

Other "swamp-like" wetlands—typified by an overstory of trees and periodically saturated soils—occur in Vermont, providing an extra dimension of plant community and wildlife diversity.

Floodplain Forests: Along many of our larger rivers are extensive sections of floodplain where the soils are subjected to occasional flooding, often every year during spring runoff, but become drained and relatively dry in summer. Additionally, the flooding waters bring with them and deposit great quantities of clays and silts (alluvium), which mix with the organic matter there. These events, then, create special environmental conditions that support distinctive "floodplain forests" of silver maple, cottonwood, willows, and various others (white ash, butternut, slippery elm). In the Champlain Valley, Connecticut River Valley, and southern Vermont, sycamore and hackberry sometimes occupy the floodplains, as well.

Most floodplain forests are almost without a shrubby understory; instead, the herbaceous ground layer is often thick and lush, with ostrich fern, wild leeks, nettles, and many others making a sea of green in spring and summer. Many mammals use these zones for travel or as homes (muskrats and beaver in bank dens, for example), while birds such as northern orioles, warbling vireos, warblers of many species, and others remain concealed in the protection of the high canopies.

Woodland Seeps: In spring-fed, permanently wet areas in the forest conditions may be right for a fairly common, but always small (sometimes tiny), type of wetland, characterized (variable, depending on location) by water cress, golden saxifrage, horsetails, sensitive fern, and several species of moss. Seeps are also important as a source of food and water for woodland animals, especially in winter when they may remain open and free of ice and snow. In fact, they may help wild turkeys survive deep-snow winters by offering places for them to scratch and peck for food.

(Woodland seeps are quite different in plant species composition from the more open, exposed seeps sometimes found along river banks in calcareous bedrock regions. In such "riverine seeps" grow such species as grass-of-Parnassus, Kalm's lobelia, cotton grasses, and a variety of other sedges.)

Vernal Pools: Seeming to blend with the hardwood forests surrounding them, and undetected by the casual eye in summer, fall, and winter, vernal pools are small, discrete, yet critical wetlands whose presence becomes obvious in early spring after the snow melts.

Then, in various places one can see where water rests in little ponds among the trees, pools of perhaps 1500 square feet and from one to three feet deep. These are the vernal (named for the time of their occurrence), or ephemeral (for their duration), pools, without inlet or outlet, whose source of water is the winter snow, ice, or rain. Except for the trees that ring them, they are generally devoid of rooted vegetation, but have a rich layer of organic matter at the bottom.

The pools look quiet and empty, but upon closer inspection (aided by a microscope), one may be startled by the life that teems within: mosquito and midge larvae wriggle at the surface; translucent fairy shrimp flip around in the deeper parts; copepods (a tiny crustacean) cruise throughout; larvae of salamanders, mayflies, caddisflies, and damselflies crawl about the bottom; fingernail clams, no bigger than their name describes, reside in the bottom muck. Fortunately for all, there are no fish to prey on them.

The first nocturnal spring rain after the air temperature reaches at least 40 degrees Fahrenheit (usually late March or early April) marks an important time in the life of vernal pools. Then, under cover of night, spotted and Jefferson salamanders emerge from their underground habitation and, using traditional routes and often over considerable distances, migrate en masse to the pools—the same ones they and their predecessors have used for generations. There, by the tens or sometimes hundreds, they breed and lay eggs.

By summer the vernal pool will have disappeared, its waters dried up, its residents either entering dormant phases as eggs or larvae in the leaf litter or soil (e.g., many invertebrates) or by dispersal to other areas (salamanders, adults of insects).

Being small, not obviously wetlands nor manifestly critical to an important group of wildlife, and occurring in widely scattered locations, vernal pools have not often received the protection they need. Logging, road building, and residential or commercial development have taken their toll. On the other side of the coin, knowledge of them has also been a problem: being so concentrated at these sites at one particular time of year, spotted salamanders have been subject to heavy collection for the biological supply houses. Therefore, education and awareness must go hand in hand to afford these places adequate protection. By such means will we realize that a vernal pool is really an oasis in both time and place.

13

Ponds and Lakes

We sail out into open water. We have come to where the current stops and the water is gathered into reservoirs of many sizes and shapes, the receivers of the water from the uplands before it continues on its way to the ocean.

These reservoirs are usually classified as ponds or lakes, but the distinction is not always clear. Ponds are on the whole smaller and shallower than lakes, and have more extensive bottom vegetation. Since ponds are shallow, their waters are heated uniformly in summer or cooled uniformly in fall, whereas lakes are deep enough to develop thermal layers. In summer, a warm layer lies above a cool one; in winter, cool above warm (in reality, the lower layer remains more constant in relation to the changeable upper layer). As we shall see later, this stratification, or lack of it, determines to a great degree the types of fish that inhabit each body.

Some lakes occupy sites that have been around for millennia, dating back to geological processes associated with crustal movements and plate tectonics more than 500 million years ago. Lake Champlain, as we mentioned before, sits in a deep, long trench thought to be created when a massive block of bedrock dropped down more than 700 feet between the Adirondacks and the Green Mountains; Lake Dunmore, near Brandon, is a low place in a series of metamorphic-rock folds on the western side of the Green Mountains. Of course, these ancient sites subsequently were much modified by the glaciers, and most of the lakes we see today owe at least part of their character in one way or another to the ice sheets.

The glaciers made lakes in one of two different ways: by gouging out ("overdeepening") preexisting basins, valleys, or pockets, or by depositing material they had eroded and transported, blocking old drainages and building new basins.

Most of the gouged basins contain deep, clear, cold, and highly stratified water. Lake Willoughby is a classic example: the rock between the masses of Mounts Pisgah on the east and Hor on the west was ground out and eroded by an ancient river that ran between the two peaks, which had probably begun by following a long crack (fault) in the rocks. The river and glaciers enlarged and deepened this trough until it became one of the deepest lakes in New England, dropping to more than 300 feet in some places. Glacial till from the outwash

A Vermont Lake. The contemplative time of sunset fishing, at Great Averill Pond in extreme northeastern Vermont. Photo courtesy Vermont Department of Tourism and Marketing.

plugged the north and south ends, creating the long, scenic lake we now see. Also in the northern part of Vermont, Crystal Lake, Great Averill Pond, Maidstone Lake, and Lake Seymour exhibit features of gouged basins. So, in more southern parts of the state, do portions of Lakes St. Catherine and Bomoseen.

Though lakes lying in gouged basins usually have cliffs and other tourist-drawing postcard-pretty scenery, they are in a minority in Vermont. Those made by the deposition of glacial till and damming are far and away the most common here. These are ordinarily rather shallow, have a sandy-gravelly floor overlaid with muds and silts, feature much vegetation at the edges, and do not become thermally stratified. Lake Carmi, Lake Elmore, Emerald Lake, and parts of Lake Champlain well illustrate these attributes.

Kettles, mentioned earlier, are a special class of depositional ponds, beginning as depressions in the land where an isolated block of glacial ice was trapped and melted, and where no proper inlet or outlet existed. Kettles are usually fairly symmetrical in shape, often nearly round and small. Many of them have become bogs, as perhaps

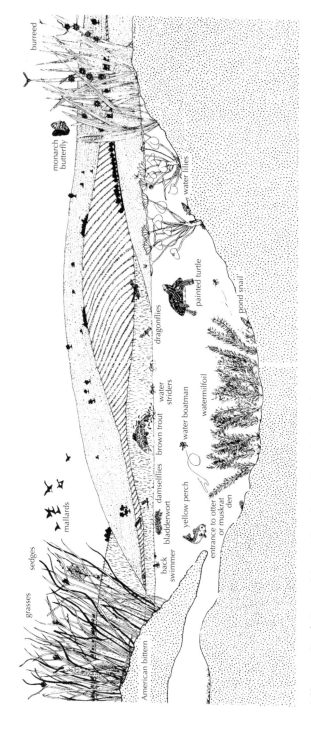

A Vermont Pond. Some of the activity of a small pond, depicted in cross-section. Drawing by Ann Pesiri Swanson.

burreed

monarch butterfly

water lilies

grasses

sedges

mallards

American bittern

back swimmer

bladderwort

damselflies

brown trout

water striders

dragonflies

painted turtle

yellow perch

water boatman

watermilfoil

entrance to otter or muskrat den

pond snail

will many more of them. Spectacle Pond at Brighton State Park near Island Pond is a large kettle, only 8 to 10 feet at the deepest, with a thick bottom of muck. Silver Lake in Barnard is another fine example of a large kettle pond.

Size, however, is not always a good criterion for determining whether a basin was gouged or was formed in a depositional moraine. Many of the small high-elevation ponds in the Green Mountains, such as Bear Pond, Lake of the Clouds, and Sterling Pond (all in the Mount Mansfield State Forest), are shallow and nearly filled with organic matter, but they are gouged basins. On the other hand, some or portions of some of our larger lakes are depositional, such as Island Pond and Lake Bomoseen.

Like any of the ecosystems we have talked about, ponds and lakes are not static: they are constantly evolving. They pass through stages of vegetation development as surely and predictably as grasslands or forests, only in the case of these bodies of water they are in the process of being filled in, with sediments brought by rivers and matter from dying organisms, to become dry land at some future time. Centimeter by centimeter, year by year, century by century the lake bottom builds. Finally, the lake is shallow enough for the sun to call forth plants, and then as plants die, the soil accumulates even faster. The lake thus transforms into a marsh (or perhaps a bog), next into a swamp, finally into the familiar forest. The lake by then has died and land has been born. It seems to be a one-way journey to extinction, but future lakes may come from the mighty movements of continents, the warping of mountains to make valleys, and, perhaps in the distant future, more glaciers.

Many outside influences can change the course of development of a pond or lake. The rate of sedimentation, water quality, basin depth, and the speed of water flowing through them are all important factors. Great quantities of fertilizers coming from agricultural runoff and phosphates from detergents have resulted in abnormally fast and luxuriant plant growth in many lakes (eutrophication), causing clogging of the shallower bays with water weeds and premature aging of the lakes. This is a great problem in portions of Lake Champlain and other water bodies.

Intentional or inadvertent introduction of exotic (nonnative) plants and animals can have devastating effects. We have mentioned earlier the unfortunate and ominous entry of zebra mussels into Lake Champlain and its tributaries.

Since its first appearance in St. Albans Bay of Lake Champlain in 1962, Eurasian watermilfoil has spread to 38 other lakes, up and down the length of the state and across its width. Once in a body of water, it spreads quickly by vegetative reproduction (pieces breaking off and rooting), and becomes prolific and virtually impossible to control. At its worst, it clogs shallows and bays, making them impassible to boats

A Beaver Pond. Beavers, once almost extirpated from Vermont, are now abundant and can change the character of many a forest stand through their construction of dams and impounding of brooks an streams. Backwoods beaver ponds often remain good trout fishing areas for many years, if the water stays cool enough in summer, oxygenated, and not loaded with silt. Photo by John Hall.

and totally unattractive to swimming and fishing. It displaces more beneficial native aquatic plants and degrades fish spawning areas. It is worthless as food for aquatic or water-oriented animals.

It is also virtually impossible to control by mechanical or chemical methods. However, a native aquatic insect may be coming to our rescue: a tiny weevil within the last few years has been discovered feeding extensively on the watermilfoil without harming other species. If, perhaps bolstered by artificial propagation, the weevil proves an effective and appropriate "grazer," it might help bring this wild ecological swing back in balance.

The modern phenomenon of acid rains—the turning of our rainwater into mild (and sometimes not so mild) acids by the reaction of industrial air pollutants, particularly sulfur, with atmospheric moisture—has altered the basic water chemistry of many lakes and adversely affected the wildlife populations within them. The problems are most severe in the Adirondacks, where lakes have become "acid baths" and entire fish populations have been wiped out. Vermont, being somewhat protected from the prevailing winds by the Adirondacks to the west, so far seems to be suffering less, though there is mounting evidence that our bodies of water—and mountain vegetation—are indeed being affected.

Lake Champlain ("the sixth Great Lake") is one of the largest freshwater lakes in the country, 120 miles long and with 435 square miles of surface water, 587 miles of shoreline, and over 70 islands. Over 8,000 square miles of land in Vermont, New York, and Quebec drain into it. It has great depth, too, plunging over 400 feet in places (with perhaps another 300 feet of sediment beneath the water). For its impressive physical dimensions, biological diversity, attractiveness for recreation, economic importance, and sheer beauty, it is of regional, national, and indeed international importance.

For years, the Lake Champlain Basin Program has been working on ways to conserve the special qualities and features of the big lake through education, planning, and application of appropriate management techniques. However, the program received a big boost in 1990 with the passage of the federal Lake Champlain Special Designation Act, which recognized the lake as a resource of national significance and provided funds for a comprehensive plan to protect the lake and its watershed into the future. So began one of the state's major conservation planning efforts, involving hundreds of people in the basin, untold hours of work, and volumes of information and data. Five years later, the report "Opportunities for Action: An Evolving Plan for the Future of Lake Champlain" presented facts about the lake (physical, biological, social, economic) and outlined twelve key areas for action (e.g., reducing nutrients, pollution prevention, managing fish and wildlife, protecting wetlands, managing recreation).

While it concluded that the lake is generally healthy now, much preparation, attention, and work needs to be done to insure it stays that way into the future.

Despite its wealth of information and well-honed recommendations, the report is, after all, but a plan on paper. It will be up to us and those who follow to provide the energy, will, and dedication to take words and ideas, and translate them into deeds.

Lake Zones

Most lakes are divided into zones based on physical dimensions and biological characteristics. Each zone has a distinct identity and figures importantly in the dynamics of lake life. Nearest the shore is the littoral zone, where shallowness and light penetration allow plants to root and grow making it the most biologically productive area. A marsh is really a highly developed littoral zone of a wide, slow-moving river that is, for all intents and purposes, a long lake (the outstanding marshlands on the eastern side of Lake Champlain are, in effect, part of that lake's littoral zone that has been cut off from direct contact with the lake). Though often called the shore zone, the littoral zone is not just shoreline; some shallow ponds have nothing but littoral zone, since vegetation grows out to the deepest middle parts, covering the entire surface of the water.

The littoral zone, whether a marsh or a portion of a pond or lake, teems with insects and other invertebrates. The large nymphs of some dragonflies (e.g., green darner), highly predatory, propel themselves through the tangle of vegetation in pursuit of other aquatic insects and even small fish. Backswimmers, water boatmen, giant water bugs, and predaceous diving beetles, all free-swimming as adults, carry an air supply down with them on their dives underwater for prey. Whirligig beetles, also free-swimming, are mostly seen gyrating around on the surface, but they quite readily dive for prey; they have two sets of eyes, one below the surface, one above, with which they can spot prey in either place. Water striders (sometimes known as Jesus bugs, for their ability to "walk on water") hunt for other invertebrate prey on the surface, being able to stand and move about on the film with specially adapted feet. Also working the surface by virtue of their thick, water-repellent hairs, fish spiders are also able to dive and stay submerged for many minutes, sometimes more than half an hour. On the underside of the film flatworms and tiny snails are able to glide and move about in their scavenging. Hanging down from the surface film are mosquito larvae, their minute breathing tubes poking through to the air. These various invertebrates and many others represent an important component of the productivity of the lake, as they are a major source of food for many larger insects, amphibians, reptiles, fish, and birds that cruise in and over the area in search of meals.

The open water beyond the littoral zone—and including the bottom only to a depth where light still reaches—is referred to as the limnetic zone. This is the realm of plankton, the floating, microscopic organisms, both plants and animals, the former of which are able to use the sun to manufacture their food. This is an important hunting ground for some larger predatory fish: such warm-water species as largemouth bass, northern pike, and walleye spend much time here, although they also move into the outer limits of the littoral zone in search of other game.

The benthic zone is the bottom beyond the littoral and beneath the limnetic zones. It contains numerous creatures in the sedimentary muds, many more than the littoral mud, for it is better aerated than the highly organic, poorly oxygenated bottom closer to shore. Clams, crustaceans, worms of many kinds, and other invertebrates live off decayed matter lying there or the dead plankton that "snowfalls" from the waters above. These bottom animals, in turn, become food for diving ducks and bottom-scouring fish. The brown bullhead ("horned pout," alluding to the poisonous spines on its pectoral and dorsal fins) is a native catfish in many of Vermont's warm-water ponds and lakes, where at night it uses its "whiskers" in these muds to feel out its slow-moving prey.

Finally, the deeper, colder lakes have a fourth zone, the profundal.

This is the region of open water below the limnetic zone into which insufficient light penetrates for plants to grow. Because no plant plankton can live there, the few bottom-dwellers below this zone obtain food solely from what drifts down from the limnetic zone. Since this zone is far from the air, insulated by the waters above it, it remains cool in summer and thus may harbor some cold-water species of fish. There is not enough food here, however, so the fish travel elsewhere to hunt. These fish may roam the various lake levels and zones during the temperate times of the year, but during the hot days of summer and the ice-covered months of winter they retreat to the profundal zone.

Fish

More than 80 species of fish inhabit Vermont ponds and lakes, from the tiny minnows to one of the largest freshwater fish in the world, the lake sturgeon. Most of these species are the so-called warm-water variety, those that prefer ponds and shallow lakes, where the waters are uniformly heated in summer and abundant vegetation grows at shoreside.

Of these warm-water fish, the yellow perch is, by far, the most common. It is often ignored by sport anglers but it actually constitutes, in total pounds taken, the most important food fish in Vermont. It can be caught almost any time, anyplace, and is most popular in winter, when it can be taken through the ice and its flavor seems best. Chain pickerel, northern pike, largemouth bass, sunfish, bullhead, suckers, and several others are also common warm-water fish in these waters. Some people regard these as "trash" fish, worthless for sport and harmful to game species, but others value them. For example, northern pike have long been considered by many to be vicious predators; some people will take every opportunity to eliminate them, including shooting them in flooded fields, marshes, and shallows as they spawn in the early spring. Other people, however, look at the northern pike as a fine sport fish, with a spirited fighting nature and a good trophy size; many come miles just in search of the pike.

In the lakes where the lower layer of water remains cool or cold the year round, the cold-water species are to be found: trout of several kinds, smelt, and, in special places, salmon. These fish, strongly associated with the north country, spend most of their time in the depths, although in some cases they may move into shallower water or even into rivers to feed or spawn.

Rainbow trout are often found in the cold waters, as are the lake trout. The latter, largest of our trout species, prefers the very deep lakes where there is a high dissolved-oxygen content. It is a nonmigratory native species, feeding and spawning in the deepest parts of the open water (unaccountably, however, in some lakes outside Vermont it spawns in shallow areas). A fine sport fish summer or winter, the lake trout may weigh 25 pounds or more and maintains stable populations in such cool northern lakes as Willoughby, Maidstone, and Seymour, and Great and Little Averill ponds. It is known to have inhabited Lake Champlain in fair numbers before 1880 but, for as yet unexplained reasons, has virtually disappeared from there. There are several hypotheses for the fish's decline, among them severe depredation on young trout by the smelt (a species that shares its region of the lake) and a general worsening of conditions in Lake Champlain. These, however, seem implausible, given the general good health of Lake Champlain today. The most likely principal cause, say many fisheries biologists, is the sea lamprey.

The sea lamprey is a primitive, jawless fish of the North Atlantic that, with its round, sucker-like mouth, attaches itself to other fish (primarily salmonids), scraps away the flesh with rows of rasping teeth, and lives as a parasite on their body fluids. As an anadromous fish (living in salt water and moving up rivers for spawning), it apparently lived naturally in Lake Ontario, having gained access by the St. Lawrence River, but was stopped from reaching the other Great Lakes by Niagara Falls. However, with construction of a canal around the falls in the late 1800s, sea lampreys moved into Lake Erie, then to Huron, Michigan, and Superior. There it helped bring the salmonid sport fishery to near collapse.

The sea lamprey also apparently invaded Lake Champlain via the St. Lawrence River, and, thence Richelieu River and Chambly Canal, over the same period of time and, according to state fisheries biologists, has had a similar, long-term debilitating effect on Champlain's salmonids, most notably lake trout.

Attempts to boost the lake trout population through stocking of hatchery-raised fish could not correct what was perceived to be an unhealthy ecological imbalance. Keying off the experience in the Great Lakes, Vermont embarked on a program to reduce sea lampreys by treating feeder rivers (where lamprey spawn) with a pesticide that kills lamprey young. The program began in 1996, amid outspoken concerns over the effects of the pesticide on nontarget organisms, especially native mussels and rare fish. While the program shows early signs of success, without irreversible harm to nontarget species, future years will tell the true tale of its effectiveness.

One species of salmon lives in a few lakes in Vermont and apparently has done so since glacial times. The landlocked salmon, otherwise known as the Sebago salmon (after one of its ancestral homes, Sebago Lake, Maine), is believed to have evolved from a stock of the Atlantic salmon that was denied reentry to the sea by an intervening barrier created by the receding glacier.

The landlocked salmon retains much of its kinship with the Atlantic salmon, both in appearance and in its schooled migration from lakes upstream to spawning grounds in rivers. It is as if the species shifted its instinctive attraction to salt water to the fresh water of lakes. In Vermont its native range was traditionally restricted, a few inhabiting Lake Champlain, but mainly most of the species living in Lake Memphremagog and its major tributary, the Clyde River. There it was relatively abundant until the 1930s, but soon after that it began to fade under the developing industrialization and dams and the unstable water levels they caused. By 1950 the species was rare and by 1965 it was almost gone.

To reverse an impending permanent loss, the Vermont Fish and Game Department initiated a landlocked-salmon-restoration project in the 1960s. Young fish from a remnant population of the Lake Memphremagog strain had some years earlier been taken to Maine to be raised as brood fish. Fry from these captives were brought back to Vermont, raised in hatcheries here, and released in tributaries to various lakes that were deemed suitable for their survival and growth. The program is still under way and appears successful to date. In addition, a new hatchery on the shores of Lake Champlain may well provide the seeds for future populations of landlocked salmon in that big lake, as well as elsewhere.

Lake Champlain's 440 square miles contain rich and varied fisheries, which in times past supported a thriving industry, and which have always been a great attraction for anglers.

It has both warm- and cold-water species, depending on the geographic region and the depth of water. Perch are abundant in practically every shallow area. Smallmouth bass, typical of clearer and cooler waters, are the most common of the black bass, though largemouth bass also live here in sizable numbers. American eels spend their adult lives in the lake (as well as in most rivers of the state outside the Northeastern Highlands), then migrate out to the Atlantic Ocean for spawning—just the opposite cycle from the Atlantic salmon. The small, silvery-gray smelt is one of the cold-water species most often caught in winter; it is relished for its fine flavor.

The 1800s and early 1900s were when the lucrative commercial fishing industry existed on Lake Champlain. Walleye (pike perch) and whitefish (a relative of the trout) were the mainstays of the fishery and were principally caught in nets when they massed on their spawning runs—the walleye in spring, the whitefish in the fall. The catches were large: from 1893 to 1904, for example, yearly averages of almost 40,000 pounds of walleye and 38,000 pounds of whitefish were taken, supplying both the Canadian and the American markets.

The netting of these fish on their spawning runs and grounds created bitter controversy in those years, a controversy that has continued in various forms up to today. Walleye has always been the focus of this debate, since, as one of the finest-tasting fish, its spring migration would draw hundreds of fishermen. Walleyes schooled by the hundreds of thousands in Missisquoi Bay, coming from both the United States and Canadian waters of Champlain. They would then spawn in the bay or in the channel of the Missisquoi River, where they were netted. Public pressure resulted in 1911–12 in laws preventing the netting of walleyes in Vermont, but the Canadians continued this practice, not only for their own markets, but for the American ones as well—an added insult to the Vermont fishermen. Finally, however, in the 1960s Canada also outlawed the indiscriminate netting of spawning fish.

The walleye, being a favorite game fish, has always been in the public eye, more so than the whitefish. That species, though a substantial part of the old commercial enterprise, and though still abundant in Lake Champlain, is hardly talked about anymore. It is a resource that is almost untouched today, for reasons hard to determine.

Some fish in Lake Champlain and its major tributaries are found nowhere else in Vermont. Several are "living fossils," belonging to ancient lines of fish now extinct, and their presence here can be traced back to the effects of the Ice Age.

One such ancient species is the lake sturgeon, among the largest freshwater fish in the world. Individuals weighing more than 300 pounds have been caught, though in Vermont the biggest have been just over 125. The physical attributes of this bony (ganoid) fish testify to its antiquity: a skeleton of cartilage rather than bone, an asymmetrical tail, bony plates covering the head, and diamond-shaped scales. With these characteristics, the sturgeon reminds one of a shark, which is a primitive fish of the oceans. The comparison is further enhanced by the location of the two species' mouths on the underside of their heads—the sturgeon uses it for "vacuuming" food from the lake bottom, however, rather than attacking large prey.

The sturgeon, once an important food for the natives in Vermont and New York, later become a commercially valuable catch for white settlers. In those early years it probably lived in both the St. Lawrence and Connecticut rivers, in addition to Lake Champlain. But since it must enter main, unspoiled tributaries for spawning, it has suffered under the subsequent damming of those rivers, as well as the siltation from farmland runoff, and now it is scarce enough to be on Vermont's endangered-species list. It is so infrequently caught, and then quite by accident, that startled anglers often do not know what it is.

Patriarchs like the sturgeon, but with more sizable populations, are the bowfin and the long-nosed gar. Their primitive body characteristics are similar to the sturgeon's, but in addition they have an air bladder that acts like a lung, through which they can actually breathe air directly, much in the manner of African lungfish. This allows them to stay for extended times in oxygen-poor waters, such as in a marsh

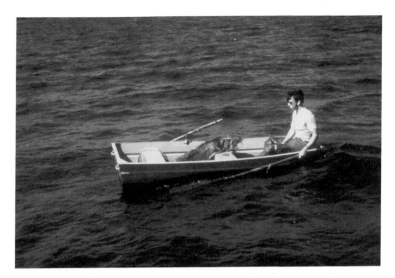

Lake Sturgeon. In his 1842 book *Natural History of Vermont*, naturalist Zadock Thompson wrote of the lake (then called round-nosed) sturgeon: "This fish is quite common in Lake Champlain, and grows to a very large size. It is frequently taken in the seine measuring more than 6 feet in length, and weighing 100 pounds or more." It is now imperiled and listed as an endangered species in Vermont. Here an angler, not knowing what he had caught, brought in this large specimen. Photo by Robert Candy.

or muddy shallows, where they swim near the surface and gulp air. Both are voracious feeders, and a turmoil witnessed at the surface of a Champlain marsh or shoreline may well involve one of these fish in action.

Of all the lakes in Vermont, Champlain alone has these ancient species. It is likely that over a long period of time its size has provided the only habitat satisfactory for the needs of such large, specialized fish. Following the glacier's retreat they probably lived in many other big lakes in the north, but as the waters receded they were unable to sustain themselves: the lakes' shrinking produced increasingly specialized local conditions that impinged on the fish more and more.

Other fish in Lake Champlain also remind us of its onetime tie, at the close of the Wisconsin glaciation, to the Atlantic Ocean through the St. Lawrence River. The fleshy, almost eellike ling is a freshwater codfish whose ancestors are thought to have come from the sea, entered the basin during the era of the Champlain Sea, and been subsequently cut off from egress to the ocean. They adapted totally to life in fresh water, have since evolved in that setting, and have even moved into many rivers adjoining the lake. The sheepshead, so-called for the appearance of its blunt head, has a similar history, as we believe does the smelt, a cold-water species that normally migrates from salt to fresh water to spawn, like the salmon or shad. Smelt have been taken by people to many other lakes in Vermont, where for the most part they have evidently done very well.

Birds

On Vermont lakes in summer, especially the large ones, the "sea gulls" are ever-present in greater or lesser numbers. The ring-billed gull is the species seen most often in the state now, as it also feeds in the smaller lakes, swarms around town dumps, and follows the plow in many a farmer's field. It is interesting to note that it had not even been sighted in Vermont until the 1940s, at which time its population exploded everywhere in the East and moved inland. It even outnumbers the herring gull on Lakes Champlain and Memphremagog, and may, in fact, be driving that gull out. The competition focuses on the shared breeding sites: both species nest on islands in Lake Champlain, some of which are really no more than rocky emergences from the lake. Here ringbills form large colonies and the herring gulls smaller, more isolated groups on the fringes of the ringbills', where they seem barely able to hang on. Over 7,000 pairs nest (1997) on Young Island (off Grand Isle), and on one of the Four Brothers Islands more than 12,000 ringbills now nest each year. Elsewhere on the lake small colonies of them are also scattered, occasionally sharing the sites with colonies of the common tern.

The Four Brothers Islands, technically in New York and owned by The Nature Conservancy, are a preservation area, home to other interesting birds, some not strictly "water" or lake birds at all. There the black-crowned night-heron has a rookery of 30 to 35 individuals that nest and roost in scraggly cedar trees growing over the island. As their name implies, these herons are busy mostly at night, sleeping during the day. In summer evenings you may hear their hoarse "wok-wok" as they fly with slow wings to feed in outlying marshes and swamps. The cattle egret, closely related to the herons, is an interesting newcomer to the Four Brothers, in fact, to the United States. It made its first appearance in the Western Hemisphere sometime between 1920 and 1930 in South America, having wandered or been blown in a storm from its native home, Africa. From South America, it got to the West Indies, thence to Florida, where the first breeding was recorded for the country in the 1950s. Since then it has moved north, breeding on the Four Brothers Islands for the first time in 1973. More recently it has been seen in other areas, occasionally a good distance from Lake Champlain. This white egret is a bird of the open fields, where it follows cattle and other farm animals here as it does wild animals in Africa, picking up insects and worms that their hooves stir up.

A more recent immigrant is the double-crested cormorant, the black "shag" of the Atlantic coast, familiar to most there as it sits in groups on rocks and small islands, flies singly or in small flocks low over the water, or dives for fish. This long-necked, colonial-nesting bird, now so prevalent along the coast, ironically was near extinction earlier in the century due to persecution, loss of habitat, and heavy pesticide use. Since the 1970s, however, it has made a remarkable comeback (estimated 96,000 breeding pairs). It made its appearance in Vermont in the 1960s, and bred first in 1982 on Young Island in Lake Champlain. Since then its population has exploded, with an estimated 1,500 to 2,000 pairs nesting on seven islands in the lake (1994).

Cormorants' high, and growing, numbers and nesting habits (colonial, on small islands) have raised some questions and considerable concern over their impact on the lake's fish populations and on the vegetation of the small islands. The state Fish and Wildlife Department has already attempted to control numbers at some of the more sensitive sites (e.g., where they are a threat to the endangered common tern) by destroying eggs, and research is underway on food habits, population dynamics, and the likely future picture.

With the summer days shortening and blending into fall, the lakes and ponds of Vermont begin to reveal new birds, the migrants on their way south. As mentioned earlier, Lake Champlain, an important branch of the Atlantic Flyway, attracts the greatest variety and numbers, while the other main branch, the Connecticut River, draws fewer birds. Most of the larger lakes, however, have something to offer the bird-watcher at this time of year.

Earliest to appear are the shorebirds, the sandpipers and stubbier-billed plovers, as they begin passing through as early as mid-July. Shorebirds migrate over bodies of water, yet stop to rest and feed along the exposed edges, where they are most often seen. Low-water years bring down many new species, those that would normally fly over Vermont to marshes and shores elsewhere but which come down to take advantage of newly exposed flats in marshes, rivers, or lakesides. For example, an artificial drawdown in 1974 of the Dead Creek Waterfowl Area near Addison attracted great numbers of shorebirds, including species rarely, if ever, seen in Vermont.

Ducks and geese arrive in October and November, the dabblers working the perimeters and marshes, the divers heading for more open water. The geese split the difference, moving at the edges and into fields to feed, but spending much resting time in the open-water areas.

The most regularly seen diving ducks at this time are the common goldeneye, the smaller bufflehead ("butterball"), the ring-necked duck, the greater and lesser scaups ("bluebills"), three species of ocean-bound scoter, and the common merganser. A few other birds more oriented to oceans and saltwater bays appear sporadically, such as the oldsquaw, the red-breasted merganser, and the horned grebe.

The duck so prized by hunters of the prairie states, the canvasback, is sometimes seen, but its formerly more common look-alike cousin, the redhead, is now a rarity. Both are victims in the Midwest of the draining of marshlands, potholes, and other bodies of water for conversion to farmland.

Some water birds stay longer than others in the fall, being ever more squeezed into the ice-free areas of the lakes. Several even overwinter where the water remains open, such as at the base of hydroelectric dams, the mouths of fast-moving rivers, or, as at one spot in Burlington harbor, where heat from an electrical generating plant keeps warm water circulating.

At the other end of the season's pendulum, spring soothes us out of the grip of ice and the waterfowl mellow the evenings as we see and hear them heading north. They keep pace with the thaw, moving to breeding grounds in the Canadian tundra and prairies, or perhaps farther west. Only a few diving ducks remain in Vermont to breed: the mergansers (some of which have stayed the entire winter) and common goldeneyes in tree cavities and the marsh-nesting ring-necked ducks. The rest keep going to lands far away, which they reach by May.

One large diving bird comes early and some of its kind remain in Vermont to nest, but precious few. This is the common loon, whose eerie, trembling "laugh" evokes the solitude of the unspoiled lakes of the northern wilderness. The loon was at one time fairly common to the state and New England as a whole. But it has retreated from civilization, as it requires freedom from disturbance to ensure successful nesting. Lakeside cottages, motorboats, increased tourism, and the camp-following raccoon, which preys on loon eggs and young, have driven the loon out of most of the East. A 1979 survey in Vermont yielded sobering results: 18 pairs of loons attempted to nest in the state in spring and summer, with only 12 successful nestings, which produced but 14 young. However, this was good compared with Massachusetts and Connecticut, each having only one nesting pair. Since then, numbers have fluctuated, but risen slowly. In 1996 there was a record high of 31 territorial pairs, 21 nesting, and 22 surviving chicks.

Over the ice-free seasons, and by most smaller lakes and ponds, other birds are active in their daily pursuits. Early in spring one sees tree swallows practically everywhere, twisting and turning on their wings as they snap up insects close to the water surface. Later, bank swallows return to ponds and lakes with sandy banks, where they dig their nesting burrows, often bunching in huge colonies that riddle the banks with holes. A solitary sandpiper, true to its name, may appear as a lone migrant along streamsides, ponds, and lakes. Until 1976 none had ever been reported to breed in the continental United States, but in the summer of that year breeding of the species was confirmed at a pond near Groton State Forest. So Vermont boasted a first for the country!

Common Loon. "The diver with the necklace," as the French have called it, in a lake in north-central Vermont. The loon's heavy body (its bones are not hollow as in most flying birds) and powerful legs located far back on the body allow it to dive after fish—occasionally as deep as 200 feet. Formerly an abundant bird breeding on most fair- to large-sized lakes in New England, the loon has been reduced to a few breeding pairs in southern New England, over 20 in Vermont, and greater but still critically low numbers in New Hampshire and Maine. As of 1997, it remains a state endangered species. Photo by Diane Pence.

Reptiles and Amphibians

In some respects, the area of Vermont west of the Green Mountains has more biological affinity with the Midwest than it does with the rest of the state or the East, as has been seen with some plants. In theory, the height of the mountain range and different climates and soil types on either side have been deterrents to uniform distribution of many plants and animals, and this is especially so with some reptiles and amphibians. For instance, the spiny softshell turtle is an aquatic animal of the Midwest, but an isolated population exists on the eastern shore of Lake Champlain and north in the lower Ottawa River. The map turtle lives in Lake Champlain at the mouths of the larger tributaries, such the Missisquoi and Lamoille. The map turtle, named for the intricate patterns and coloration on its head, legs, and shell (carapace), occurs here only in the water of the Lake Champlain basin, with its main range through Lake Ontario, Lake Erie, and the Midwest. It searches the muddy bottoms of the lake and rivers for its food—primarily crayfish, clams, and aquatic vegetation—and comes ashore to bask and for egg laying. It is wary on land; when approached, it scoots quickly off rocks and ledges, back into the security of water.

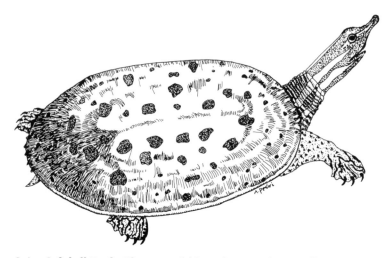

Spiny Softshell Turtle. The name of this turtle comes from small spines on the front and back of the shell that is soft at the edges and covered with a leather-like "skin"—you can see it literally bend when the turtle slides off a basking log into the water. A widely distributed reptile in the Midwest, especially the Great Plains, it barely ranges into Vermont: it usually occurs in northern Lake Champlain and major tributaries, but is not abundant even there. Adults are about a foot in length. It is primarily an aquatic animal; its long snout, like a snorkel, allows it to breathe while submerged and to root out mud-dwelling organisms to eat. Drawing by Ann Pesiri Swanson.

Vermont has one species of musk turtle, with the descriptive but not very appealing name of stinkpot (the musk is produced from glands just under the carapace and released when the animal is disturbed or frightened). It, too, is a species of primarily more western distribution, and in Vermont is limited to the Champlain Valley and southern parts of the state. It is nowhere common, preferring clear water bodies with muddy bottoms (this group is also called "mud" turtles, where they spend a great deal of time searching for food). This is a rather feisty, small turtle whose head somewhat resembles that of a snapping turtle, perhaps owing to its similar carnivorous feeding habits. Like the snapper, too, it has a long neck and can inflict a painful bite if handled carelessly. It is unusual in that it can climb trees—albeit slanting ones—where it basks on limbs overhanging the water.

Other turtles are not so restricted. The common painted turtle, for example, occurs in many ponds and lake margins throughout the state. Though it is shy, observers can often see it basking in the summer on rocks and logs at the water's edge, or its head poking up from the surface in the shallows. The snapping turtle, though equally widespread in the state, is much less in evidence, preferring to remain hidden by day in the water depths or within the shoreside vegetation,

Malformed Frogs. An array of malformations (missing limbs and eyes, deformities, etc.) in leopard frogs from the Champlain Valley. Vermont is one of very many states in which unusually high incidences of such problems occur. While a widespread environmental stress—ranging from water pollution to atmospheric ozone to ultraviolet radiation—is suspected, ongoing studies across the country have not yet pinpointed the exact cause. Photo by Richard Levey.

moving out at night to catch a fish or frog, or perhaps sample the plants. Despite its size, reputation, and rather fierce appearance, it is a reclusive creature, usually coming in contact with humans only when it comes on land for egg-laying in midsummer. The mud puppy ("proteus" to earlier naturalists) is a large, external-gilled salamander that lives in Lake Champlain and its larger tributaries, but rarely farther east. So, for many species, these east-west biological zones are as real and important as the more evident north-south ones.

Many amphibians occur over most of the state, in many types of water bodies and wetlands, among them several species of the family of "true frogs" (Ranidae), typical-looking frogs with long hind legs and toes and narrow waists, excellent jumpers and leapers. The bullfrog is the largest of all our frogs and the one least likely to be found on land, preferring the weedy margins of bigger ponds and lakes. Most people are familiar with its resounding "jug-o-rum" spring mating call, as they are with the distinctive banjo plunk of the green frog. This species is also widespread in the state, both in range and habitats (ponds, lakes, wetlands of many types), and can grow to be quite big, though not to the hugeness of the bullfrog.

Ponds and lakes are home, at least some of the year, to what might be our most common, somewhat similar-looking species of true frogs, the northern leopard and pickerel. Both breed, often in great numbers, within the littoral vegetation of ponds and lakes, as well as in other types of wetlands. They may move into open uplands—wet meadows, thickets, ditches—for the rest of the spring and summer, to return later for winter hibernation. Both are excellent leapers. Though both have large dorsal and lateral spots, the two may be distinguished by the shape of the spots: the leopard's are circular or oval, and ringed with a faint, light border, while the pickerel's are more rectangular, lined up in longitudinal rows, and without the lighter borders. Moreover, the concealed underside of the pickerel frog's hind legs is bright orange (sometimes yellow), white on the leopard.

Since the 1970s, many amphibians, even abundant species, have been showing worldwide decline, not just from polluted or overdeveloped areas, but even in remote, pristine ones. The fear is that amphibians, being especially vulnerable at various stages in their life cycles, may be the unfortunate early indicators of possible major environmental stresses, from massive changes in habitats, to global warming, to acid precipitation, to increasing ultraviolet radiation, and others.

This worry was compounded when, in 1995, reports came from Minnesota of frogs from all over the state with deformities—legs missing, fused, paralyzed, or located in odd places on the body, and even extra legs. Since then, fourteen states (Texas, California, Idaho, Montana, Colorado, North Dakota, Minnesota, Wisconsin, Kansas, Missouri, Tennessee, Ohio, Massachusetts, and Vermont) and three Canadian provinces (Alberta, Ontario, and Quebec) have reported deformed individuals of nine species of frog, one toad, and one salamander.

In Vermont in 1996 and 1997, northern leopard frogs (so far, the only species observed to be affected) from eight of the fourteen counties have shown significant deformities, from missing or stunted limbs to missing eyes, in rather alarming proportions: the incidence of deformities has average over 13 percent of all sampling, a far higher number than would be expected in normal populations. Twenty percent of them were affected in the Poultney River alone.

Researchers are grappling with the difficult task of trying to determine causes where no consistent patterns of land use or sources of pollution are evident. Theories range from airborne or water-borne pollutants, to ultraviolet radiation, bacterial or viral infection, and even larval predation by an exotic crayfish that has been discovered. Surveying, monitoring, and research on causes continue amid heightened public concern and intense media coverage.

Invertebrates

As mentioned earlier, the various zones of ponds and lakes can be amazing refuges, of sorts, for aquatic insects and other invertebrates.

Many are visible to the naked eye, but many more are microscopic. Some are highly mobile (e.g., larvae of dragonflies, water boatmen), while others are stuck in place (e.g., freshwater sponges, bryozoans, clams). See pages 205–207 for more discussion on some of these intriguing and important lives.

. . .

In a final look from lake to shore, past marshes and swamps that build to forests, we see everything reflected in the water. In the ripples the wind pushes across, we see the interplay of sun and soil, the merging of land and water. The bass below eats a perch that slid out too far from the underwater marsh. A snapping turtle lumbers out of a pond to the land to lay its eggs. A rainbow trout labors far upstream to spawn. With the ending day, a ring-necked duck coasts in from the open lake to its marshland nest, while a wood duck rises out of the marsh for the trees. And the spring peeper that greets our spring at the edge of water will be looking from the forest as we make our way through another summer.

IV Openings

And as I was green and carefree, famous among the
barns
About the happy yard and singing as the farm was
home,
   In the sun that is young once only,
     Time let me play and be
    Golden in the mercy of his means. . . .

All the sun long it was running, it was lovely, the hay
Fields high as the house, the tunes from the chimneys,
it was air
And playing, lovely and watery
     And fire green as grass.

—Dylan Thomas, *Fern Hill* (1945)

Introduction

We have come quite a way down from mountains, through forests and evergreens and broad-leaved trees, through mystical coves of bogs, down rivers to lakes and past the vital marshes. But before we leave this adventure we should step into the fields of rural Vermont, the small woodlots, or even villages. They are still much of what the state is all about—under cultivation, in pastures, managed for local wood supplies or maple syrup, cleared for houses and other buildings, or left on their own to let Nature decide.

One often hears of Vermont that it is the most rural state in the Union, meaning that it has the greatest percentage of its citizens living "in the country." This way of life leaves its personal mark on the landscape and in many ways helps make Vermont an attractive state from the tourists' point of view. It means there is a nice variety of scenery, a healthy blend of village, farm, field, and forest. Vermont is never monotonous, and the work of people often relates directly to the land.

For our varied needs in life, and in a society that is forever looking for more and more things to come out of the land, for increasing numbers of people—lumber, crops, acreage for houses, fuel, recreation—the provision for and management of the open and forested spaces are critical considerations. Now more than ever, in manipulating the environment to suit our needs we have to be careful about how, when, and where we do it, for the unanticipated or unsuspected biological and ecological consequences can be far-reaching and virtually irreversible. We must not confuse simple species diversity (more and different species) with natural diversity of native plants, animals, natural communities, and ecological processes. It is the latter, not the former, that maintains our biological heritage, richness, and integrity over the long haul.

It is estimated that 25 to 30 percent of all plant species here are not native to Vermont (including our state flower, red clover). This is also likely true to a lesser extent in some groups of animals—in particular, invertebrates (all earthworms are nonnative!), fish, and birds. Many of these species are associated in some way with human habitation, agriculture, and horticulture in its various forms. Human-created openings—fields, meadows, yards, roadsides, and others—may be the incubators where exotic species can get their start and, once established, proliferate and ultimately be able to supplant native ones, disrupt intricate ecological relationships, or weaken a system's ability to defend itself against pathogens. Their influence may go far beyond their mere presence.

A long time ago, when Indians were first made, there lived one alone, far, far from any others. He knew not of fire, and subsisted on roots, barks, and nuts. This Indian became very lonesome for company. He grew tired of digging roots, lost his appetite, and for several days lay dreaming in the sunshine; when he awoke he saw something standing near, at which, at first, he was very much frightened. But when it spoke, his heart was glad, for it was a beautiful woman with long light hair, very unlike any Indian. He asked her to come to him, but she would not, and if he tried to approach her she seemed to go farther away; he sang to her of his loneliness and besought her not to leave him; at last she told him, if he would do just as she should say, he would always have her with him. He promised that he would.

She led him to where there was some very dry grass, told him to get two very dry sticks, rub them together quickly, holding them in the grass. Soon a spark flew out; the grass caught it, and quick as an arrow the ground was burned over. Then she said, "When the sun sets, take me by the hair and drag me over the burned ground." He did not like to do this, but she told him that wherever he dragged her something like grass would spring up, and he would see her hair coming from between the leaves; then the seeds would be ready for his use. He did as she said, and to this day, when they see the silk (hair) on the cornstalk, the Indians know she has not forgotten them.

14

Fields, Farms, and Towns

It is as natural for trees to grow in Vermont as for water to run. When one is cut down twenty spring up, and the fittest survives ultimately to replace the parent tree. We need only assist nature a little, or at least give her a fair chance to assert her claims. She is a cherishing mother, and when ordinary land is protected a short time from cattle it will soon have a growth out of their reach.

—Vermont Commissioners on Forestry, 1884

Being basically a forested state, Vermont does not come easily by its open spaces. It takes work to maintain a field here. A clearing will not long remain if untended, for the natural momentum is toward building the forest, following the various paths of succession: field to shrubs to forest is a continuous evolution, set back only by fire, flood, wind, mowing by people, and grazing by animals, or else the replacement of the earth with concrete and steel.

The stone walls, often coursing mile upon mile through mature woodlands or along backroads overarching with trees, are testimony to this resiliency; they are the former definers of fields and meadows. The stone walls persist, though moss-covered and collapsing in places. But the split-rail fences of an earlier era of land clearing (1700s) have disappeared, while barbed wire running through the middle of trees is rusty evidence of yet a later one (late 1800s). The trees grow back, and the forests return as they have time and again through our history, as well as many more times on their own.

Plants of the earliest field stages must be able to tolerate the full sun and wind—the drying effects of these forces during the growing season. They must endure widely fluctuating temperatures from day to night and from season to season. They must have the means to survive the months of ice and snow, and they must have ways to reach and colonize new openings quickly.

Field plants have met those demands in many ways. The first to appear on bare soil are the annuals, growing rapidly from seed to flower in one season and releasing multitudes of seeds the same fall or winter. Fireweed is one of these, a hardy plant whose name belies its role as a colonizer of burned-over areas, but which also grows prolifically along roadsides.

Following the groundbreaking of the annuals are the biennials, which take two years to flower, then the perennials, living many years

225

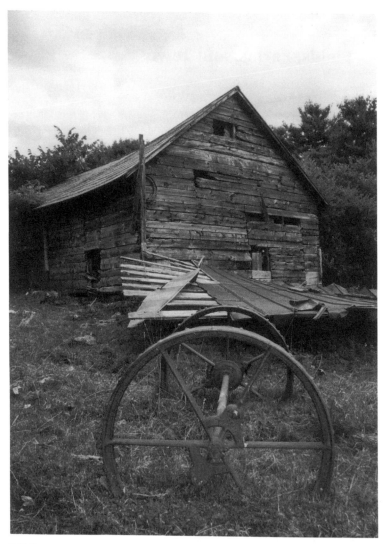

Old Farm. Photo by Brian MacDonald.

and flowering each year after reaching maturity. These two groups usually have deeper root systems than the annuals and a variety of means to retain water and endure desiccating conditions. Perennial grasses are clumped and bunched into water-holding mats and have narrow bladelike leaves with tough outer coats. The milkweeds store water in the milky sap of leaves and stems, and the fine coat of hairs covering the common mullein reflect light rays, thereby lowering leaf temperatures and evaporation rates.

These plants have effective methods of reaching new territories, and once there, of spreading rapidly. Structures attached to the seeds of milkweeds, dandelions, goldenrods, thistles, and many grasses—usually in the form of little "parachutes"—allow them to be carried away by the wind. The tough, indigestible seeds of many fruits—raspberries and blackberries, for example—are eaten by birds and mammals and then deposited elsewhere in their excrement. Other seeds, such as those of burdock and beggarticks, hitchhike by sticking to fur, feathers, or clothing.

The perennials have extensive subterranean rootstocks, from which the colony quickly expands. Above ground, the sensitive growing tips of the stems often are protected under a shield of leaves or buried in the tangle of a vegetative mat. The basal growth of grasses and the rosette of winter cress well illustrate these forms of protection.

Summer and early fall are the time for the field flowers to show their riches. The names and hues seem to come without end: the clovers and cinquefoils, a yellow snapdragon called butter-and-eggs and the sweet-smelling milkweeds, birdfoot trefoil, chicory, and bedstraws, the aggressive purple loosestrife, black-eyed Susans, Queen Anne's lace, yarrow, the many goldenrods, asters, and thistles.

Ironically, most of the pioneer plants of the fields and meadows are not native to the United States. They have come from other countries, mostly European, in the plant food for human beings or livestock, in clothing or fur, by ship or plane. Or sometimes they have been introduced intentionally, as food crops and pasturage, or simply out of a person's nostalgia for his or her homeland. The Vermont state flower, red clover, was brought over from England in 1747, for use as cattle fodder and a soil enricher; burdock and devil's paintbrush (orange hawkweed), so prevalent along almost any summer roadside, are both originally from Europe. Once early Europeans in this country had incorporated their methods of farming and way of life here, these species and many others of the field found the newly cutover eastern America similar to their original environment and much to their liking, so that, thus encouraged by the re-creation of their former habitats, they easily outcompeted the American natives, which were more at home in the woodlands.

As succession advances beyond the fields, shrubs and brambles appear, such as meadowsweet, steeplebush, alternate-leaved dogwood, blackberries, and raspberries. Small trees soon follow—staghorn sumac with its clumps of velvet red seeds, hawthorns, pin cherry, beaked hazelnut, and shadbush. In areas that have been burned, the pioneer trees may sidestep this sequence: quaking aspen and paper birch may grow from bare ground directly into the mature

Shepherd's Purse. A nonnative species now very common in the United States, this field plant is well equipped for life in the often dry open, by virtue of a deep taproot that pulls moisture and nutrients from far underground. In addition, the basal rosette of leaves can overwinter and thus initiate plant growth quickly in the spring. Drawing by Ann Pesiri Swanson.

forest and, where white pine grows nearby, it may enter the fields early and quickly take over from the herbaceous plants.

Particularly in the Champlain and Connecticut River Valleys, on moderately dry sites, red cedar may have persisted through years of grazing and grown to be a dominant species when pastures are abandoned. This is due to its general poor palatability as food for cattle (or other animals): it has prickly, juniper-like leaves when young (it is a kind of juniper), which deter would-be browsers. Only when it grows tall enough to be out of mouth's reach does it produce the more typical, soft, cedar-like needles.

This shrub stage, intermediate between open field and closed for-

Bindweed. Bindweeds, along with their fellow family members the morning glories, open their flowers in the morning, to be pollinated by bees, then usually close by noon for the rest of the day. The flowers are typical of the family, with flaring, funnel-shaped, fused petals. The species shown, field bindweed, is nonnative and occurs in many overgrown meadows. Drawing by Ann Pesiri Swanson.

est, is a habitat all its own, a productive mixing zone usually classified by ecologists as an "edge," connoting a place of great diversity and wildlife activity. Animals such as the white-tailed deer, wild turkey, and even some birds of the deeper forest come to the edge to feed. Certain birds move from the forest to openings for their territorial displays and mating—the ruffed grouse and woodcock, for example. And the edge is a home for a whole group of living things, especially birds, that neither venture far out into the open nor drop back deep into the woods.

Finally, beneath the shrubs and the rapidly growing pioneer trees, the seedlings of a new forest appear, protected in the shade of the

The Edges. Where forest meets field are often places of considerable plant and wildlife diversity. On the other hand, if penetrating into dense forest, they may also be easy avenues for predators of vulnerable deeper-woods birds. Photo by John Hall.

older growth, awaiting their turn for dominance. For most of Vermont, it is young sugar maples, beeches, ashes, and others of the northern hardwoods that make up this vigorous understory and one day will be the mature forest of the region (if the landowner lets the process to go that far).

Today's fields, thickets, and smaller woodlots of the Vermont hillsides and valleys still largely owe their existence and character to the farmer. Though farming has dwindled greatly in the past few decades—down from when it was the most important industry in Vermont to now, when many homesteads are falling into abandonment or being converted to country houses for people employed elsewhere—agriculture is still a substantial part of Vermont's economy. Nearly 6,000 farms continue in operation, and farming as a business ranks third, behind manufacturing and tourism. Dairy farming, based on mixed-grain croplands and pasturage, accounts for 90 percent of all agriculture in the state: it is the natural form of farming in the Vermont terrain, with its rocky soils and short growing season. Most are small farms, averaging less than 300 acres and supporting a variety of side activities to supplement the primary work, including the cultivation of honey, the supplying of firewood and lumber, and the production of something for which Vermont is world-famous—maple syrup. In addition, the 40,000 acres of Vermont Christmas tree plantations supply an average million trees each year, while 5,000 acres of apple

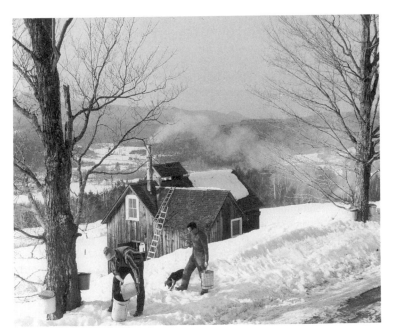

Maple Sugaring. Learned from Native Americans, sugaring in spring remains a strong ritual in the rural areas of Vermont. Traditional method involving spouts, buckets, wood fires for boiling down, and horse-drawn sleds are still very much in evidence despite the increasing use of such labor-saving devices as plastic tubing and oil burners. Vermont ranks first in the nation in maple syrup production. Photos courtesy Vermont Department of Tourism and Marketing.

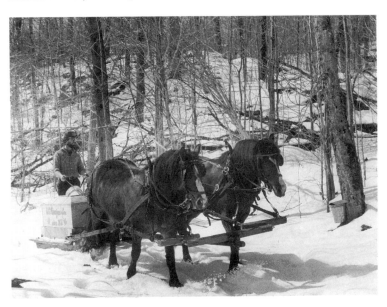

orchards annually yield 14 million dollars-worth of the sweet fall fruit. The term "woodlot" generally refers to a tract of privately owned forestland, of various sizes and shapes, managed or held by the landowner for personal reasons, including firewood, timber, wildlife, recreation, maple syrup, and solitude. Since the vast majority (85%) of all Vermont forestland is in such woodlots, to a great degree they determine the ecological and scenic character of the state. And while such patterns may contribute to an attractive and diverse landscape, depicted so memorably in magazines and calendars, such checkerboarding of the land is a great, sometimes frustrating, challenge for conservationists: it makes it very difficult to ensure adequate—and properly managed—habitats for such species requiring large, relatively contiguous forest tracts as black bear, lynx, and forest-interior birds. However, some landowners have banded together for this very reason, agreeing to manage their woodlots for a common conservation goal.

The picture may be changing. Since the energy crises of the 1970s, particularly the high cost of home-heating fuels, Vermonters have been increasingly looking to their forests for firewood. Now more than 60 percent of the state's residents use wood as their primary or secondary source of heat. More than ever woodlot owners are turning to foresters for information on putting their land into production for their own wood supplies. Even the scope of wood for energy is expanding: a few industrial plants in the state now use wood chips instead of coal or oil to generate electricity, and several institutions have installed wood-chip burners for heat.

The movement toward wood for energy raises many questions: how much can the woodlots produce; what are the long-term effects of continually taking many "cull" trees; and so forth. But for now, the possibilities of wood for energy have meant not only a cheaper and more local source of fuel for Vermonters, but also a way for forestry to become visible—to show its purpose and improve the timber quality of the state's woodlands.

In addition to supplying firewood and lumber, many of Vermont's woodlots have been used for generations for the production of maple syrup. Vermont is the country's leading maple-syrup producer, averaging 500,000 gallons a year. The tradition here is still strong, though ever more difficult to maintain from an economic standpoint, despite modern, labor-saving innovations. Nevertheless, maple-sugaring time in March and April remains a cherished rite of a new season, which will not soon be allowed to disappear, for it means much more than money to those involved in it.

Birds

The spring and summer fields are places of busy bird activity in Vermont. But though many species visit the fields for hunting or picking at seeds and fruits, few actually nest there, for the open space affords limited protection, and there is a lack of plant diversity and only a few "levels" of vegetation here.

The killdeer is one of the most widely recognized of the birds that do succeed in raising a brood under these conditions. It is also one of the earliest migrants to return after winter, often arriving when snow is still on the ground. This plover (the family of short-billed shorebirds) lays its eggs in completely exposed areas—plowed fields, gravel parking lots, grassy knolls, and the like. To deter predation, its eggs are nearly invisible, as they blend perfectly with the background. In addition, its young are able to run and fend for themselves soon after they hatch, and when predators are near the parents can call them to cover or else distract the enemy by ostentatiously pretending to be injured. Predators and human activity in the spring do take their toll on this bird, but the killdeer seems nonetheless to be doing very well as a Vermont species.

Out of the mountains, in grassy pastures, hay fields, and the flatlands of river valleys and lakes, bobolinks and meadowlarks nest, the males of which have pleasant bubbling territorial songs in the spring. The Savannah sparrow is one of the most common sparrows that nest within the grasses of our western lowlands. A much rarer open-field bird is the upland sandpiper, its decline over the years probably owing to the gradual replacement of fields by forests and the haying earlier in the year of the places it uses to nest.

Many of the birds that hunt over the fields nest and spend their inactive hours in a nearby forest, forest edge, or tree cavity. From above, the red-tailed hawk winds high, ready to descend upon its prey, which is working through the grasses below. The more agile and darting kestrel ("sparrow hawk"), a kind of falcon, comes in low like a boomerang for insects or small birds, or hovers over a crouching mouse. The tilting and gliding turkey vulture—once rare in Vermont but now seen regularly over many fields all over the state—looks for dead animals in the open, but retires to the seclusion of cliffs, swamps, or deep forests for nesting and roosting. (The first record of the turkey vulture's breeding in Vermont came in 1979, when mating and young were observed on a cliff in a forest near Rutland.)

With night a great horned owl or a screech owl may soar out from the trees, where it has spent the day, and on silent wings directed by great, staring eyes and large, sensitive ears, glide toward its prey. In the mornings and evenings of a fall, winter, or early spring, the short-eared owl is seen once in a while, especially in the broad valley of the Lake Champlain basin. This visitor from the north is the most open-oriented of owls seen in Vermont, frequenting the fields for both hunting and nesting (although nesting is very sporadic in Vermont).

Several smaller birds require the fields they hunt in to be near the shrub thickets or forest edges in which they nest. The bluebird, one welcome early sign for us that spring has really arrived, is one of these, eating the insects of the field but nesting in the cavities of trees nearby. In addition to fields, it is especially fond of orchards, where it finds an abundance of insects to eat.

The bluebird is Vermont's smallest species of thrush, and though popular with people it has gone through difficult periods in its history here, as well as in other places in the country. It became scarce early in this century for lack of suitable cavity-bearing trees for nesting and owing to its inability to deal with the house sparrow and the starling. The latter two were brought to the United States—the house sparrow in 1850 and the starling in 1890—by well-intentioned people, but the consequences have been disastrous. These two aliens have moved into every state in the Union, traveling east to west, and have driven the bluebird from its nest sites, preempting them for their own broods. The decline of the bluebird population reached a low in the 1960s, perhaps at that time aggravated by the use of the pesticide DDT, but with the construction of nest boxes, the leveling off of sparrow and starling numbers, and the cessation of the use of DDT bluebirds have struggled to a minor comeback.

Other small birds are busy in the shrubs that border the fields, but they often come out where they can be easily seen. The male indigo bunting, looking much like a bluebird but without the brown breast, is a common songster that perches high (telephone wires are a favorite stakeout), although the less brilliantly colored female stays down near the nest she has built in blackberries, raspberries, or other thick low shrubs. The yellow warbler, one of the most widespread of all warblers, lives in bushy areas, streamsides, river bottomlands, and other semi-open habitats in Vermont, as it does throughout North America. Its counterpart in wetter areas is the handsome common yellow-throat. The nests of both warblers are targets of the brown-headed cowbird, a "brood parasite" that lay its eggs in the nests of others, leaving the eggs to be incubated and the young cared for by the foster parents. The cowbird is often seen following in the footsteps of cows, picking up insects stirred up by the hooves, much as they did, it is thought, when bison and other large wild mammals roamed the plains of this country.

Cowbird nest parasitism clearly is one ecological indicator, but only one, associated with "forest fragmentation" and its effects on forest interior bird species (see page 131). Others are the usurping of cavity nesting sites (old snags, etc.) by starlings, house sparrows, and other nonnative species, and increasing predation and harrassment by edge species (raccoons) and domestic animals (particularly cats).

Several bird species spend most of their time in the shrubs and small trees of the forest edge, coming into the open only infrequently; they are nevertheless familiar in the fields through their songs. The song sparrow flits about from shrub to shrub, and the rufous-sided towhee scratches in the dead leaves, singing its "drink-your-TEEE," or sharply warning "chee-wink." There are also the "mimic thrushes," a family of birds that resemble thrushes and have the ability to imitate the songs of many birds. The two most common mimics are the catbird and the brown thrasher, but the best imitator is also the rarest in Vermont, being a bird of Southern origin: the mockingbird, of residential areas, farms, and orchards of the milder lowlands, sings more than 35 different songs of other species, repeating each phrase several times and continuing at length without a pause. This species, once restricted to the South and southern Midwest, has moved north within the last 10 to 20 years. The first breeding in Vermont occurred in 1973, in Pownal, near the Massachusetts line, and since then it has progressed steadily northward, now spending summers beyond midstate.

The mockingbird is but one of several "rural" species that only recently have moved into northern territories. The cardinal is another—heretofore a very common bird in almost every Eastern and Midwest state outside northern New England. It is being seen more and more regularly in Vermont, especially in its new range of the northern half of the state, and now even overwinters two-thirds the way up. The reasons for its range expansion are not entirely clear, but a combination of factors seems responsible: the proliferation of bird feeders, the planting of ornamental and shade trees that offer an abundance of seeds and fruits, and an absence of major predators in their favored rural or urban environments.

Some birds have even adapted to the most urban of environments, cities. Robins hop on lawns; house finches (originally a western bird) sing from ornamental trees. Chimney swifts circle about, then drop down unused chimneys for roosting or nesting. Nighthawks, not hawks at all but insect-eating birds related to whip-poor-wills, nest on flat roofs and fly high over the buildings in the evening in search of moths and other insects, their electric buzzing strangely insect-like.

In the protection of the less dense woodlands, in tall trees at the forest edge, or even in urban situations, live many of Vermont's attractive and vocal birds. The male rose-breasted grosbeak has a striking coloration and a long whistle-warble song. Though one of the finches, normally vegetarians, it feeds extensively on beetles and other insects, a reason we see it near gardens, orchards, and other open areas. In fact, one of the favorite foods is the Colorado potato beetle, and by eating it the bird provides a valuable service to farmer and home gardener, whose plants are attacked by the beetle. Most people know of the northern oriole (formerly called the Baltimore oriole), dressed in vibrant orange-on-black, whistling loud and clear, and constructing intricate nests high in elms and other trees. The nest is truly a work of art, finely woven, shaped like a gourd, and featuring a side entrance.

The breeding activity of small birds continues in the weedy fields, forest edges, and thickets throughout the spring and sometimes into summer. A late-nesting field species is the common goldfinch, the "wild canary" that seems to time its nesting to the maturation of the seeds it feeds its young and the appearance of the thistledown with which it lines its nest. The handsome cedar waxwing, crested and buff-colored, is one of the latest in the season to nest, even though it arrives in Vermont early or sometimes stays here throughout the winter. The young waxwings are fed regurgitated fruit (cherries, berries, and so forth) that have ripened in the summer. When the young have fledged and begin to be on their own, one becomes more conscious of the waxwings, as they flock in sizable numbers and move quickly overhead, stripping the trees and bushes of their fruits.

As winter layers its cold and snow over the fields, sealing them off, and as the winds rattle the stalks of goldenrod and sumac, the birds of summer give way to those that will manage an existence off the meager remaining food supplies. Although they stay, some species, such as the goldfinch (the males of which have now molted to a plainer color), move more to the open woods and thickets, where seeds are still to be found on the trees, and they join forces with other finches—the redpolls, purple finches, and pine siskins that have come down from farther north. These and other northern visitors appear unpredictably from year to year: flocks of snow buntings, like flecks of white on white, swirl along roads or farmyards, searching manure piles for seeds; tree sparrows and dark-eyed juncos hop from shrubs or woodland margins for leftover grains, or visit bird feeders for their offering; and the ever-present blue jays canvas the areas for just about anything to eat—seeds, hibernating insects, buds, or the remains of dead animals.

The bugle call of the jay often is a warning that a predator is near, and to be watched. One is the northern shrike, a bird about the size of a robin, but ounce for ounces one of the toughest of all predators, eating other birds, as well as small mammals (shrews, deer mice). Shrikes—the northern and the rarer summer visitor, the loggerhead— are called butcher-birds for their macabre habit of hanging prey they have killed on thorns, barbed wire, or other sharp objects, apparently to store them for future use. The northern shrike is usually unable to kill its victim in the air, so it pulls the prey to the ground, where it batters the animal to death with its heavy hooked bill.

We human beings have created most of the fields we see, have made the edges that lead us into forest, and Nature has responded to what we have done: our work has discouraged some species and encouraged others. At the time of the virgin forests, edges and fields were uncommon, and so were the birds of those habitats—the chestnut-sided warbler, for example, one of the most familiar birds of

Northern Shrike. A usual perch of this winter visitor is at the top of a tree, on a telephone wire, or at some other high vantage point where it can keep an eye out for small birds and mammals of the open country. The northern shrike is one of the most skillful fliers in tight spaces. It kills prey with its heavy bill and may impale the victims on thorns or similar sharp objects, apparently to store them. The bird nests in the spruce forests of Canada. Drawing by Ann Pesiri Swanson.

shrubby areas today, but very rare in the early years of Vermont settlement. On the other hand, the untouched forest was ideal for the passenger pigeon, a species long since gone to extinction but once probably the most abundant bird on the North American continent. The bobwhite quail that now thrives on small grains of Midwestern grasslands no longer lives wild in predominantly forested Vermont, but it came to the state in the mid-1800s, after the woods had been cut over. Today this quail is "replaced" by its more woodland relative, the wild turkey, an early native that became extinct and then was brought back. What changes we bring to our future landscapes will surely be reflected in the birds that use them.

Mammals

Except for a few species of bats that fly over in search of insects, or some large mammals, such as deer, that wander in to graze or hunt, most of the mammals residing in the open areas, thickets, and woodlots are small and remain within the shelter of the vegetation, or else go below ground.

The meadow vole is a little vegetarian rodent with sunken eyes, short tail, small ears, and a loose skin—all of which allow it to move freely and quickly in its tight runways through the grasses. The short-tailed shrew hunts the field for ground insects, worms, grubs, or even small mammals in an endless search to satisfy its burning hunger; this little insectivore is busy all year, and its winding tunnels through the snow seem to be everywhere. Another field insectivore, the hairy-tailed mole, uses its spadelike front paws to excavate its way through the soil. Like the shrew, it has an extremely high metabolism and must eat constantly to fuel its body; in winter the mole moves deeper into the soil, below the line of frozen ground, to hunt a variety of organisms. This species is one of only two moles in Vermont, the other being the peculiar star-nosed mole (so called for the fleshy projections on its snout) of wetter and more forested habitats.

Some mammals live completely within the bounds of a field, others combine the fields and forest edges as home or feeding ground. Many, because of their catholic preferences, are often the unwanted companies of human beings, and may in certain situations become pests. The nighttime foraging of the raccoon and the striped skunk, Vermont's only skunk species, are all too well known to campers and homeowners of every corner of the state. Deer mice may move into country or village houses in the winter, and actually supplant the house mouse of more urban areas. Mice, chipmunks, and red squirrels have become a problem in sugar bushes that employ the relatively new method of plastic tubing to collect sap—the rodents eat into the tubing, whether to taste the sap or merely sharpen their teeth, causing considerable loss of time, money, and effort of those working the trees in the spring. And to many gardeners trying to raise vegetables, the woodchucks, deer, mice, voles, raccoons, skunks, and rabbits are an ever-present threat, the source of much annoyance.

In summer nights, bats take to the air over towns, fields, and other open areas, such as marshes, rivers, and lakes. They are out to catch their meals of insects, which they locate with the sensitive "sonar" equipment of their mouths and ears, and capture in the webs between their legs. All the bats in Vermont are insect-eating, and for all the loathing heaped on them because of their appearance, their nocturnal activities, and their reputation as carriers of rabies, in reality bats do a great service by consuming vast quantities of insects. Estimates run as high as a single bat's eating half its weight in mosquitoes each night; one researcher found that 100 little brown bats ate 42 pounds of insects over a summer.

Most bats in Vermont are nonmigratory, roosting and hibernating here in often large groups in barns, attics, and caves. The big and little brown bats are two of the most common hibernating species, and are usually the subject of most concern when they congregate by the hundreds in people's attics for their winter dormancy. A few species, such as the red bat, are more solitary and roost by day in trees, then migrate out of state as the fall and freezing temperatures approach. One species, the Indiana bat, is of particular interest. It spends summer out of state but in winter moves to Vermont, where it hibernates in only one or two caves. Such a "reversed" migration, up from more southern states in New England, departs from the normal pattern. However, its migratory habits are not the only reason for interest in this species. Inexplicably, it is becoming scarcer over all its natural range, from the East Coast to the Midwest, so much so that it has been placed on the federal endangered-species list and is the subject of much research and rehabilitation work. The Indiana bat is likewise on the endangered-species list of Vermont, where its presence is further threatened by much vandalism of its primary place of hibernation while the animal is in residence.

Winter for most field or forest-edge mammals means retirement to semi- or total hibernation underground or in other protected places, or else removal from the exposed open spaces. True hibernation is experienced in Vermont only by the woodchuck, woodland and meadow jumping mice, and some bats—whether in underground chambers, as in the case of the woodchuck and mouse, or in colonial "dormitories" or caves of bats. Other Vermont mammals, such as the skunk, raccoon, and squirrels, move into nests or dens, where they fall into deep slumber but are able to wake in winter's warmer spells, to venture out to scrounge for food.

A few field animals will move into the winter shelter of the shrubs and trees, from where they will occasionally steal out to the open, snowswept spaces for foraging or to get from place to place. The New England and eastern cottontails, both true rabbits (compared to hares, they build nests and care for helpless young, and have smaller ears and hind feet), are residents of the open, brushy country—edges of woods, shrubby areas, rural pastures, and urban yards. The New England cottontail apparently had been in southern Vermont prior to European settlement, but in low numbers. Today it is considered rare (if present at all), likely because of the extensive regrowth of forest, which by degrees eliminated its habitat. Its close look-alike, the nonnative eastern cottontail, is now the more common. An abundant species over much of North America east of the Rockies, the eastern cottontail was stocked into New England in the 1800s and has spread its range northward, in Vermont mostly into the farmlands and forest edges of the Champlain and Connecticut River valleys.

Other smaller rodents scurrying around on top of the snow become the winter targets of hungry mammals, especially the red fox and weasels, in addition to the hawks and owls. The short-tailed and long-tailed weasels are perhaps the most deadly of these predators,

Weasel. Vermont has both the long-tailed and short-tailed weasel, the first being larger and living more in the forests, the second inhabiting forest edges and openings. In winter both change into coats of white (except for the black tips of their tails), at which time they are called ermine. Young are born in the spring, after about 9 months of gestation. Weasels are very energetic hunters, as one can easily see from their zigzag prints in the snow. Drawing by Ann Pesiri Swanson.

small but extremely efficient, able to kill animals much larger than themselves. They are called ermine in winter, when they have changed their coats from brown to white.

The winter is long and bitter for Vermont's mammals, and it is the time of greatest mortality, be they predators or prey. But when the spring finally comes and the fields rise up with new foods and homes, many of the mammals will have already mated, and the young will be brought forth In the welcoming season in preparation for their own winters.

Insects

Insects play an enormous role in the workings of the field and forest. Whether in their pollination of the myriad wild flowers or in their attacks on valuable timber trees, we often measure the effect of insects in economic terms. But the small organisms, unnoticed in many instances, are also of great importance ecologically.

The display of wild flowers, pretty and perfumed as it is, is intended for eyes and "noses" other than ours. It is for the insects that have also blossomed in summer. The flowers' colors and smells attract the insects, the agents of their pollination, thus providing for the plants' posterity. The insects, in turn, find in the flowers food for themselves and their newly hatched young, or secure places in which to lay eggs. They appear in many sizes, shapes, colors, and styles of flight, giving life and vibrancy to the fields. They may be identified any number of ways: by their color and markings (from the plain white cabbage butterfly to ornate, multicolored flecks and spots of tortoise shells); size (from tiny hairstreaks to the giant silkworm moths—the largest, cecropia, with a wingspan up to 6 inches); habitat (the open grassy fields for skippers and sulphurs, the brushy edges for fritillaries and satyrs); pattern of flight (quick and jerky in skippers; slow, bouncy for monarchs); time of activity (butterflies mostly by day, moths mostly by evening or night); season (or even week) of appearance (spring azures in spring, white admirals in summer, monarchs in fall); food of their caterpillars (Baltimore on turtlehead).

One of the most familiar yet remarkable butterflies is the monarch, or milkweed, butterfly, which performs a unique migration. The species lives in Vermont all summer long, but individuals that emerge from metamorphosis late in the season make an epic journey to the mountains of central Mexico. Migration begins here in August and September—earlier in Canada—as they glide and kite their way south from high in the mountains to the expanses over Lake Champlain and other lakes. At night they congregate in trees or on rock ledges—the same places from year to year, though these individuals have never been there before. They take flight again by day. After thousands of miles of travel they arrive at the same wintering grounds their ancestors have always used. Here they mate. Months later with the spring they drift north again, although without the massed push of the autumn migration. Most do not make it all the way back to where they hatched the preceding year, but stop along the way to lay eggs and die. The new butterflies from these eggs complete their parents' trip north and they, in turn, mate and lay eggs late the same summer. The population of monarchs from this last hatch repeats the extraordinary cycle. It is interesting to speculate on the origin of—the "need" for—this migration, and on the mysterious mechanisms that allow the insects to find their way to places they have never been before.

When one mentions pollination, one automatically thinks of bees. Bees are some of the most prevalent and important insects as far as human beings are concerned, having played key roles throughout history, besides being critical to the success of many plants. Though most people equate *bee* with *honeybee* and *bumblebee*, these are only two among many thousands of kinds worldwide and hundreds in this part of the continent. But because the honeybee has for so long been linked with the lives of human beings, it has attracted the most attention and garnered the most laurels: it was sacred to the ancient Babylonians, the Incas, the Egyptians, and others. Until sugar cane was brought to Europe from the Near East, honey was the sole sweetener on that continent and the main fermenting agent in liquors. So missed was it by transplanted Europeans in the New World that the Massachusetts Bay Colony brought the honeybee here in 1638 so that colonists could begin enjoying what they once had back home. From that modest start, honeybees have become the base of a major agricultural industry in this country, worth millions every year. The honeybee became

Honeybee: The Vermont State Insect.
A honeybee colony is highly organized, with one queen laying all the eggs, drones (males) fertilizing the eggs, and workers (sterile females) carrying out the work of the hive—gathering pollen and nectar, building the comb, feeding the young and queen, and defending the hive. Drawing by Ann Pesiri Swanson.

"sacred" to Vermont, also. In 1978 it was proclaimed the state insect, owing to its value as a producer of honey and as a pollinator of apple trees, many farm crops, and countless other plants that have less commercial importance but are aesthetically important as wild flowers. It and all its later imported strains have spread across every state in the Union, working the flowers of the fields, gathering pollen and nectar for hives in the hollows of trees and other places. The honeybee has been one of our most welcome and productive immigrants.

But after being a relatively secure resident here for more than 350 years, the honeybee in the 1980s and 1990s ran into trouble. Two kinds of nonnative mites (tiny tick-like parasites), one infesting the tracheas of adult bees, the other the bee larvae, together have devastated colonies across the country, some areas losing as much as 80 percent of all their bees within two short years. This, naturally, has caused honey producers great concern; equally troubled are many fruit and vegetable growers whose crops depend on the bees for flower pollination. While some research now is directed at controlling the mites and restoring honeybee populations, other research is aimed at possible natural solutions, such as using mite-resistant native bees as pollinators.

Like the honeybee, the Vermont bumblebee is a social insect—this habit is rare, however, among bees in general. The bumblebee's nest is usually underground, whereas the hive of the honeybee is above ground; but unlike the latter, the bumblebee colony does not live through the winter. Except for new queens hatched late in summer, the entire bumblebee colony dies in autumn. These queens, having earlier mated with drones, move to subterranean seclusion to spend the winter. Though impregnated, the queens are able to delay egg laying until the following spring, at which time they emerge—often very early—to gather pollen and nectar to make into honey, which will be stored in wax cells they have just constructed. The queens then lay a few eggs in the wax cells, and when these larvae hatch they eat the stored food. Later these young bees take over tending the new young hatched from eggs the queen has laid throughout the rest of the spring and summer.

Thus, the survival of the bumblebee as a species depends upon a relatively few individuals, the queens, making it through the long winter.

The bumblebee has played a decisive part in the fertilization of the nonnative clovers in this country—the ordinary white and red clovers, in particular. It performs the same function here that the various European species of bumblebee do for clover overseas, in that it is one of the few insects with tongues long enough to reach into the deep recesses of clover flowers and thereby insure pollination. Without the bumblebee the clover could not be pollinated, and thus would not have become the highly important agricultural plant it is today in the United States.

Besides such helpful behavior on the part of insects there is activity that is "neutral," though fascinating, as well as activity that harms the environment—from our point of view. The caterpillars of moths and butterflies have mouth parts designed for chewing leaves (the adults have only sucking mouth parts). Ahead of one's footsteps in the summer grass jump the short-horned grasshoppers, insects that also graze on vegetation and later inject their eggs into plant stems to hatch. In the evenings of late summer one hears the steady buzzing of a green long-horned grasshopper—the katydid ("long-horned" and "short-horned" refer to the length of their antennae). The larvae of the spittlebug ("froghopper," similar to the leafhopper) feed on the juices of goldenrod and other plants, producing as a by-product a frothy protective envelope, from which they acquire their name. Ground beetles scurry among grasses in search of other insects to eat, which they grab with large pincers and devour with strong, sharp jaws.

The leaf-chewing caterpillars of some moths, butterflies, and sawflies have become serious pests for the Vermont woodlot owner, the maple-syrup producer, the apple grower and even the average small landowner. In a few cases, when they have reached epidemic proportions, they have menaced the state's forests.

One, the gypsy moth, is not part of our original fauna. A tussock moth, it was brought over from Europe in 1869 by a researcher who was attempting to produce silk from its cocoon-weaving caterpillar. Several moths escaped and 20 years later the population of moths had exploded across New England, the larvae defoliating hundreds of thousands of acres in their advance. This range extension is apparently still going on, even after millions of dollars have been spent in attempting to check it. Vermont is on the edge of its advance north, and places such as Maryland are on its southern limit.

It is not yet clear what will happen to the gypsy moth over the long term, whether it will continue to run rampant for some time to come or else soon reach saturation and be brought under control by disease or new predators or artificial methods.

Eastern Tent Caterpillar. Two tent caterpillars live in Vermont. The eastern tent caterpillar, shown here, concentrates on apple and other fruit trees, eating the leaves and laying eggs in a varnished brown case near the end of a twig. The young caterpillars emerge from small cells in the case, eat their way down the twig, and finally weave a "tent" in which they pupate before changing into adult moths. The other species, the forest tent caterpillar (not shown), eats leaves of a variety of commercially important deciduous trees. Unlike the eastern tent caterpillar, this one does not spin a web tent. It is called a tent caterpillar because of its other characteristics and life cycle, which resemble those of the eastern tent. Drawing by Ann Pesiri Swanson.

Reptiles and Amphibians

As many parents can attest, small children find a treasury of wild creatures in the fields and woodlots near their homes. From the many insects that go into collections, to the amphibians placed in terraria, to the reptiles that are occasionally stumbled upon in a child's room, the animals of these areas are a never-ending source of fascination.

Vermont's field snakes, all harmless to people, slide through the grasses, sensing their way toward insects or other small animals to eat. The smooth green snake (usually wrongly called "grass snake") is between 1 foot and 2 feet long, but because it is so perfectly camouflaged it is rarely seen. It is sometimes found crawling out on the branches of shrubs, where it has gone after insects or is seeking warmth from the sun. The smaller redbelly snake prefers the security of fallen logs and woodpiles; people often discover these snakes curled up in the warm spaces between logs, or find their shed skins draped over the bark. The redbelly snake usually eats small "game"—insects, slugs, earthworms, and the like. The larger and much more common garter snake, undoubtedly the most widespread and abundant snake in the United States, goes after rodents. Known to almost everyone, it is especially remembered by those who have grabbed it—from the foul-smelling oil it leaves on the hands.

Also quite common is the milk snake, a medium-sized reptile of wide distribution in forests, forest edges, meadows, and the lawns of rural houses. It has the local name checkered adder, "checkered" for its pattern and "adder" for the false fancy that it is poisonous. Even the common name milk snake is misleading, for it alludes to the myth that the snake slithers into barns and milks cows with its mouth. However, its presence around barns and houses should be encouraged rather than feared, since the snake is in fact there to capture mice and rats.

Several amphibians are field dwellers in the summer. The leopard frog is probably the most obvious as it leaps out from underfoot, in some areas seemingly with every step. It is the most land-bound of the large frogs in Vermont, a fact noted in its other common name, meadow frog. But like the other amphibians, it requires to some extent a moist environment and wet areas for egg laying in the spring. In late summer one may easily see hundreds of leopard frogs in the fields and crossing the roads, along with many other species, such as treefrogs

Milk Snake. This medium-sized snake lives in many natural habitats and is also often seen around houses and farm buildings, where it eats rodents. Despite a bad reputation as the "checkered adder," it is harmless to humans (it does not, as myth and its name allude to, milk cows) and in fact is quite docile. Drawing by Ann Pesiri Swanson.

and American toads, as they work their way inexorably toward water, wetlands, and protected forest areas, where they will dig down into the soil to spend the winter.

And when winter comes the snakes and other cold-blooded animals of these regions will have gone into hibernation. The small snakes often take up communal residence in underground dens, apparently to pool their slight body heat. The amphibians are buried in the muds underground, underwater, or under logs. Some, such as the spotted salamanders, have moved into the foundations or basements of houses, to spend a secure and slightly warmer winter.

This time of quiet will last until some signal, unknown to us, tells the animals of spring outside. From out of the muds, from under the trees and rocks will come these lives brought over from darkness. No sooner out of that darkness they will create, with the sounds we associate with rising spring or else silence, the new lives to carry on.

V Ending

I could not hope
to touch the sky
with my two arms

—Sappho Greek poem (ca. 550 B.C.)

As we walk from that final field perhaps we can see the crusting of the first frost upon the mountain. Or in another season, the touch and ripple of a swallow's wing upon the water. Or hear the deep-February bark of foxes. Or smell the spring come out of violets.

These are all part of this time and place, Vermont's own place, fixed for our lives on earth, but hardly more than an illusion in the timeless memory of shifting continents. We have no recollection of Vermont as an ocean bottom heaving up into Green Mountains, only the evidence of it. We see our time in its passing, but we also see its accumulation, whether in the ribboned rocks or the thin trees sprouting up from cellar holes.

It is all so simple. Change is our continuum, and how different the land is from when it was next to Africa, and the Atlantic Ocean but a trickling stream between them. How different from when the glacier smoothed down this valley, and laid it open for the first human beings.

Photo courtesy Vermont Department of Tourism and Marketing.

How different from when the last passenger pigeon flew away from the forests, forever. How different now that tracks of skis cross roads and melt within the settlement of houses.

The natural world of Vermont does not stop with borders. But borders let us comprehend this one part of our world a little better.

Our arrival to this day makes sense only when we try to imagine years by the millions. The changes over days will mount to years, then to eons. There will be a future time when mountains are worn to plains and lakes are dried to land. Yet mountains will then come to other places, the rivers will cut new ways to other lakes. One hundred million years may make another earth.

And for the moment, the sun will set beyond Lake Champlain tonight and be born again to Mansfield in the morning. The brook will glaze the rocks before it slides under the snow. A bird will be ready for daybreak. May will come as it does.

And some lives will awaken to it.

Appendixes

Appendix I

Areas to Visit

The areas are listed numerically corresponding to their initial entries in the following section: refer to the page number in parentheses for descriptions of sites. The map is to be used in conjunction with the official Vermont state map, published by the Vermont Agency of Transportation and Agency of Development and Community Affairs, Montpelier, Vermont 05602. It is available at many locations throughout the state.

58. Little Otter Creek Marsh (273)
59. Maquam Bay Waterfowl Area (273)
60. Missisquoi National Wildlife Refuge (273, 275)
61. Mud Creek Waterfowl Area (273)
62. Sand Bar Waterfowl Area (273, 276)
63. South Bay Wildlife Management Area (273)
64. Lucy M. Bugbee Natural Area (274)
65. Morristown Bog (275)
66. Snake Mountain Wildlife Management Area (275)
67. Cornwall Swamp Wildlife Management Area (275)
68. Fairfield Swamp Wildlife Management Area (275)
69. North Hero State Park (276)
70. Vernon Black Gum Swamps (276)
71. Amity Pond Natural Area (277)
72. Great Averill Pond (277)
73. Bill Sladyk Wildlife Management Area (277)
74. Lake Bomoseen (277)
75. Lake Champlain (278)
76. Lake Memphremagog (279)
77. Lake Seymour (279)
78. Lake Willoughby (279)
79. Maidstone Lake (279)
80. Pine Mountain Wildlife Management Area (279)

Descriptions of Areas to Visit

The areas listed below are illustrative of what is discussed in the text. In some cases they are among the best examples of these natural features, in others merely representative of many such places in Vermont. Locations are not pinpointed, but are generally indicated by large dots on the map on page 252. In the case of small or delicate environments, the interested reader will have to go to some effort to find them.

Most of the areas listed are publicly owned and open at all times of the year. Maps and other descriptive material are available through state or federal agencies that administer the areas in question. A list of these agencies is included in Appendix II. For information on state parks and forests, contact the Vermont Department of Forests, Parks, and Recreation; for wildlife management and waterfowl areas, contact the Vermont Fish and Wildlife Department. The addresses of these departments are given in Appendix II.

Certain critical areas, such as some waterfowl management refuges and breeding-bird islands, are closed to the public at particular times of the year or in certain sections (for example, during the nesting period or in special study areas). The reason for this is that human visitation could jeopardize breeding or interfere with scientific research. These areas are specified. Permission from the refuge manager or other appropriate authority is absolutely required for entry.

Many excellent natural areas are in private ownership, and out of respect for the owners are not listed here. For those who wish to go farther afield in search of such areas, research of the literature will lead them in the proper direction. But before attempting to enter new regions, everyone should be mindful of the rights and wishes of the landowner. The privately owned sites where visitors are welcome are listed here, with sources for additional information on them.

A special note of *caution*. Alpine areas and bogs are among the state's most fragile natural communities and need to be treated with respect. When you visit such an area please be aware of your presence and actions. As explained in the chapters on these environments, the picking of plants or careless footsteps may destroy valuable components of the communities or even change their composition permanently. Many of the plants are endangered and are protected by state and, in some cases, federal laws. Furthermore, it is illegal to pick or uproot any plant on state property without a permit. But beyond its illegality, taking from these unique areas for selfish reasons robs both ourselves and our children of a beautiful, priceless, rightful inheritance.

Archaeological sites are also very sensitive, as areas of personal importance to Native Americans, for the information they contain about the past and for the artifacts within. For these reasons, specific sites are not given here; contact the Division for Historic Preservation (see Appendix II) for more information.

Chapter 1. To Move the World

Barre Granite Quarries (1)*. The Rock of Ages quarry is the largest granite quarry in the world, extracting this important igneous rock down to 350 feet. The granite here is older than most found in the Northeastern Highlands or the White Mountains, and of special quality. The quarry may be viewed from an observation platform or on a short train ride. Literature and other information on the rock, its geology and uses, and the industry based upon it are available. For more information contact the Rock of Ages Corporation, Barre, Vermont 05641.

Bomoseen State Park and Half Moon State Park (20). 2,879 acres. The parks are within the former slate-producing capital of the East. There are many abandoned slate quarries in the area. Bomoseen State Park has a "Slate History Trail" that takes visitors on a self-guiding tour of an old quarry, remains of a water-powered slate finishing mill, and the former residences of slate workers.

Button Bay State Park (2). 236 acres. Fossilized corals, snails, and other prehistoric animals are present in the limestones of Button Island Natural Area and on the mainland shore. The nature center (open summer only) has exhibits of many geological items and formations. The name Button Bay comes from the peculiar button-shaped rocks formed in the clays of the area.

D.A.R. State Park (3). 96 acres. Fossil trilobites, brachiopods, and bryozoans can be seen in the beach limestones, along with good examples of shale.

*The number in parentheses following each entry refers to the dot on the map.

Groton State Forest. A view from Owl's Head toward Kettle Pond, showing the Piedmont peaks, smooth valleys the glacier helped shape, and long ponds so prevalent in east-central and northern Vermont. Photo courtesy Vermont Department of Tourism and Marketing.

East Woods Natural Area (4). 100 acres. This is an important research and education site, used primarily by the University of Vermont as an example of a mature northern-hardwood forest, but the area is actually composed of great sand dunes that once were on the shore of the Champlain Sea. Owned by the University of Vermont. No large groups permitted. For more information contact the Environmental Program, University of Vermont, Burlington, Vermont 05405.

Groton State Forest (5). 26,153 acres. This large forest contains abundant evidence of the glaciers: north-south elongated ponds and lakes, till, erratics, blocked drainages giving rise to wetlands, U-shaped valleys, and rounded peaks. *Noyes Pond* (*Seyon Ranch Fishing Area*, 4,000 acres) is an excellent example of the work of a valley glacier, active after the continental glacier left the area. Such features as the cirque (carved basin), tarn (lake at the bottom of the basin—dammed and modified in this case), and outwash plain are all evident.

Isle La Motte (6). One of the most important geological areas of the state, containing the oldest fossil coral reef in the world. This 500-million-year-old reef can be seen from the island roads, as it outcrops smoothly in the fields. All the areas are on private property, and permission to enter is required. Inquire at the Town Clerk's Office, Isle La Motte, Vermont 05463.

Kingsland Bay State Park (7). 286 acres. Fossils occur in the limestone ledges along the shore. The park is at present undeveloped. The peninsula is a natural area.

Lone Rock Point (8). 100 acres. One of the best views of thrust-fault formations in the eastern United States is at this site. Here the Champlain Thrust Fault outcrops into the lake, showing the older dolostone lying on the top of the younger shale. The best panoramas are from the lake. The land is owned by the Vermont Episcopal diocese and visitors are requested to obtain prior approval before entering the property. Write the Episcopal Diocesan Center, Rock Point, Burlington, Vermont 05401.

Maidstone State Forest (9). 475 acres. This heavily glaciated area has a great deal of deposition, owing to the activity of the last glacier. An unsorted collection of boulders, gravel, sand, and erratics are everywhere in evidence.

Mount Mansfield State Forest (10). 37,242 acres. This very large state forest comprises many interesting features. *Little River State Park* sits atop a large, sandy delta formed in a glacial lake. *Nebraska Valley*, some of it in private ownership, contains fine examples of the work of a valley glacier that existed here after the continental glacier left. The cirque and associated features are from a geologist's point of view among the best in the eastern United States. The large delta, kame terrace, lateral and terminal moraines (formed by the valley glacier), tarn (Lake Mansfield, privately owned), and the beautifully sculpted cirque basin can be seen in large part on a drive up the valley road. On *Mount Mansfield* itself, the glacier left evidence that it reached that high: the large erratic "Drift Rock" perched alone on the summit, deep scratches (striae) in the bedrock where rocks were dragged over the surface, and the different topographies of the two exposures—the smoothly sloping west flank, where the glacier passed over, and the steep cliffs of the east side, where it plucked rocks away. Scenic *Smuggler's Notch* is a unique sinuous way through the Green Mountain range, carved by now defunct rivers that once flowed down either side in a series of complicated postglacial events. Most of these areas are owned by the Vermont Department of Forests, Parks, and Recreation, but the summit of Mount Mansfield is owned by the University of Vermont.

Mount Philo State Park (11). 163 acres. This "mountain" is actually an isolated part of the Champlain Thrust Fault, with older quartzite and dolostone pushed over and on top of younger shales. Evidence of the Champlain Sea is in the marine-beach gravels just west of the park,

Mount Mansfield State Forest. Looking east from near Underhill Center. The long ridge is supposed to represent a person's face in profile, looking up. The peaks, from right to left, are the forehead, nose, and chin. Two smaller bumps (not so apparent from this angle) between the nose and chin are the upper and lower lips. The chin is the highest point in Vermont, at 4,393 feet. The Abenakis call this mountain Mozondebiwadzo, meaning "Moose Head Mountain"—see page 24 for the Abenaki story of the making of the mountain. Photo by Brian MacDonald.

and of Lake Vermont in lake-beach gravels on both east and west sides of the mountain. These features indicate that Mount Philo in prehistoric times was an island, with waves lapping its shores. Excellent views of the Champlain basin can be seen from the summit, reached via a toll road.

Redstone Quarry Natural Area (12). 3 acres. This unused quarry within the city limits of Burlington is now an education and research site owned by the University of Vermont. The red quartzite once quarried here for building material, along with the lighter-colored dolostone, represents the time 400 to 500 million years ago when this area was a seashore beach or estuary, then the bottom of a shallow sea. The rocks exposed in some places show pits, ripples, and holes where rain once fell, the currents passed, and worms lived. No large groups permitted. For further information contact the Environment Program, University of Vermont, Burlington, Vermont 05405.

Vermont Marble Exhibit (13). Displays of both local and foreign marble can be seen here, with information given on the rock's formation, uses, and Vermont's industry based on it. Marble is the important rock

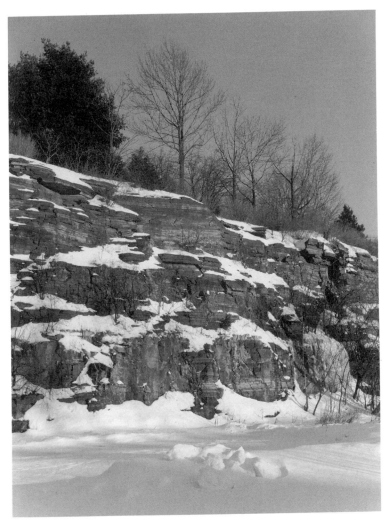

Redstone Quarry Natural Area. This area has some of the oldest fossil forma-tion in the state, dating back over 500 million years when "Vermont" was part of a shallow marine estuary. Photo by Louis Borie.

of this region of Vermont, along with slate. Operated by the Vermont Marble Company. For more information contact the company in Proctor, Vermont 05765.

Weybridge Cave Natural Area (14). 97 acres. The large cave in the un-developed state park was formed by the dissolving of limestone bedrock. Interesting geological formations are associated with the cave, and it is possible (we don't know for certain) that this is an important roosting and hibernating place for bats. *Caution*: This cave is suitable for exploration only by expert spelunkers, as no provisions for public access have been made: it is deep and very dangerous. Owned by the Vermont Department of Forests, Parks, and Recreation.

Chapter 2. *Physiographic Regions of Vermont*

THE GREEN MOUNTAINS

The entire length of the Green Mountains may be traveled on Route 100, with many fine views along the way. In addition, on the western side of the range Routes 7 and 116 offer similar vistas.

Camel's Hump State Park (15). 18,153 acres. This important segment of the Green Mountain range contains Camel's Hump, the fourth-highest peak in Vermont, and provides excellent views of the state. Many hiking trails to the summit, including the Long Trail.

Elmore State Park (16). 755 acres. This park is at the north end of the Worcester range, an important subrange of the Green Mountains. From the summit of Mount Elmore are good views of this range, more of the Green Mountains, and the White Mountains of New Hampshire.

Camel's Hump. Looking east, from near Hinesburg. The distinctive profile of Vermont's fourth highest peak, called Dawabodiiwadzo by the Abenakis ("Seat Mountain"—see page 24 for the Abenaki story about its creation). This 17,000-acre park has many faces. The forest below 2500 feet is managed for multiple uses, while above that elevation it is preserved as a natural area. The 10-acre summit, containing many rare arctic-alpine plants, is patrolled by ranger-naturalists. Photo by Louis Borie.

Green Mountain National Forest (17). 366,000 acres. This extensive forest encompasses much of the southern half of the Green Mountain range. The Long Trail runs its entire length and the Appalachian Trail goes as far north as Route 4. Many interesting natural features occur along its length.

Jay State Forest (18). 1,319 acres. The northernmost state forest in this range through which the Long Trail passes.

Mount Mansfield State Forest (10). 37,242 acres. Many hiking trails in this region go to the summit of Mount Mansfield and give overviews to the state. The toll road and privately run gondola operate in the summer, taking visitors on a scenic ride to near the summit. Summit owned by University of Vermont, Burlington, Vermont 05405, but open to the public.

Putnam State Forest (19). 13,397 acres. A hiking trail to Mount Hunger and White Rocks leads to excellent views of other parts of Vermont, including the wide glacier-carved valley between the Worcesters and Green Mountains.

THE TACONIC MOUNTAINS

Bomoseen and Half Moon State Parks (20). 2,879 acres. Situated at the extreme northern end of the Taconics, these parks provide views of the gentle old mountains and of the abandoned slate quarries so extensive in the region.

Emerald Lake State Park (21). 908 acres. The western portion of the park is in the Taconics, and Dorset Peak, the highest in that range, can be seen nearby.

Lake St. Catherine State Park (22). 128 acres. The park offers good views of the mountains.

THE VALLEY OF VERMONT

The Valley of Vermont can be traveled in its entirety along Route 7.

Emerald Lake State Park (21). 908 acres. This park is situated at the narrowest place in the valley, where the Green Mountains and Taconics rise sharply within a few hundred yards of each other.

Shaftsbury State Park (23). 102 acres. This park lies within the Valley of Vermont, and the calcium-based rocks of the area are reflected in the kinds of vegetation growing, which can be well observed along a pleasant nature trail that goes around the lake.

THE CHAMPLAIN LOWLANDS

Many state parks and other public property display the low relief and topography of this region. Most are within or near the agricultural

The Taconics. The peak of Mount Aeolus in southwestern Vermont. From percolating water over great expanses of time, the limestone in this range has dissolved to form many caves and springs. The stone is also an important source of rock for industry (the white areas are limestone quarry sites). Photo by Brian MacDonald.

The Champlain Lowlands. A view of land-use patterns and, in the distance (top right), of Snake Mountain, from Bristol Cliffs in the Green Mountain National Forest. Snake Mountain is part of the Champlain Thrust Fault, the line of which can be seen running south here (to the left). Photo by John Hall.

lands the area is known for, featuring its heavy clayey soils. For other parks in the region, consult the various guides and maps.

Mount Philo State Park (11). 172 acres. This park probably gives the best overall view of the lowlands, reached by the way of a toll road.

THE VERMONT PIEDMONT

Allis State Park (24). 487 acres. An excellent panorama of the Piedmont can be seen from the summit of Bear Mountain, within the park, where a fire tower stands.

Calvin Coolidge State Forest (25). 18,511 acres. This large forest area shows typical Piedmont characteristics, with smaller monadnocks, worn relief, and valleys filled in with glacial till. The forest is within easy reach of the asbestos, talc, garnet, and other igneous-mineral deposits that are found in the Piedmont.

Darling State Park (26). 1,998 acres. Burke Mountain, within the park, is a granitic monadnock of 3,244-foot elevation, up which a privately maintained toll road runs. This road and the mountain's many hiking trails offer good views north to the gouged basin of Lake Willoughby. Although state owned, the park is leased to a private ski company.

Groton State Forest (5). 26,153 acres. The views from Owl's Head (reached via a dirt road and a short, easy trail) and other peaks within this area show many of the Piedmont features—worn hills and mountains, numerous small ponds and lakes, and so on.

Mount Ascutney State Park (27). 2,187 acres. The mountain itself is a fine example of an igneous monadnock, 3,144 feet high. A toll road and hiking trails take the visitor to fine views of the surrounding countryside and the Connecticut River Valley.

THE NORTHEASTERN HIGHLANDS

Vermont Route 105 passes through the scenic beauty of these lands.

Brighton State Park (29). 152 acres. One of two state parks in the region, Brighton shows kettles and other works of glaciation, and one can see the granite hills of the surrounding area.

Maidstone State Forest (9). 475 acres. More remote than Brighton State Park, this forest offers ample evidence of the structure and formation of the "Granite Hills" of Vermont.

Willoughby State Forest (28). 7,300 acres. Trails to the summit of Mount Pisgah on the east side of Lake Willoughby offer outstanding views of the area and show typical Highland structures in a more northern environment.

Lake Willoughby. The cliffs of Mount Pisgah rise dramatically on the left, and those of Mount Hor on the right. This view is from the northern end of the lake, looking south. Photo courtesy Vermont Department of Tourism and Marketing.

Chapter 3. Before We Came

This chapter sets the stage for what is to follow in greater detail in subsequent chapters. Old-growth forests mentioned in the text are listed under the coniferous and hardwood categories in the material accompanying chapters six and seven.

Chapter 4. People Arrive in Vermont

Most Native American sites in the state have vanished and are known only through the evidence uncovered by archaeological excavations or the occasional discovery of artifacts; the digs are not suitable for the casual visitor. Later Vermont civilization, especially as it relates to impacts on the natural resources, can be studied largely by "reading the landscape." Many areas have noteworthy local histories. Community historical societies as well as the Vermont Historical Society in Montpelier are most helpful holders of this information.

The Division for Historic Preservation maintains and operates several historic sites that give excellent insights into Vermont's past: Chimney Point, Crown Point, Mount Independence. Also, there are current five underwater historic preserves maintained by the division, where divers can explore sunken boats and ships of Lake Champlain and learn about this important component of our history.

Brighton State Park (29). 152 acres. In the heart of the spruce-fir country. The park shows evidence of logging of the great white pines in the huge stumps standing throughout the park.

Fort Dummer State Park (30). 217 acres. This was the site of the first permanent white settlement in Vermont in 1724. The fort was built to protect what was then a Massachusetts colony from invasion by the French and Native Americans.

Groton State Forest (5). 26,153 acres. Old mill sites, railroad beds, and other remnants of an earlier time show the extent of a great logging industry here. Remains of Civilian Conservation Corps (CCC) camps and buildings are in the forest. A brief account of its history, along with some spots to visit, are contained in a self-guiding booklet available at the various campgrounds in the forest.

Jamaica State Park (31). 758 acres. Archaeological evidence of native settlements.

Lake Carmi State Park (32). 588 acres. There is evidence of Native American settlements near the lake, and an old railroad bed in the park indicates a former route to Canada. Some of the land is private.

Mount Mansfield State Forest (10). 37,242 acres. *Little River State Park* especially (the southern portion, off the campground) has many old stone walls, foundations of farmhouses and barns, cemeteries, and other indications of the past uses of this forestland. An extensive self-guiding trail from Little River State Park visits some of the farm sites, which are now grown to woodland. The work of the Civilian Conservation Corps is evident at many places in the forest: the stone hut near the summit of Mount Mansfield, many trails around Mount Mansfield, remains (big stone fireplaces and building foundations) of its camps at Moscow and Little River State Park, lean-tos at Smuggler's Notch State Park, and the huge dam at Waterbury Reservoir on the way to Little River State Park (built following the disastrous flood of 1927).

Victory Bog Wildlife Management Area (33). 4,970 acres. Evidence is plentiful here of an extensive old logging operation, as seen in the extant railroad beds, camps, and mill sites.

Chapter 5. Alpine Communities

Caution: As stated earlier, to protect these environments all visitors should exercise good judgment and extreme care. You are asked to stay on the rock trails, off the vegetation, and to disturb no living thing. Only this way can the plants have a chance to survive.

Camel's Hump State Park (15). 17,356 acres. The Camel's Hump summit of only 10 acres contains the second-largest area of tundra in Vermont, one of only two. Access is by hiking trails only.

Mount Mansfield Summit (within Mount Mansfield State Forest, 10), 250 acres. This highest peak in Vermont holds the largest tract of tundra in the state. It can be reached by hiking trails, a toll road, or, part way, by gondola (the last two means are privately operated). Owned by the University of Vermont, Burlington, Vermont 05405, but open to the public.

Mount Pisgah (within Willoughby State Forest, 28). 500 acres. The cliffs here harbor many alpine plants. No trails lead directly to this area, but a hiking trail to the top of the cliffs allows for a view of the habitat, as well as spectacular surrounding scenery.

Smuggler's Notch (within Mount Mansfield State Forest, 10). 20 acres. This part of the state forest is home to many rare alpine plants and is a great tourist attraction. No trail access, but many pull-offs along the road offer views. Most of the cliffs are owned by the Vermont Department of Forests, Parks, and Recreation.

Chapter 6. Coniferous Forests

Brighton State Park (29). 152 acres. The huge stumps in the park are evidence of an old-growth white-pine forest that existed until 1900. *Spectacle Pond Natural Area* is an excellent stand of red pine on the sandy east side of Spectacle Pond. The area north and east of the park—most of it owned by timber companies—is the most extensive spruce-fir forest of lower elevations in Vermont.

Calvin Coolidge State Forest (25). 18,511 acres. In this predominantly hardwood forest *Tinker Brook Natural Area* is a 15-acre old-growth stand of red spruce and hemlock, growing on the banks of the brook ravine.

Cambridge State Forest (34). 25 acres. This small area contains a splendid stand of old-growth white pine and hemlock on both sides of a stream, where the banks are deep and drop off sharply.

Fisher-Scott Memorial Pines (35). 22 acres. Another fine old-growth stand of white pine, on a slope. This area was the retreat of the well-known Vermont writer Dorothy Canfield Fisher. Owned by the Vermont Department of Forests, Parks, and Recreation.

Granville Gulf Reservation (36). 1,171 acres. A small section of 6 acres here supports an old-growth, or near old-growth, stand of red spruce and hemlock, located on the cool, steep eastern slopes. Owned by the Vermont Department of Forests, Parks, and Recreation.

Quechee Gorge (37). 10 acres. A portion of the gorge contains untouched mixed forest, with many boreal species of plants growing below it or on the near-vertical ledges. Owned by the U.S. Army Corps of Engineers, regional office in North Springfield, Vermont 05150.

Roy Mountain Wildlife Management Area (38). 1,515 acres. A fine 57-acre stand of native red pine is located within this Fish and Wildlife land, and is a registered natural area of the Society of American Foresters.

Victory Bog Wildlife Management Area (33). 4,970 acres. This is a region of wild swamps, forests, and a few boglike sections. It is one of Vermont's best, most extensive boreal-forest realms.

The alpine boreal forest is well developed and in many cases along mountain ranges has not been touched by human beings. It can be seen particularly well at *Mount Mansfield State Forest* (10), *Camel's Hump State Park* (15), *Putnam State Forest* (19), and *Willoughby State Forest* (28), as well as in the *Green Mountain National Forest.*

Chapter 7. The Northern Hardwoods

The bulk of state and national forests in Vermont are of the hemlock—northern-hardwood association, or hardwoods and softwoods mixed. Hence a visit to areas mentioned previously as well as many others will reveal the ecology and natural history of these environments. The places listed below have some special attributes beyond the "generalized" forest, most being undisturbed old-growth tracts.

Bomoseen and Half Moon State Parks (20). 2,879 acres. Sections on the hills within the parks have stands of oak-hickory climax, with elsewhere much red cedar, common juniper, and the more standard northern hardwoods.

Downer State Forest (39). 705 acres. Though small this is an operating model for forest management, with plantations (mostly in softwoods), timber-stand improvement, research projects, and the demonstration of various silvicultural techniques.

Gifford Woods State Park (40). 114 acres. A 5-acre parcel on the east side of Route 100 has a stand of old-growth hardwoods, including sugar maple, white ash, yellow birch, American beech, and many others. This is one of the very few such stands left in the state, and it has been designated a National Natural Landmark by the National Park Service.

Green Mountain National Forest (17). 366,000 acres. Forests of many characters are represented in this large, complex system, and much of it is managed for multiple use. *Lookoff Mountain Maple-Beech Forest* (41) is a 100-acre tract within it that has been registered as a natural area; old hardwoods grow on the west slope of the mountain. Though not strictly virgin, some forests here have been designated wilderness areas, to be left untouched except for hiking, backwoods camping, hunting, fishing, cross-country skiing, and other compatible recreational uses: two are *Bristol Cliffs* (42), 4,495 acres in the northern section and *Lye Brook* (43) 14,300 acres in the southern. A permit to use these areas is mandatory and may be obtained from the U.S. Forest Service offices listed in Appendix II.

Groton State Forest (5). 26, 153 acres. Part of this forest is an isolated 25-acre tract on Lord's Hill, where impressive old-growth hardwoods and some conifers exist—one of the best stands in the Northeast. Access to this area is by logging road and foot only.

Chapters 8 and 9. Brooks and Streams; Rivers

It is impossible here to list all the significant waterways of Vermont, so just the most noteworthy appear. In addition, some waterfalls and gorges are pointed out, for their beauty and because they serve to indicate youthful streams and rivers. *Caution*, however: these features are dangerous areas for climbing—visitors should not attempt to hike up or beside the falls. For a thorough delineation of the distribution of the state's fish species, the reader may refer to the Vermont Fish and Wildlife Department's map "Vermont Guide to Fishing," which shows all the rivers and streams and their game fish. All navigable waters are state owned, though access to them may be restricted by private ownership of the surrounding land.

Barton River (44), running north-south, is a major tributary of Lake Memphremagog, having important wetlands associated with it as it enters the lake.

Batten Kill (45) in southern Vermont is famous for trout fishing. It is a subsequent river for part of its course, and superimposed through the Taconic Mountains.

Connecticut River (46). This is the largest, longest river associated with Vermont, but it actually controlled by New Hampshire. It has been a major waterway for transportation to and through Vermont throughout human history, with the state's first white settlers from the south inhabiting its shores. It is geologically significant for the glacial record it has kept.

Lamoille River (47) is another major river on the west side of the state. It is superimposed on the Green Mountains. Marshes and swamps at the Sand Bar Waterfowl Area occupy the site of old-river delta deposits into Lake Champlain. It is used by some overwintering ducks where the waters stay open.

Missisquoi River (48). This superimposed river in the northern

Little Otter Creek. Looking across the waters, wetlands, and shore of the South Slang, Little Otter Creek, near Ferrisburgh. This is important as a wildlife refuge and for the long archaeological record of Native American habitation. Photo by Brian MacDonald.

reaches of the Green Mountains is especially important for the large delta formed at its mouth, which supports an extensive wetland area. It is also the principal spawning ground in the northern part of the state for muskellunge and walleye.

Nulhegan River (49). A northern tributary of the Connecticut River, the Nulhegan and the smaller streams that drain into it from the north are integral to the moist, boggy, swampy areas of boreal forest in the region. This is the river the famous Rogers' Rangers traveled down in their escape from the St. Francis Indians, before Vermont was settled by whites.

Otter Creek (50) is the longest river within Vermont's borders, known by early natives as one of the best fishing areas in the state. It was also an important Native American passageway and a transportation route for early white trappers. The present river was preceded by an ancient one before glaciation, which left great deltas near Brandon. The modern Otter Creek is a meandering subsequent river with major wetlands at its lower end, near Lake Champlain.

White River (51) is a long, winding river that flows east from the Green Mountains to the Connecticut River. Its valley was once a long arm of the post glacial Lake Hitchcock.

Winooski River (52). Natives considered this an excellent river for fishing and a major way into the interior of Vermont. (They called it Winooski, meaning "onion," supposedly because of the great numbers of wild leeks growing on its rich banks.) It is a splendid example both of a superimposed river and of a U-shaped valley that was re-formed by the continental glacier. Valuable and extensive wetlands lie at its mouth as it enters Lake Champlain, where some ducks and other water birds remain in winter. Much of the area of Colchester sits on a massive delta formed when the river dumped its sands into Lake Vermont and the Champlain Sea. Interstate Route 89 travels through this valley, affording good views of the river.

Granville Gulf Reservation (36). 1,171 acres. *Moss Glen Falls* can be seen here, on the west side of Route 100, cascading down the sheer rock face. Owned by the Vermont Department of Forests, Parks, and Recreation.

Green Mountain National Forest (17). 325,000 acres. The *Falls of Lana* are long, sinuous, and precipitous; they can be reached by trails from Silver Lake and Branbury State Park, near Lake Dunmore. *Texas Falls* is another scenic attraction, also in the northern sector of the National Forest.

Moss Glenn Falls (53). Near Stowe, this is a long, picturesque series of falls through a forested region. The falls are part of *Putnam State Forest* (19).

Quechee Gorge (37). The gorge is an outstanding example of a river's (the Ottauquechee) cutting its way through metamorphic bedrock (schist), making a spectacular steep-walled valley more than 160 feet deep. Owned by the U.S. Army Corps of Engineers, regional office in North Springfield, Vermont 05150.

Willoughby Falls Wildlife Management Area (54). 130 acres. The Willoughby River in this section, owned and managed by the Vermont Fish and Wildlife Department, is where the spectacular spawning runs of the steelhead rainbow trout may be observed and fished in early spring.

Chapter 10. Marshes

Visitors to marshes should keep two things in mind: the need to be well prepared for the special physical conditions, and the necessity of not disturbing the birds during their nesting season. The first requirement includes equipping oneself with information about the area, maps, and a canoe (essential in many marshes), and learning of any special precautions to take. Observing the second requirement is simple, since spring and summer are the critical times for nesting and the rearing of young birds—it is then that care should be taken when

Quechee Gorge. A dramatic example of rock cutting by the Ottauquechee River, which courses through the bottom of the deep cleft. Photo courtesy Vermont Department of Tourism and Marketing.

visiting, for human traffic can disrupt breeding cycles, even causing the failure of birds to nest.

The Vermont Fish and Wildlife Department owns and manages 17 waterfowl areas, mostly marshes, comprising more than 8,000 acres. The U.S. Fish and Wildlife Service has one area in the state, of 5,661 acres.

Most marshes of substantial acreage are attractive to bird-watchers and waterfowl hunters. For more information on species and good areas for birding, consult *Birds of Vermont* (See Appendix III); for rules and regulations regarding hunting, contact the Vermont Fish and Wildlife Department and the Missisquoi National Wildlife Refuge.

Black Creek Waterfowl Area (55). 158 acres. A relatively small marsh, located near St. Albans Bay State Park, accessible only by water.

Dead Creek Wildlife Management Area (56). 2,858 acres. The lengthy impoundments are maintained, regulated, and managed by the Fish and Wildlife Department, and part of the river is free-flowing. The marsh complexes are among the most important in the state for waterfowl of many kinds and other species. Numerous access points are available by water, but most of the area can be seen from lookout stations and roadside pull-offs at several places. Part of the area requires permission from the year-round manager for visitation. There is also a controlled goose-hunting area near the headquarters. Office: R.F.D.#1, Box 130, Vergennes, Vermont 05491.

Dead Creek Waterfowl Area, Near Addison. Snow and Canada geese converge on the fields of Dead Creek Waterfowl Area in the fall. The slow-moving river and associated wetlands and uplands, adjacent to Lake Champlain, are one of the state's most important regions for migratory and nesting birds. Photo by John Hall.

East Creek Waterfowl Area (57). 398 acres. This shallow marsh is visible from several locations along roads, and portions are boatable by canoe only.

Little Otter Creek Marsh (58). 1,097 acres. This highly valued area is one of the most extensive unspoiled marshes in Vermont. Many species of waterfowl and water-based birds nest here, including the black tern. The marsh can be well explored only by boat or canoe, though it can be reached via fishing-access areas or through private fields. Much of the marsh is owned by the Vermont Fish and Wildlife Department, but some of it is in private holdings.

Maquam Bay Waterfowl Area (59). 829 acres. A medium-sized marsh adjacent to the Missisquoi National Wildlife Refuge, it augments the marshlands of this northern area. It is accessible by boat or canoe only.

Missisquoi National Wildlife Refuge (60). 5,839 acres. This refuge contains great expanses of marsh and swamp associated with Lake Champlain, the Missisquoi River, and its delta. Large numbers of migratory and nesting birds have been recorded here. Most of the refuge is accessible only by boat or canoe, and visitors must have permission from the refuge manager before entering. (R.F.D. #2, Swanton, Vermont 05091). Some of the marshland is private property, but most of it is federally owned.

Mud Creek Waterfowl Area (61). 1,019 acres. An important impoundment on Mud Creek has created good habitat for waterfowl and other birds. It can be reached on foot as well as by canoe.

Sand Bar Waterfowl Area (62). 1,560 acres. One of the state's most important refuges for nesting waterfowl and other birds, as well as for migrating species. The marshes are only part of the whole wetland area. Some of the area can be viewed from Route 2, which travels through the refuge, although canoeing provides the best observations. Visitors must obtain permission to enter from the refuge manager, R.D., Sand Bar, Milton, Vermont 05468.

South Bay Wildlife Management Area (63). 1,641 acres. The large Coventry Marsh occupies the mouth of the Barton River where it empties into South Bay of Lake Memphremagog. The marshlands are best seen from the water but a road that parallels the marsh on the east side and railroad tracks through the area offer excellent hiking possibilities. One of the finest marshes outside the Lake Champlain region, it features many boggy characteristics.

Chapter 11. Bogs

Bogs are some of the most interesting yet delicate of our natural areas. Visitors are therefore implored to remember the fragility and irreplaceable beauty there, and leave everything as it lives. *Caution*: because of the floating mat, many bogs present tough going for hikers—

people have trouble getting through the thick tangle of shrubs or may sink down into the mat and find it difficult to walk. In view of this, it is a good idea not to go alone into bogs and when there to watch one's footing at all time.

The Nature Conservancy and a few other organizations own peatlands (bogs and fens), some of which are open to the public. For more information, contact the organizations listed in Appendix II.

Green Mountain National Forest (17). 366,000 acres. *Lost Pond Bog* is a 10-acre bog within the national forest, near the Long Trail, and has a quaking sphagnum-moss mat and some open water.

Groton State Forest (5). 26,153 acres. 200-acre *Peacham Bog* is one of the more extensive treed bog systems in the state, where black spruce and tamarack dominate, with shrubs underneath. Trail access is from the nature center in the forest. Part of a 750-acre state natural area.

Lake Carmi State Park (32). 588 acres. *Lake Carmi Black Spruce-Tamarack Bog* covers more than 200 acres; much of it is on private land but a portion of it is part of the state park, though which a road passes. This is a mature bog with abundant tree cover in black spruce and tamarack, many shrubs, and typical bog plants.

Lucy M. Bugbee Natural Area (64). 12 acres. The limestone-bearing bedrock makes this less acid than many other bogs, encouraging a dif-

Moose Bog. This large bog is part of the Wenlock Wildlife Management Area, east of Island Pond. Besides the expected array of bog plants, it and the adjacent softwood swamps and uplands support populations of spruce grouse, gray jays, and other boreal species. Photo by Charles W. Johnson.

ferent type of bog flora. The trees are mostly tamarack and white cedar, with a rich understory. No open water in the bog, and no trail access. Named after a champion of wildflower protection in Vermont. Owned by the Vermont Department of Forests, Parks, and Recreation.

Missisquoi National Wildlife Refuge (60). 5,839 acres. *Maquam Bog*, the state's largest peatland (1,000 acres), is within the refuge, occupying a former shallow bay of Lake Champlain. It contains many heath shrubs, including abundant rhodora, and pitch pine, growing on a hummocky mat of sedges and sphagnum. Permission from the refuge manager is required before entering (see Appendix II).

Morristown Bog (65). 30 acres. This is a predominantly black-spruce bog with a sphagnum mat, Labrador tea, pitcher plants, and other bog plants. No trail access. Owned by the Vermont Department of Forests, Parks, and Recreation.

Snake Mountain Wildlife Management Area (66). 1,194 acres. The 10-acre *Cranberry Bog* sits within this high-elevation area, near the summit of Snake Mountain. A more or less typical kettle bog, with no open water but trail access from the base of the mountain.

Chapter 12. Swamps

The same words of warning apply here as in marshes: know where you are going, be prepared for adverse conditions, and do not disturb breeding birds in season. In addition, most swamps are without trail systems, so it is easy to become disoriented and even lost. A compass and map are good tools to take along.

Cornwall Swamp Wildlife Management Area (67). 1,392 acres. This wild red-maple and cedar swamp along Otter Creek has best access by foot, off a road that passes east-west through the forest. The large swamp lacks well-defined trails.

Fairfield Swamp Wildlife Management Area (68). 1,363 acres. This extensive swamp was created by a dam impoundment and is composed mostly of white cedar. It is a good area for herons and ducks. Best access is by canoe, but Route 36 crosses it from east to west.

Lake Carmi State Park (32). 588 acres. A hemlock—red-maple-tamarack swamp lies within the park, adjacent to the bog. It can be seen easily and "dryly" from the abandoned railroad bed that runs its entire length. Although situated in a state park, much of the swamp is privately owned. In another area of the park, a fine cedar swamp borders Lake Carmi.

Missisquoi National Wildlife Refuge (60). 5,839 acres. A fine silver maple—swamp-white-oak swamp grows at the edges of the marshes and in the impounds where they are subject to seasonal flooding.

Missisquoi National Wildlife Refuge. This aerial view is of Missisquoi Bay, an area of Lake Champlain shared by the United States and Canada in northwestern Vermont, showing the distinctive "bird's-foot" delta, where sediments—carried by the Missisquoi River and deposited into the bay—grow into flat islands which in turn divert the river, and the process continues. Various types of wetlands—swamps, marshes, and bogs—occupy many of the low areas here. Photo by Louis Borie.

The swamp is alive in summer with wood and numerous other ducks, black-crowned night-herons, great blue herons, and countless songbirds. Permission from the refuge manager (R.F.D. #2, Swanton, Vermont 05091) is required for entry, and the best views are from boat or canoe. A nature trail near the headquarters leads visitors through a small sample of the forest. Many areas are off-limits to visitors during waterfowl breading season.

North Hero State Park (69). 401 acres. Part of the park near Lake Champlain contains a silver-maple—swamp-white-oak swamp that can be reached by a hiking trail.

Sand Bar Waterfowl Area (62). 1,560 acres. Another excellent silver-maple—swamp-white-oak swamp grows in conjunction with the Lamoille River, its delta, and the marshes of the waterfowl area. This important area for a great many birds and mammals can be seen best from a boat or canoe, but the general lay of the land can be gathered from the road. Permission from the refuge manager is necessary for entry: R.F.D., Sand Bar, Milton, Vermont 05468.

Vernon (Maynard Miller) Black Gum Swamps (70). 60 acres. A series of four black-gum swamps are the best stands in the state, containing aged specimens of the black gum and other more southern species of plants. The swamps are owned by the town of Vernon and maintained as a natural area; no large groups are permitted, and visitors are asked to inquire of the Vernon town clerk for directions to swamps: Town Clerk's Office, Vernon, Vermont 05354.

Victory Bog Wildlife Management Area (33). 4,970 acres. Within this area are extensive tracts of spruce–fir–tamarack–red-maple swamps, mixed with more upland forest types, boggy areas, and some marshlands.

Chapter 13. Ponds and Lakes

As in the case of rivers, the important ponds and lakes in Vermont are simply too numerous to mention in their entirety here. Again, consult the "Vermont Guide to Fishing" for the spectrum of bodies of water and the species of fish living in them. All navigable waters are owned by the state, but often access to them is privately controlled, except where the state has purchased or been granted right-of-way.

Amity Pond Natural Area (71). 182 acres. This very small pond and surrounding land have been designated a natural area of the Vermont Department of Forests, Parks, and Recreation, which owns it.

Bill Sladyk Wildlife Management Area (73). 9,386 acres. This large area encompasses many ecosystems and provides important habitat for black bear and other animals. Included are fine examples of unspoiled ponds and lakes, some prime natural areas of Vermont. *Beaver Pond, Duck Pond, Round Pond*, and *Turtle Pond* are all small (40 acres or less), in the northern sector of the management area.

Green Mountain National Forest (17). 366,000 acres. The forest contains several natural and unspoiled lakes and ponds, many of which are within close hiking distance of the Long Trail. Several are high-elevation ponds with boglike characteristics and shore vegetation. *Wallingford Pond* (81 acres), *Bourn Pond* (65 acres), *Fifield Pond* (20 acres), *Griffith Lake* (18 acres), and *Branch Pond* (53 acres) are all splendid natural areas here.

Great Averill Pond (72). 847 acres. This and its close companion, *Little Averill Pond* (482 acres), are important deep-water lakes of the Northeastern Highlands, containing lake trout and other cold-water species. State-owned fishing access.

Groton State Forest (5). 26,153 acres. The state forest contains several nice undeveloped lakes (called ponds): *Marshfield Pond, Kettle Pond*, and *Osmore Pond*. All have rocky shorelines.

Lake Bomoseen (74). 2,364 acres. The largest lake wholly within Vermont, Bomoseen contains both warm- and cold-water species of fish, including pike, large and smallmouth bass, and rainbow trout. State-owned accesses, including Bomoseen State Park.

Lake Champlain (75). 172,032 acres. An extremely important body of water for many reasons, not only because of its biological features, but also owing to its richness of geological information. Vermont shares it politically with New York and Canada. People interested in pursuing its history are directed to the references in Appendix III.

Several islands in the lake are noteworthy for the birds that nest on them in summer. The *Four Brothers Islands*, across from Shelburne Bay, technically in New York, are a natural area owned by The Nature Conservancy and are used by ring-billed and herring gulls, black-crowned night-herons, cattle egrets, ducks, cormorants and other birds for nesting. West of Grand Isle is *Young Island*, a 10-acre site for nest-ing gulls and common terns (owned by the Vermont Fish and Wildlife

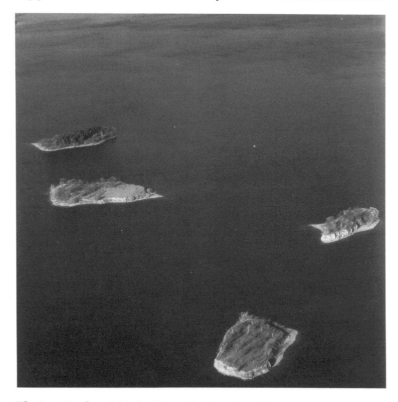

The Four Brothers Islands. These islands, technically in New York State, are an important natural area for colonial nesting birds in the Lake Champlain region. They are owned and managed by The Nature Conservancy. Photo by Robert Candy.

Department). North of St. Albans Bay is *Popasquash Island*, a 1-acre rocky emergence where common terns—which are actually uncommon in Vermont—nest annually (owned by the Vermont Fish and Wildlife Department). Several other public and private islands and rock outcrops serve as breeding places in Champlain for these colonial species.

Caution: because of the small size of these islands and their critical importance to the nesting birds, people should not visit them in summer. Good observation may be made from a distance.

The book *Birds of Vermont* (see references, Appendix III) lists principal areas on the lake for birds and what may be expected there at various times of the year. The "Vermont Guide to Fishing" shows the distribution of game fish in the lake.

Lake Memphremagog (76). 6,317 acres. This is the second-largest lake with which Vermont has contact (it is shared with Canada). It is a major area for various species of gull and tern, with other waterfowl and many land birds living in the wetlands at the southern end. It may be viewed well from South Bay and from paved roads that run along much of its perimeter. There are several state-owned access points.

Lake Seymour (77). 1,732 acres. This is the second-largest lake entirely within Vermont. It possesses fine populations of lake trout and smelt. State-owned access areas.

Lake Willoughby (78). 1,692 acres. One often hears this lake referred to as the Lake Lucerne of Vermont, and indeed it is a uniquely beautiful area. Spectacular views of this deep, long body of water are reached by hiking trails in *Willoughby State Forest* (28) or by road (Route 5A). It is one of the deepest lakes in New England, having been carved by the glacier in a preexisting valley. It contains a large variety of cold-water fish. A few state-owned accesses.

Maidstone Lake (79). 748 acres. Home of lake trout, landlocked salmon, and smelt, this deep lake also supports loons, an occasional moose coming in to drink, and other, wilder animals. State-owned accesses, including Maidstone State Park.

Mount Mansfield State Forest (10). 37,242 acres. The high-elevation ponds are of interest as glacial relicts and for the plant life within them. They are small, shallow, and eutrophic. The largest is *Sterling Pond*, in the section of the forest north of Route 108. South of the road, nearer Mount Mansfield's summit, are *Bear Pond* and *Lake of the Clouds*. *Goose Pond*, a beaver-influenced, boggy pond, is in the southern portion of the forest, off the main trail. The rest of the ponds are reached by the Long Trail or other hiking trails.

Pine Mountain Wildlife Management Area (80). 2,271 acres. Within this land are two undeveloped connecting ponds, totaling 70 acres. Trail access on state-owned property.

Unknown Pond, Ferdinand. This small, shallow lake in the Northeast Kingdom has a boggy shoreline, thick with boreal plants. Photo by Charles W. Johnson.

Chapter 14. Fields, Farms, and Towns

The plants and wildlife of meadows, woodlots, woodland edges, and urban areas can be observed the length and breadth of the state, for the human presence, which created these spaces, is felt throughout. Most clearings for agriculture occur in the Champlain Valley, the Valley of Vermont, and the Connecticut River Valley, and there we expect to find the greatest array of field flora and fauna; in addition, the milder climates of these areas encourage more southerly species to infiltrate, both plants and animals.

Many of the state's farms and their operations can be viewed by the public, with prior arrangements. The Vermont Department of Commerce and Community Development supplies brochures on these and related places and events. A sample of the selections includes "Red Clover Trail" (operating farms), "Maple Sugar Houses Open to Visitors," "Morgan Horse Farm of the University of Vermont," and "Vermont Agricultural Fairs and Field Days." There are also many apple orchards and Christmas tree plantations where visitors may go to purchase the products and learn about the operations.

For more information, contact either the Department of Commerce and Community Development or the Vermont Department of Agriculture.

Appendix II

Conservation and Environmental Organizations

The following private, state, and federal organizations are the major ones in Vermont that engage in statewide programs related to conservation, environmental protection, and environmental/natural resources education. Many others not listed here operate at the local and regional levels. Trade organizations are not included. For more information or details, consult the Vermont Environmental Directory, published by the Vermont Natural Resources Council, 9 Bailey Avenue, Montpelier, VT 05602.

Private Organizations

Appalachian Trail Conference, New England Regional Office, 18 On the Common, Unit 7, Lyme, NH 03768-0312. Seeks protection and proper management of the 2,100-mile Appalachian Trail and associated corridor lands.

Arctic to Amazonia Alliance, P.O. Box 73, Strafford, VT 05072. Facilitates better communications and understanding between indigenous and nonindigenous peoples, particularly regarding human rights, social justice, economics, and the environment.

Association of Vermont Conservation Commissions, HCR 32, Box 36, Adamant, VT 05640. Promotes municipal conservation commissions in Vermont.

Association of Vermont Recyclers, P.O. Box 1244, Montpelier, VT 05601. Promotes waste reduction, reuse, recycling, and buying recycled in Vermont.

Atlantic Center for the Environment, P.O. Box 217, Montpelier, VT 05601. A division of the Quebec-Labrador Foundation. A joint Canadian-U.S. organization that provides social and environmental services for rural communities in northern New England and eastern Canada.

Audubon Council, Vermont, P.O. Box 9, Fiddler's Green, Waitsfield, VT 05673. Advances protection and wise use of Vermont's wildlife and other natural resources and encourages coordination and information exchange among member organizations. Also responsible for Bluebirds Across Vermont.

Audubon Society, National: Vermont State Office, 9 Bailey Avenue, Montpelier, VT 05602. Facilitates coordination and cooperation between Audubon's state chapters, regional, and national offices, regarding environmental education, research, and advocacy.

Audubon Society, National: Vermont Chapters. There are currently eight local chapters of the Audubon Society throughout Vermont, which meet on a regular schedule to promote local, state, and national conservation and environmental education through a variety of activities. Contact the Vermont State Office (above) for details.

Birds of Vermont Museum, 900 Sherman Hollow Road, Huntington, VT 05462. Displays (currently 170) of Robert Spear's hand-carved wooden birds in their habitats. Includes Vermont nesting species and winter visitors, and North American endangered species. Offers educational programs, demonstrations, field trips, gifts.

Bonnyvale Environmental Education Center, 1221 Bonnyvale Road, West Brattleboro, VT 05301. Offers environmental education programs at its facility and 100 acres in West Brattleboro.

Catamount Trail Association, P.O. Box 1235, Burlington, VT 05402. Manages, promotes, and protects the 300-mile cross-country ski trail running the length of Vermont from Massachusetts to Canada.

Connecticut River Watershed Council, 1 Ferry Street, East Hampton, MA 01027. Works to maintain and improve water quality, protect key river-related lands, and bring varied interest together to resolve issues and plan for the future of the Connecticut River Valley in Vermont, New Hampshire, Massachusetts, and Connecticut.

Conservation Law Foundation, Inc., 21 East State Street, Montpelier, VT 05602. Promotes and advocates for environmentally responsible and economically sound conservation law.

Discovery Museum, 51 Park Street, Essex Junction, VT 05452. A hands-on science and children's museum for people of all ages, with natural and physical science exhibits and workshops, planetarium shows, and gift store.

Ducks Unlimited, RR 2, Box 205AA, St. Johnsbury, VT 05819. Promotes conservation of wetlands and habitats for birds through use of easements, leases, and restoration projects.

Earth First! (*Vermont Group*), P.O. Box 85, Sharon, VT 05065. Protects wilderness and biodiversity, restores healthy ecosystems in Vermont, and promotes deep ecology, through activism.

Environmental Law Foundation of Vermont, P.O. Box 8, Montpelier, VT 05601. Helps people participate in the creation, implementation, and enforcement of sound environmental laws and policies.

Fairbanks Museum and Planetarium, Main and Prospect Streets, St. Johnsbury, VT 05819. Houses the largest collection of natural science specimens and exhibits in northern New England. Conducts science and environmental education throughout Vermont. Home of the Northern New England Weather Center, which broadcasts daily. Gift shop.

Federated Garden Clubs of Vermont, Inc., P.O. Box 376, Manchester, VT 05254-0376. Promotes protection of state forests, rural areas, and pristine natural areas. Provides education on conservation ecology and horticulture.

Federation of Lake Associations: Northern Vermont, West Road, P.O. Box 131, Derby, VT 05829. Comprised of twenty-two lake associations in northern Vermont that have united to protect their lake resources.

Federation of Lake Associations: Southern Vermont, HCR 62, Box 136, Bomoseen, VT 05732. Comprised of thirteen lake associations in southern Vermont, interested primarily in maintaining and improving the quality of lakes in the region.

Green Mountain Audubon Nature Center, 255 Sherman Hollow Road, Huntington, VT 05462. A 300-acre sanctuary operated by the Green Mountain Audubon Society (see above), providing trails, special habitats, an active 700-tap sugarbush, natural history education programs, presentations, and special events.

Green Mountain Club, Inc., Route 100, RR 1, Box 650, Waterbury Center, VT 05677. Manages, maintains, and protects the 440-mile Long Trail System. Ensures public access to the Long Trail. Educates hikers about backcountry activities, conservation, and the environment.

Green Mountain Forest Watch, 48 Elliot Street, Brattleboro, VT 05301. Works to preserve and restore eastern native biodiversity and habitat from Canada to Florida.

Hulbert Outdoor Center, RR 1, Box 91A, Fairlee, VT 05045. Offers outdoor/environmental programs for schools and youth groups, training programs for adults, Elderhostel programs, and wilderness trips for people of all ages.

Keeping Track, Inc., RFD 1, Box 263, Jericho, VT 05465. Works on ways to conserve wildlife habitat in Vermont. Trains groups of volunteers to participate in community and regional habitat monitoring programs.

Keewaydin Environmental Education Center, RD 1, Box 88, Salisbury, VT 05769. Provides residential environmental education programs for Vermont school groups in winter, spring, and fall. Spring and fall sessions are at Keewaydin Camps in Salisbury, winter sessions at Seyon Ranch, Groton State Forest.

Lake Champlain Basin Program, Gordon House, 64 West Shore Road, Grand Isle, VT 05458. A collection of individuals, agencies, and organizations working together to develop a plan for the future of Lake Champlain. Works to ensure that Lake Champlain and its drainage basin will be protected, restored, and maintained.

Lake Champlain Committee, Inc., 14 South Williams Street, Burlington, VT 05401-3400. Works to protect the natural resources and aesthetic beauty of Lake Champlain and its watershed, through research, advocacy, and public education programs.

Lake Champlain Maritime Museum, Basin Harbor Club, Vergennes, VT 05491. Offers exhibits, displays, educational materials, programs, and special presentations on the maritime history of Lake Champlain.

Land Trusts: Local and Regional. Many local and regional land trusts operate in Vermont, serving to protect agricultural land, forest land, public access and trails, and natural areas, through conservation easements, donations of land, landowner agreements, and other methods.

Lamoille County Nature Center, RR 4, Box 932, Professional Drive, Morrisville, VT 05661. Provides education on natural history, the diversity of Vermont's habitats, animal and bird behavior, and ecology, though workshops, lectures, field trips, and school programs.

Merck Forest and Farmland Center, Route 315, P.O. Box 86, Rupert, VT 05768. A 2,820-acre forest preserve in the Taconic Mountains managed for public education and outdoor recreation. Includes a solar-powered visitors center, small diversified farm, sugarbush, rustic cabins and shelters, and 26 miles of trails. Provides environmental and resource management programs for the general public and school groups, summer camp, and special events.

Montshire Museum, P.O. Box 770, Montshire Road, Norwich, VT 05055. Provides displays, exhibits, and educational programs for the public, schools, and communities in Vermont and New Hampshire, in all areas of the natural and physical sciences.

National Wildlife Federation: Northeast Natural Resource Center, 58 State Street, Montpelier, VT 05602. Undertakes a comprehensive conservation education program. Distributes periodicals and educational materials. Sponsors outdoor education programs in conservation. Litigates environmental disputes on behalf of natural resources and wildlife.

The Nature Conservancy: Vermont Chapter, 27 State Street, Montpelier, VT 05602. Preserves biodiversity through purchasing, managing, researching, and providing education about special ecological areas, and assisting other conservation organizations and agencies to do so.

New England Forestry Foundation, Inc., P.O. Box 1099, 283 Old Dunstable Road, Groton, MA 01450-3099. Focuses on the practical, scientific management of private New England woodlands. Conserves over 16,000 acres in ninety-seven private New England forests.

New England Society of American Foresters, Green Mountain Division, c/o Vermont Dept. of Forests, Parks & Recreation, 103 S. Main Street, Waterbury, VT 05671. Promotes local and state awareness of forestry, through opinions on legislative issues and with policy statements.

Northern Forest Alliance, 43 State Street, Montpelier, VT 05602. A coalition of regional, state, and national organizations united to protect the 26-million-acre Northern Forest of Vermont, New York, New Hampshire, and Maine, through education, advocacy, and research and by the establishment of wild areas, well-managed forestlands, and healthy, viable human communities.

Preservation Trust of Vermont, 104 Church Street, Burlington, VT

05401. Assists in statewide efforts to protect Vermont's special architectural resources, cultural landscape, and fabric of communities, through educational, technical, and financial assistance to other groups, communities, and individuals.

River Watch Network, 153 State Street, Montpelier, VT 05602. Strives to restore and protect the water quality of the nation's rivers. Coordinates volunteer efforts to scientifically evaluate river health and use findings for river protection and improvements. Creates partnerships for river protection. Works with students and teachers on applications for river protection and management.

Rural Vermont, 15 Barre Street, Montpelier, VT 05602. Promotes healthy farms, healthy food, and a healthy rural environment through rural and agricultural policy, education, and advocacy.

Shelburne Farms Resources, 102 Harbor Road, Shelburne, VT 05482. Located on a 1,400-acre working farm and historic site on Lake Champlain. Teaches and demonstrates stewardship of natural and agricultural resources, through school field trips, educator workshops, summer camp, the Children's Farmyard, walking trails, guided tours, internships, and volunteers. Gift shop.

Shelburne Museum, Shelburne, VT 05482. Vermont's largest museum, including many outdoor displays and structures. Offers exhibits and artifacts on all aspects of Vermont history, including arts, crafts, agriculture, architecture, industries, and commerce. Gift shop.

Sierra Club: Vermont Chapter, P.O. Box 5568, Essex Junction, VT 05453-5568. Seeks to preserve, protect, and enable the enjoyment of the natural environment, through lobbying, public education, and electoral politics.

Soil and Water Conservation Society: NH/VT Chapter, 69 Union Street, Winooski, VT 05404. Promotes the conservation and wise use of land and water, through workshops and conferences of natural resources problems and solutions.

Statewide Environmental Education Programs, 9 Bailey Avenue, Montpelier, VT 05602. Coalition of individuals and organizations promoting environmental education in Vermont. Fosters environmental appreciation and understanding. Provides a resource network for educators, organizations, schools, and state agencies. Offers an annual conference and periodic workshops.

Trout Unlimited: Vermont Council, P.O. Box 266, Jonesville, VT 05466. Participates actively in river cleanups, erosion prevention, and protection of cold-water fisheries.

Trout Unlimited: Regional Chapters. Six active regional chapters report to the Vermont Council and conduct a variety of projects of particular concern and interest to the geographic area. Contact the Vermont Council for details.

Vermont Association of Conservation Districts, P.O. Drawer B,

Montpelier, VT 05601. Fosters public awareness of the value of conservation education by providing advice on land management and financial aid for land use practices.

Vermont Archaeological Society, P.O. Box 663, Burlington, VT 05402. Promotes all aspects of Vermont archaeology through educational materials and programs, field trips, newsletter, and other activities.

Vermont Botanical and Bird Club, Warren Road, Box 327, Eden, VT 05652. Pursues scientific interests in plants and birds, through meetings, field trips, and newsletter.

Vermont Current Use Tax Coalition, 9 Bailey Avenue, Montpelier, VT 05602. Coalition of twenty groups to ensure the continuation and improvement of Vermont's Use Value Appraisal program, providing equitable property taxation on productive agricultural and forest land in Vermont.

Vermont Farm Bureau, RR 2, Box 123, Richmond, VT 05477-9605. Directs lobbying efforts at the state and national levels for the benefit of agriculture.

Vermont Federation of Sportsmen's Clubs, P.O. Box 756, Colchester, VT 05446. Represents Vermont's hunting and fishing clubs. Sponsors hunter safety programs, conservation projects, presentations, and special projects. Engages in legislative and policy issues.

Vermont Geological Society, Department of Geology, Perkins Building University of Vermont, Burlington, VT 05405-0122. Promotes all aspects of the science of geology through educational materials and programs, field trips, and professional meetings.

Vermont Green Up, Inc., 1 Baldwin Street, Montpelier, VT 05602. Sponsors annual Green Up Day in May, the statewide campaign of volunteers to clean up roads, rivers, and other areas of Vermont. Provides antilitter information.

Vermont Historical Society, Pavilion Building, 109 State Street, Montpelier, VT 05602-0901. Collects, preserves, and interprets Vermont history for the use, education, and enjoyment of present and future generations. Operates a museum, research library, and gift shop. Publishes periodicals and books. Presents public programs statewide. Provides assistance and resources.

Vermont Institute of Natural Science, RR 2, Box 532, Woodstock, VT 05091. Implements statewide programs in environmental education and research, focusing on natural history, animal and bird behavior, and ecology. Offers workshops, lectures, field trips, and courses for all age groups. Head office is the 70-acre Bragdon Nature Preserve and Vermont Raptor Center. Two branch offices: Montpelier North Branch, 713 Elm Street, Montpelier, VT 05602. Manchester Office, Equinox Hotel, Manchester Village, VT 05255.

Vermont Land Trust, Inc., 8 Bailey Avenue, Montpelier, VT 05602. Engages in land protection and encourages its productive use. Protects

(1997) over 90,000 acres of farm land, forest land, natural habitat areas, recreation lands, and historic lands. Several branch offices statewide (contact main office).

Vermont Leadership Center, HCR 61, Box 26, Island Pond, VT 05846. Promotes stewardship of human and natural resources through experiences that build leadership and ignite the personal potential of each individual. Offers year-round educational programs for all ages, a summer nature camp, facilitation services, a Youth Conservation Corps, community development, and recreational opportunities. Includes a conference center, cabins, wilderness campsites, ropes courses, cross-country trails, canoeing, a small farm, and active sugarbush.

Vermont Natural Resources Council, 9 Bailey Avenue, Montpelier, VT 05602. Protects Vermont's natural resources and environment through research, education, and advocacy. Focuses on protecting and restoring rivers, streams, and wildlife; shaping land and water use policies; preserving forest and agrarian heritage; involving citizens in issues.

Vermont Public Interest Research Group, 43 State Street, Montpelier, VT 05602. Works on consumer protection and environmental health issues in Vermont, through public education, grassroots organizing, lobbying, and research.

Vermont Recreation and Parks Association, 74 Main Street, Newport, VT 05855. Develops and promotes parks and recreation opportunities for people in Vermont. Sponsors the Annual Governor's Conference on Recreation and other events. Advocates for legislation and funding to support recreation and parks.

Vermont Trails and Greenways Council, 103 S. Main Street, Waterbury, VT 05602. Coalition of private, state, and federal organizations. Promotes recreation trails and greenways throughout Vermont, through regular meetings, educational materials, and positions on legislative and policy issues.

Vermont Woodland Association, 9 Bailey Avenue, Montpelier, VT 05602. Advocates excellent forestry that employs highly integrated management practices to provide timber, improved wildlife habitat, recreation, scenic beauty, clean air and water, and other resources.

Wild Earth, P.O. Box 455, Richmond, VT 05477. A melding of conservation biology and wildlands activism. Explores wilderness and biodiversity issues from an ecocentric perspective. Serves as sister organization to the Wildlands Project to restore and protect natural diversity on earth.

Winooski Valley Park District, Ethan Allen Homestead, Burlington, VT 05401. A coalition of seven towns along the lower Winooski River that acquires and manages parklands for conservation, environmental protection, and recreational use.

State Government

Agency of Natural Resources, State Office Complex, 103 S. Main Street, Waterbury, VT 05671. Includes the Planning Division, Administrative Service, Vermont Geological Survey, and three departments: Environmental Conservation, Fish and Wildlife, and Forests, Parks, and Recreation. Responsible for managing the state's natural resources and 295,000 acres of state-owned lands (including state forests, parks, natural areas, wildlife management areas, boating accesses, fish hatcheries, pond sites, and streambanks). Provides services, support, and education in the areas of forestry; recreation; wildlife, fisheries, and aquatic biology; rare, threatened, and endangered species, and natural communities; natural resources planning; geology; air; water resources (including ponds, lakes, rivers, wetlands, and water quality); others. Several councils, boards, and advisory committees work with the Agency on specific issues such as endangered species, trails and greenways, fish and wildlife hunting regulations, and so forth. Five regional offices: St. Johnsbury, Essex Junction, Barre, North Springfield, and Pittsford. Also, a laboratory in Waterbury. Contact the central office for details.

Department of Agriculture, Food, and Markets, 120 State Street, Montpelier, VT 05620-2901. Develops, coordinates, and administers programs for regulating and managing the state's agricultural lands, products, and livestock.

Department of Libraries, 109 State Street, Montpelier, VT 05602. Loans books, periodicals, magazines, and audiovisual material on all subjects. Provides services of many kinds: general information, reference and law, technical processing, and special services. Includes several regional libraries.

Division for Historic Preservation, 135 State Street, Drawer 33, Montpelier, VT 05633-1201. Responsible for identifying, protecting, promoting, interpreting, and enhancing the historic, architectural, and archaeological resources of Vermont. Maintains an underwater historic preserve system (can be visited by divers).

Vermont Housing and Conservation Board, 149 State Street, Drawer 20, Montpelier, VT 05620-3501. Administers the Vermont Housing and Conservation Trust Fund, providing loans and grants to nonprofit organizations, municipalities, and certain state agencies to develop, preserve, and rehabilitate affordable housing and conserve and protect agricultural land, historic properties, important natural areas, and public recreational lands.

University of Vermont Extension System, 601 Main Street, Burlington, VT 05401-3439. Provides to the general public information, education, and applied research on forestry, agriculture, horticulture, nutrition, and other areas. Fourteen county field offices. Contact the central office for details.

Vermont Colleges and Universities

Bennington College, Natural Science Division, Bennington, VT 05201. Courses in environmental studies, ecology, botany, biology, physical sciences, and others. Environmental studies through the Division of Natural Sciences and Mathematics. Students combine work in the sciences with appropriate work in other disciplines.

Burlington College, 95 North Avenue, Burlington, VT 05401. Courses, independent studies, and internships in ecology, geography, natural sciences, and others.

Castleton State College, Castleton, VT 05735. Courses in physical sciences, zoology, botany, ecology, aquatic biology, and others. Offers bachelor of arts degree in natural sciences.

Center for Northern Studies, Wolcott, VT 05680. Courses in polar biota, indigenous cultures of the circumpolar north, northern resource management issues, winter ecology, and others. Offers a comprehensive undergraduate and graduate program in northern studies, including field work.

Community College of Vermont, P.O. Box 120, Waterbury, VT 05676. Courses in environmental studies, biology, forest ecology, botany, ornithology, natural history, and others.

Environmental Law Center, Vermont Law School, South Royalton, VT 05068. Courses in environmental law, in various disciplines. Offers a master of studies in law in environmental law.

Goddard College, Plainfield, VT 05667. Courses in ecology, agriculture, herbal botany, and others. Offers a bachelor of arts and master of arts in environmental arts and sciences.

Johnson State College, Department of Environmental and Health Science, Johnson, VT 05656. Courses in water resources, energy and mineral resources, agriculture, land use, environmental law, ecology, ornithology, field geology, and others. Offers a bachelor of science degree in environmental science.

Lyndon State College, Department of Natural Science, Lyndonville, VT 05851. Courses in physical sciences, conservation biology, ecology, and others. Offers a bachelor of arts degree in environmental science.

Marlboro College, Marlboro, VT 05344. Courses in ecology, limnology, silviculture, natural resources policy and administration, wildlife management, geography, and others. Offers undergraduate programs in environmental science or natural resource management.

Middlebury College, Program in Environmental Studies, Middlebury, VT 05753. Courses in environmental geology, ecology, environmental and natural resources policy, and others. Offers a bachelor of arts degree in environmental studies.

Norwich University, Math and Sciences Division, Northfield, VT 05663. Courses in geology, mineralogy, ecology, biology, ornithology, plant taxonomy, invertebrate zoology, and others. Offers a bachelor of science degree in geology, biology, and others.

Saint Michael's College, Winooski Park, Colchester, VT 05439. Courses in ecology, environmental research, physical sciences, biology, and others. Programs are geared toward physical and biological sciences coupled with socioeconomic influences.

Southern Vermont College, Department of Environmental Studies, Bennington, VT 05201. Courses in water quality, forest ecology, ecology, environmental law, and others. Environmental studies are a part of a liberal arts program.

Sterling College, Craftsbury Common, VT 05827. Courses in ecology, geography and history of land use, forestry, woodlot harvesting, wildlife biology, and others. Offers one- and two-year programs in environmental studies and natural resources management.

University of Vermont, Environmental Studies Program, 153 South Prospect Street, Burlington, VT 05405. Courses in environmental studies, environmental law, environmental policy, and others. Offers majors with an interdisciplinary emphasis in the College of Arts and Sciences, the College of Agriculture and Life Sciences, and the School of Natural Resources.

University of Vermont, School of Natural Resources, Burlington, VT 05405. Offers courses in forest genetics, geographic information systems, park and recreation design, wildlife habitat and population management, fisheries biology, wetlands ecology, forest pathology, and others. Offers a bachelor of science degree in forestry, environmental studies, recreation management, resource economics, wildlife and fisheries biology, and natural resources.

Vermont Technical College, Department of Agriculture and Business, Randolph Center, VT 05061. Courses in soils and fertilizers, landscape design, botany, zoology, physical sciences, and others. Offers horticulture science and management courses.

United States Government

University of Vermont Extension System (see Vermont State Government).

Green Mountain National Forest, Forest Supervisor's Office, P.O. Box 519, 151 West Street, Rutland, VT 05702. Administers and manages over 325,000 acres of national forest system land in Vermont, for back-country recreation, wildlife and fish habitat, scenery, and production of wood fiber and high quality sawtimber. Three district offices: Manchester Center, Middlebury, and Rochester. Contact the central office for details.

Missisquoi National Wildlife Refuge, RR 2, Box 163, Swanton, VT 05488. Manages the 5,839-acre refuge to provide breeding, migration, and wintering areas for migratory birds. Provides public recreation and information.

Northeastern Forest Experiment Station, George D. Aiken Forestry Sciences Laboratory, P.O. Box 968, 705 Spear Street, Burlington, VT 05402. Conducts research on environmental stress on tree growth; human dimensions of tourism, fish and wildlife, and outdoor recreation; integrating ecological and social dimensions of forest ecosystem management.

Natural Resources Conservation Service (formerly Soil Conservation Service), 69 Union Street, Winooski, VT 05404. Provides technical and, in some cases, financial assistance for soil and water conservation, natural resources surveys, and rural community protection and development. Twelve county regional offices. Contact the central office for details.

Resource Conservation and Development Area, George D. Aiken, P.O. Box 411, Route 66, Professional Center, Randolph, VT 05060. *Resource Conservation and Development Area, Northern Vermont*, RR 4, Box 2293, Comstock Road, Berlin, VT 05602-8927. RC&Ds offer rural programs to help local people develop, use, and renew their natural and human resources. George D. Aiken Area serves six southern counties (Orange, Windsor, Windham, Addison, Rutland, and Bennington); Northern Vermont Area serves eight northern counties (Caledonia, Chittenden, Essex, Franklin, Grand Isle, Lamoille, Orleans, and Washington).

U.S. Environmental Protection Agency (EPA): *Region I*, John F. Kennedy Building, 1 Congress Street, Boston, MA 02203. Provides technical, financial, and enforcement assistance to Vermont in air management, environmental services, planning and management, waste management, water management, wetlands protection, toxic substance control, pesticides, pollution prevention, and oil spills.

U.S. Fish and Wildlife Service, Lake Champlain Complex, 11 Lincoln Street, Essex Junction, VT 05452. Protects, enhances, and conserves fish and wildlife resources in the Lake Champlain watershed, through restoration, technical expertise, interagency cooperation and partnerships, and public information. Includes Lake Champlain Fish and Wildlife Resources Office in Essex Junction and the Bethel and Pittsford National Fish Hatcheries.

U.S. Forest Service (see Green Mountain National Forest; Northeast Forest Experiment Station).

Appendix III

References

Due to the great number of magazine and journal articles on all topics covered in this book—many of them excellent and informative—regrettably I have had to include only books and booklets in the references listed here. Readers wishing to go into more depth on a subject should review the bibliographies in these references, contact the relevant organizations in Appendix II, or consult with libraries.

Geology and Earth Resource

Christman, Robert A. 1956. *The Geology of Mt. Mansfield State Forest.* Vermont Geological Survey, Vermont Development Commission, Montpelier, Vt.

Christman, Robert A. 1956. *The Geology of Groton State Forest.* Vermont Geological Survey, Vermont Development Commission, Montpelier, Vt.

Dodge, Harry W., Jr. 1959. *The Geology of Calvin Coolidge State Forest Park.* Vermont Geological Survey, Vermont Development Commission, Montpelier, Vt.

Dodge, Harry W., Jr. 1962. *The Geology of Button Bay State Park.* Vermont Geological Survey, Montpelier, Vt.

Dodge, Harry W., Jr. 1967. *The Geology of Darling State Park.* Vermont Geological Survey, Montpelier, Vt.

Dodge, Harry W., Jr. 1969. *The Geology of D.A.R. State Park, Mt. Philo State Park, and Sand Bar State Park.* Vermont Geological Survey, Vermont Development Commission, Montpelier, Vt.

Doll, Charles G. (ed.). 1961. *Centennial Map of Vermont.* Vermont Geological Survey, Vermont Development Department, Montpelier, Vt.

Doll, Charles G. (ed.). 1970. *Surficial Geologic Map of Vermont.* Vermont Geological Survey, Department of Water Resources, Montpelier, Vt.

Jacobs, Elbridge Churchill. 1950 (reprinted 1969). *The Physical Features of Vermont.* Vermont Geological Survey, Vermont Development Department, Montpelier, Vt.

Ludlum, David M. 1985. *The Vermont Weather Book.* Vermont Historical Society, Montpelier, Vt.

McPhee, John. 1981. *Basin and Range.* Farrar, Straus & Giroux, New York.

Stewart, David P. 1961. *The Glacial Geology of Vermont.* Vermont Geological Survey, Vermont Development Commission, Montpelier, Vt.

Van Diver, Bradford B. 1987. *Roadside Geology of Vermont and New Hampshire.* Mountain Press Publishing Company, Missoula, Mont.

Welby, Charles W. 1962. *Paleontology of the Lake Champlain Basin in*

Vermont. Vermont Geological Survey, Vermont Development Department, Montpelier, Vt.

Archaeology, History, and Land Use

Allen, Ira. 1798. *The Natural and Political History of the State of Vermont.* J. W. Meyers, London.

Calloway, Colin G. 1989. *The Abenaki.* Chelsea House Publishers, New York.

Calloway, Colin G. 1990. *The Western Abenakis of Vermont, 1600–1800.* University of Oklahoma Press, Norman, Okla.

Calloway, Colin G. 1991. *Dawnland Encounter: Indians and Europeans in Northern New England.* University Press of New England, Hanover, N.H.

Cronon, William. 1983. *Changes in the Land: Indians, Colonists, and the Ecology of New England.* Hill and Wang, a division of Farrar, Straus, and Giroux, New York.

Dobbs, David, and Ober, Richard. 1995. *The Northern Forest.* Chelsea Green Publishing Company, White River Junction, Vt.

Hagermann, Robert L. 1975. *Mansfield: The Story of Vermont's Loftiest Mountain* (second ed.). Phoenix Publishing, Canaan, N.H.

Haviland, William A., and Power, Marjory W. 1994. *The Original Vermonters: Native Inhabitants, Past and Present* (second ed.). University Press of New England, Hanover, N.H.

Hill, Ralph Nading. 1978. *Lake Champlain: Key to Liberty.* Vermont Life Magazine, in cooperation with the Burlington Free Press, Montpelier, Vt.

Huden, John C. (ed.). 1971. *Archaeology in Vermont.* Charles E. Tuttle Company, Rutland, Vt.

Irland, Lloyd C. 1982. *Wildlands and Woodlots: The Story of New England's Forests.* University Press of New England, Hanover, N.H.

Matthiessen, Peter. 1978. *Wildlife in America.* Viking Press, New York.

Nash, Roderick F. 1982. *Wilderness and the American Mind* (third ed.). Yale University Press, New Haven, Conn.

Pike, Robert E. 1984. *Tall Trees, Tough Men.* W. W. Norton and Company, New York.

Rolando, Victor. 1992. *200 Years of Soot and Sweat: The History and Archaeology of Vermont's Iron, Charcoal, and Lime Industries.* Vermont Archaeological Society, Burlington, Vt.

Russell, Howard S. 1982. *A Long Deep Furrow: Three Centuries of Farming in New England.* University Press of New England, Hanover, N.H.

Vermont, State of. 1994. *Stonewalls and Cellarholes: A Guide for Landowners on Historic Features and Landscapes in Vermont's Forests.* Department of Forests, Parks and Recreation, Agency of Natural Resources, Waterbury, Vt.

Williams, Samuel. 1794. *The Natural and Civil History of Vermont.* (n.p.), Walpole, N.H.

Natural History and Ecology, General

Bennett, Dean B. 1996. *The Forgotten Nature of New England: A Search for Traces of the Original Wilderness.* Down East Books, Camden, Me.

Caduto, Michael J. 1985. *Pond and Brook: A Guide to Nature Study in Freshwater Environments.* University Press of New England, Hanover, N.H.

DeGraaf, Richard M., and Rudis, Deborah D. 1983. *New England Wildlife: Habitat, Natural History, and Distribution.* Publication GTR NE-144. USDA Forest Service, Washington, D.C.

Farb, Peter. 1963. *Face of North America: The Natural History of a Continent.* Harper & Row, New York.

Hunter, Malcolm L., Jr. 1990. *Wildlife, Forests, and Forestry: Principles of Managing Forests for Biological Diversity.* Prentice Hall, Englewood Cliffs, N.J.

Johnson, Charles W. 1985. *Bogs of the Northeast.* University Press of New England, Hanover, N.H.

Jorgensen, Neil. 1977. *A Guide to New England's Landscape.* Pequot Press, Chester, Conn.

Marchand, Peter J. 1987. *Life in the Cold: An Introduction to Winter Ecology.* University Press of New England, Hanover, N.H.

Marchand, Peter J. 1987. *North Woods: An Inside Look at the Nature of Forests in the Northeast.* Appalachian Mountain Club, Boston.

Odum, Eugene P. 1971. *Fundamentals of Ecology* (third ed.). W. B. Saunders Company, Philadelphia.

Palmer, E. Laurence, and Fowler, H. Seymour 1975. *Fieldbook of Natural History* (second ed.). McGraw-Hill Book Company, New York.

Pielou, E. C. 1991. *After the Ice Age: The Return of Life to Glaciated North America.* University of Chicago Press, Chicago.

Thomson, Betty F. 1958. *The Changing Face of New England.* Macmillan Company, New York.

Watts, May Theilgaard. 1957. *Reading the Landscape.* Macmillan Company, New York.

Wessels, Tom. 1997. *Reading the Forested Landscape: A Natural History of New England.* Countryman Press, Woodstock, Vt.

Whitney, Gordon G. 1996. *From Coastal Wilderness to Fruited Plain: A History of Environmental Change in Temperate North America from 1500 to the Present.* Cambridge University Press, Cambridge, England.

Wilson, Edward O. 1992. *The Diversity of Life.* W. W. Norton and Company, New York.

Natural History, Vermont

Borie, Louis. 1977. *University of Vermont Natural Areas.* Environmental Program, University of Vermont, Burlington, Vt.

Foote, Leonard E. 1946. *A History of Wild Game in Vermont.* Vermont Fish and Game Service Bulletin, Montpelier, Vt.

Hard, Walter, Jr. (ed.). 1967. *Vermont Life Book of Nature.* Stephen Greene Press, Brattleboro, Vt.

Meeks, Harold A. 1986. *Vermont's Land and Resources.* New England Press, Shelburne, Vt.

Thompson, Elizabeth. 1996 (May). *Natural Communities of Vermont: Uplands and Wetlands.* Nongame and Natural Heritage Program, Vermont Fish and Wildlife Department, Waterbury, Vermont, in cooperation with the Vermont Field Office, The Nature Conservancy, Montpelier, Vt.

Thompson, Zadock. 1853. *Natural History of Vermont.* Originally published by the author, 1853. Reprinted in 1972 by Charles E. Tuttle Company, Rutland, Vt.

Vermont, State of. 1995. *A Landowner's Guide: Wildlife Habitat Management for Vermont Woodlands.* Departments of Fish and Wildlife and Forests, Parks, and Recreation, Waterbury, Vt.

Vogelmann, Hubert W. 1964 (reprinted 1971). *Natural Areas in Vermont: Some Ecological Sites of Public Importance.* Report 1. Vermont Agricultural Experiment Station, University of Vermont, Burlington, Vt.

Vogelmann, Hubert W. 1969. *Vermont Natural Areas.* Report 2. Central Planning Office and Interagency Committee on Natural Resources, Montpelier, Vt.

Young, Augustus. 1856. *Report on the Natural History of the State of Vermont.* Chauncy Goodrich, Burlington, Vt.

Plants

Appalachian Mountain Club. 1964. *Mountain Flowers of New England.* Appalachian Mountain Club, Boston.

Burns, G. P., and Otis, C. H. 1916 (reprinted 1979). *The Handbook of Vermont Trees.* Originally published by Free Press Printing Company, Burlington, Vt. Reprinted by Charles E. Tuttle Company, Rutland, Vt.

Clark, Anna M. 1899. *Trees of Vermont.* Free Press Association, Burlington, Vt.

Harlow, William M. 1957. *Trees of the Eastern and Central United States and Canada.* Dover Publications, New York.

Jones, L. R., and Rand, F. V. 1909 (reprinted 1979). *The Handbook of Vermont Shrubs and Woody Vines.* Originally published by Vermont Agricultural Experiment Station, Burlington, Vt. Reprinted by Charles E. Tuttle Company, Rutland, Vt.

Magee, Dennis W. 1981. *Freshwater Wetlands: A Guide to Common Indicator Plants of the Northeast.* University of Massachusetts Press, Amherst, Mass.

Newcomb, Lawrence. 1989. *Newcomb's Wildflower Guide.* Little, Brown and Company, Boston.

Seymour, Frank C. 1969. *The Flora of Vermont.* Bulletin 660. Vermont Agricultural Experiment Station, University of Vermont, Burlington, Vt.

Slack, Nancy G., and Bell, Allison W. 1995. *AMC Field Guide to New England Alpine Summits.* AMC Books, Boston.

Steele, Fredric L., and Hodgdon, Albion R. 1971 (second ed.). *Trees and Shrubs of Northern New England.* Society for the Protection of New Hampshire Forests, Concord, N.H.

Mammals

Godin, Alfred J. 1977. *Wild Mammals of New England.* Johns Hopkins University Press, Baltimore, Md.

Vermont, State of. 1973–1975. *Vermont Game Annuals.* Bulletins 73-2 through 75-2. Vermont Fish and Game Department, Agency of Environmental Conservation, Montpelier, Vt.

Willey, Charles H. 1978. *The Vermont Black Bear.* Vermont Fish and Game Department, Agency of Environmental Conservation, Montpelier, Vt.

Birds

Bent, Arthur C. 1919–1958 (reprinted 1961–1968). *Life Histories of North American Birds.* Originally published as a 21-part series of bulletins by the United States National Museum. Reprinted as a 26-volume set by Dover Publications, New York.

Farrar, Richard B., Jr. 1973. *Birds of East-Central Vermont.* Vermont Institute of Natural Science, Woodstock, Vt.

Forbush, Edward H., and May, John B. 1939. *A Natural History of American Birds of Eastern and Central North America.* Houghton Mifflin Company, Boston.

Laughlin, Sarah B., and Kibbe, Douglas P. (eds.). 1985. *The Atlas of Breeding Birds of Vermont.* University Press of New England, Hanover, N.H.

McElroy, Thomas P., Jr. 1974. *The Habitat Guide to Birding.* Afred A. Knopf, New York.

Spear, Robert N., Jr. 1976. *Birds of Vermont* (third ed.). Green Mountain Audubon Society, Burlington, Vt.

Fish

Coker, Robert E. 1954. *Streams, Lakes, Ponds.* University of North Carolina Press, Chapel Hill, N.C.

Eddy, Samuel. 1969. *The Freshwater Fishes* (second ed.). William C. Brown Company, Dubuque, Iowa.

Everhart, W. Harry. 1958. *Fishes of Maine.* Maine Department of Inland Fisheries and Game, Augusta, Me.

Halnon, Leonard C. 1963. *Historical Survey of Lake Champlain Fishery.* Vermont Fish and Game Department, Montpelier, Vt.

Hubbs, Carl L., and Lagler, Karl F. 1949. *Fisheries of the Great Lakes Region.* Bulletin 26. Cranbrook Institute of Science, Bloomfield, Mich.

Scarola, John. 1987. *Freshwater Fishes of New Hampshire.* New Hampshire Fish and Game Department, Concord, N.H.

Vermont, State of. 1973–1975. *Vermont Fisheries Annuals.* Bulletins 73-1 through 75-1. Vermont Fish and Game Department, Agency of Environmental Conservation, Montpelier, Vt.

Amphibians and Reptiles

Andrews, James S. 1995 (April). *A Preliminary Atlas of the Reptiles and Amphibians of Vermont.* The Vermont Reptile and Amphibian Scientific Advisory Group of the Vermont Endangered Species Committee, in cooperation with the Vermont Field Office of The Nature Conservancy, Montpelier, Vt., and the Nongame and Natural Heritage Program, Vermont Fish and Wildlife Department, Waterbury, Vt.

Babcock, Harold L. 1971. *Turtles of the Northeastern United States.* Dover Publications, New York.

DeGraaf, Richard M., and Rudis, Deborah D. 1985. *Amphibians and Reptiles of New England: Habitats and Natural History.* University of Massachusetts Press, Amherst, Mass.

Oliver, James A. 1955. *The Natural History of North American Amphibians and Reptiles.* Van Nostrand Company, Princeton, N.J.

Invertebrates

Borror, Donald J., and DeLong, Dwight M. 1964. *An Introduction to the Study of Insects.* Holt, Rinehart and Winston, New York.

Fichtel, Christopher, and Smith, Douglas G. 1995. *The Freshwater Mussels of Vermont.* Technical Report 18. Nongame and Natural Heritage Program, Vermont Fish and Wildlife Department, Waterbury, Vt.

Frost, S. W. 1959. *Insect Life and Insect Natural History.* Dover Publications, New York.

Hanson, Trish, and Walker, E. Bradford. 1996. *Field Guide to Common Insect Pests of Urban Trees in the Northeast.* Vermont Department of Forests, Parks and Recreation, Forest Biology Laboratory, Waterbury, Vt.

Parker, Bruce L., McGrath, Katherine E., Moulton, Sara, and Teillon,

H. Brenton. 1989 (December). *History of the Major Forest Insect Pests in Vermont.* Research Report 57. Agricultural Experiment Station, University of Vermont, Burlington, Vt., and Department of Forests, Parks and Recreation, Waterbury, Vt.

Pennak, R. W. 1989. *Fresh-Water Invertebrates of the United States.* John Wiley and Sons, New York.

Teillon, H. Brenton, Burns, Barbara, and Kelley, Ronald S. 1996. *Forest Insect and Disease Conditions in Vermont: 1996.* Department of Forests, Parks and Recreation, Agency of Natural Resources, Waterbury, Vt.

Conservation

Carson, Rachel. 1962. *Silent Spring.* Houghton Mifflin Company, Boston.

Graham, Frank, Jr. 1971. *Man's Dominion: The Story of Conservation in America.* M. Evans and Company, New York.

Hunter, Malcolm L., Jr. 1995. *Fundamentals of Conservation Biology.* Blackwell Science Publications, Cambridge, Mass.

Klyza, Christopher McGrory, and Trombulak, Stephen C. (eds.). 1994. *The Future of the Northern Forest.* University Press of New England, Hanover, N.H.

Lake Champlain Basin Program. 1996 (October). *Opportunities for Action: An Evolving Plan for the Future of the Lake Champlain Basin.* Lake Champlain Basin Program, Grand Isle, Vt.

Leopold, Aldo. 1949. *Sand County Almanac and Sketches Here and There.* Oxford University Press, New York.

Marsh, George Perkins. 1864. *Man and Nature.* Scribner's, New York.

Northern Forest Lands Council. 1994 (September). *Finding Common Ground: Conserving the Northern Forests—Recommendations of the Northern Forest Lands Council.* Northern Forest Lands Council, Concord, N.H.

Udall, Stewart. 1963. *The Quiet Crisis.* Avon Books, New York.

U.S. Fish and Wildlife Service. 1995 (October). *Final Action Plan and Environmental Impact Statement for the Silvio O. Conte National Wildlife Refuge.* U.S. Fish and Wildlife Service, Turners Falls, Mass.

Vermont, State of. 1997. *A Plan for a Decade of Progress: Actions for Vermont's Economy—1996 Report.* Vermont Economic Progress Council, Agency of Commerce and Community Development, Montpelier, Vt.

Vermont, State of. 1997. *Vermont Historic Preservation Plan: Planning for the Future of Vermont's Heritage.* Division for Historic Preservation, Agency of Development and Community Affairs, Montpelier, Vt.

Field Guide Books

There are many field guides published on a wide variety of natural history topics, including groups of organisms (birds, reptiles and amphibians, insects, etc.), behavior and life histories, tracks and signs, landscapes, habitats, and so forth. The appeal and utility of guides is a matter of personal preference. Many of the popular guides are published in series:

Audubon Society Field Guides. Many topics; color photographs for identification. Alfred A. Knopf, New York.

Golden Field Guides. Many topics; drawings and paintings for identification. Golden Press, New York.

Peterson Field Guides. Many topics; drawings and paintings for identification. Houghton Mifflin Company, Boston.

Sierra Club Naturalist's Guides. Guides on the natural history of areas and regions in the country (e.g., Southern New England, North Woods). Sierra Club Books, San Francisco.

Smithsonian Guides to Natural America. Guides on parks, preserves, sanctuaries and scenic wonders in regions of the country (e.g., Northern New England). Smithsonian Books, Washington, D.C., and Random House, New York.

Stokes Nature Guides. Many topics; many on behavior and life histories (e.g., birds, insects). Little, Brown and Company, Boston.

Appendix IV

Common and Scientific Names of Plants and Animals Listed in the Text*

Plants, Herbaceous Flowering

Arbutus, trailing—*Epigaea repens*

Arethusa (Dragon's mouth)—*Arethusa bulbosa*

Arrowhead, common (Duck potato)—*Sagittaria latifolia*

Arrowhead—*Sagittaria spp.*

Aster, white wood—*Aster divaricatus*

Aster, whorled—*Aster acuminatus*

Bedstraws—*Galium spp.*

Beggarticks—*Bidens frondosa*

Bilberry, alpine (bog)—*Vaccinium uliginosum*

Bindweed—*Convolvulus spp.*

Black-eyed Susan—*Rudbeckia serotina*

Bladderwort, horned—*Utricularia cornuta*

Bloodroot—*Sanguinaria canadensis*

Blue flag (Iris)—*Iris versicolor*

Bunchberry—*Cornus canadensis*

Burdock—*Arctium minus*

Burreed—*Sparganium spp.*

Butter-and-eggs—*Linaria vulgaris*

Butterwort—*Pinguicula vulgaris*

Calopogon (Grass-pink)—*Calopogon pulchellus*

Calypso (Fairy-slipper)—*Calypso bulbosa*

Cattail, common—*Typha latifolia*

Chestnut, water—*Trapa natans*

Chicory—*Cichorium intybus*

Cinquefoil, three-toothed—*Potentilla tridentata*

Cinquefoils—*Potentilla spp.*

Clintonia (Bead lily)—*Clintonia borealis*

Clover, red—*Trifolium pretense*

Clover, white—*Trifolium repens*

*Many common and scientific names have changed since publication of the first edition.

Cohosh, blue—*Caulophyllum thalictroides*
Cotton grass—*Eriophorum spp.*
Cranberry, large—*Vaccinium macrocarpon*
Cranberry, mountain—*Vaccinium vitis-idaea*
Cranberry, small—*Vaccinium oxycoccus*
Crowberry, black—*Empetrum nigrum*
Daisy, ox-eye—*Chrysanthemum leucanthemum*
Dandelion, common—*Taraxacum officinale*
Diapensia—*Diapensia lapponica*
Devil's paintbrush (Hawkweed)—*Hieracium aurantiacum*
Duckweeds—*Lemnaceae* (family)
Dutchman's-breeches—*Dicentra cucullaria*
Elodea (Waterweed)—*Elodea canadensis*
Fireweed—*Epilobium angustifolium*
Foamflower—*Tiarella cordifolia*
Gentian, bottle (closed)—*Gentiana clausa*
Ginger, wild—*Asarum canadense*
Goldenrods—*Solidago spp.*
Goldthread—*Coptis groenlandica*
Grass-of-Parnassus—*Parnassia glauca*
Grasses—*Poaceae* (family)
Hepatica, round-lobed—*Hepatica americana*
Hepatica, sharp-lobed—*Hepatica acutifolia*
Indian pipe—*Monotropa uniflora*
Jack-in-the-pulpit—*Arisaema atrorubens*
Jewelweeds—*Impatiens spp.*
Lady's-slipper, pink—*Cypripedium acaule*
Lady's-slipper, showy—*Cypripedium reginae*
Lady's-slipper, yellow—*Cypripedium calceolus*
Lady's-tresses—*Spiranthes spp.*
Leek, wild—*Allium tricoccum*
Lobelia, Kalm's—*Lobelia kalmii*
Loosestrife, purple—*Lythrum salicaria*
Marigold, marsh—*Caltha palustris*
Mayflower, Canada—*Maianthemum canadense*

Milkweed, common—*Asclepias syriaca*

Miterwort, naked—*Mitella nuda*

Morning glory—*Ipomaea spp.*

Moss, Spanish—*Tillandsia usneoides*

Mullein, common—*Verbascum thapsus*

Nettles—*Urtica spp.* and *Laportea canadensis*

Orchids—*Orchidaceae* (family)

Orchis, showy—*Orchis spectabilis*

Orchis, white bog—*Platanthera dilatata*

Partridgeberry—*Mitchella repens*

Pickerelweed—*Pontederia cordata*

Pitcher plant—*Sarracenia purpurea*

Pogonia, rose—*Pogonia ophioglossoides*

Pond lily, yellow—*Nuphar variegatum*

Pondweeds—*Potamogeton spp.*

Primrose, bird's-eye—*Primula mistassinica*

Pyrola, pink—*Pyrola asarifolia*

Queen Anne's lace—*Daucus carota*

Rattlesnake plantains—*Goodyera spp.*

Rice, wild—*Zizania aquatica*

Rushes—*Juncaceae* (family)

Sandwort, mountain—*Minuartia groenlandica*

Sarsaparilla, wild—*Aralia nudicaulis*

Saxifrage, golden—*Chrysosplenium americanum*

Saxifrage, purple mountain—*Saxifraga oppositifolia*

Saxifrage, white mountain (live-long)—*Saxifraga aizoon*

Saxifrage, yellow mountain—*Saxifraga aizoides*

Sedge, Bigelow's—*Carex bigelowii*

Sedges—*Cyperaceae* (family)

Shepherd's purse—*Capsella bursa-pastoris*

Shinleaf—*Pyrola elliptica*

Smartweeds—*Polygonum spp.*

Spatterdock (Yellow pond lily)—*Nuphar variegatum*

Spring beauty—*Claytonia virginica*

Starflower—*Trientalis borealis*

Sundew, round-leaved—*Drosera rotuntifolia*

Sundew, spatulate-leaved—*Drosera intermedia*

Sundews—*Drosera spp.*

Sunflowers—*Helianthus spp.*

Thistles—*Cirsium spp.*

Trefoil, birdfoot—*Lotus corniculatus*

Trillium, painted—*Trillium undulatum*

Trillium, red—*Trillium erectum*

Trillium, white—*Trillium grandiflorum*

Turtlehead—*Chelone glabra*

Twayblades—*Liparis* and *Listera spp.*

Twinflower—*Linnaea borealis*

Violet, dogtooth (Trout lily)—*Erythronium americanum*

Violets—*Viola spp.*

Water lilies—*Nymphaea spp.*

Watercress—*Nasturtium officinale*

Waterleaf, Virginia—*Hydrophyllum virginianum*

Watermilfoil, Eurasian—*Myriophyllum spicatum*

Watermilfoils—*Myriophyllum spp.*

Windflower (Wood anemone)—*Anemone quinquefolia*

Winter cress—*Barbarea spp.*

Wintergreen—*Gaultheria procumbens*

Yarrow—*Achillea millefolium*

Trees and Shrubs

Alder, speckled—*Alnus rugosa*

Arrow-wood—*Viburnum dentatum*

Ash, black—*Fraxinus nigra*

Ash, green—*Fraxinus pennsylvanica*

Ash, white—*Fraxinus americana*

Aspen, big-tooth—*Populus grandidentata*

Aspen, quaking—*Populus tremuloides*

Basswood (Linden)—*Tilia americana*

Bayberry—*Myrica spp.*

Bayberry family—*Myricaceae* (family)

Beech, American—*Fagus grandifolia*

Birch, black—*Betula lenta*

Birch, gray—*Betula populifolia*

Birch, heart-leaved paper—*Betula papyrifera v. cordifolia*

Birch, paper (white)—*Betula papyrifera*

Birch, yellow—*Betula alleghaniensis*

Blackberry—*Rubus allegheniensis*

Blueberries—*Vaccinium spp.*

Box-elder (Ash-leaved maple)—*Acer negundo*

Butternut—*Juglans cinerea*

Cedar, northern white—*Thuja occidentalis*

Cedar, red—*Juniperus virginiana*

Cherry, black—*Prunus serotina*

Cherry, choke—*Prunus virginiana*

Cherry, pin (fire)—*Prunus pensylvanica*

Chestnut, American—*Castanea dentata*

Chestnut, Chinese—*Castanea mollissima*

Cottonwood, eastern—*Populus deltoides*

Dogwood, alternate-leaved—*Cornus alternifolia*

Dogwood, flowering—*Cornus florida*

Elm, American—*Ulmus americana*

Elm, slippery (red)—*Ulmus rubra*

Fir, balsam—*Abies balsamea*

Fir, Fraser—*Abies fraseri*

Gale, sweet—*Myrica gale*

Gum, black (Tupelo)—*Nyssa sylvatica*

Hackberry—*Celtis occidentalis*

Hawthorns—*Crataegus spp.*

Hazelnut, beaked—*Corylus cornuta*

Heath, beach—*Hudsonia tomentosa*

Heaths—*Ericaceae* (family)

Hemlock, eastern—*Tsuga canadensis*

Hickory, bitternut—*Carya cordiformis*

Hickory, shagbark—*Carya ovata*

Hobblebush (Witch-hobble)—*Viburnum alnifolium*

Holly, mountain—*Nemopanthus mucronata*

Hophornbeam, eastern—*Ostrya virginiana*
Juniper, common—*Juniperus communis*
Labrador tea—*Ledum groenlandicum*
Laurel, bog (pale)—*Kalmia polifolia*
Laurel, great—*Rhododendron maximum*
Laurel, mountain—*Kalmia latifolia*
Laurel, sheep—*Kalmia angustifolia*
Leatherleaf—*Chamaedaphne calyculata*
Meadowsweet—*Spirea latifolia*
Maple, mountain—*Acer spicatum*
Maple, red (soft)—*Acer rubrum*
Maple, silver—*Acer saccharinum*
Maple, striped—*Acer pensylvanicum*
Maple, sugar (hard or rock)—*Acer saccharum*
Mountain ash—*Pyrus americana*
Nannyberry—*Viburnum lentago*
Oak, black—*Quercus velutina*
Oak, bur (mossy-cup)—*Quercus macrocarpa*
Oak, chestnut—*Quercus prinus*
Oak, red—*Quercus rubra*
Oak, scarlet—*Quercus coccinea*
Oak, swamp white—*Quercus bicolor*
Oak, white—*Quercus alba*
Oak, yellow (chinkapin)—*Quercus muehlenbergii*
Pine, jack—*Pinus banksiana*
Pine, pitch—*Pinus rigida*
Pine, red (Norway)—*Pinus resinosa*
Pine, white—*Pinus strobus*
Poplar, balsam—*Populus balsamifera*
Poplar, tulip—*Liriodendron tulipifera*
Raspberries—*Rubus spp.*
Redbud—*Cercis canadensis*
Rhodora—*Rhododendron canadense*
Rosemary, bog—*Andromeda glaucophylla*
Sassafras—*Sassafras albidum*

Shadbush (Serviceberry)—*Amelanchier spp.*

Spruce, black—*Picea mariana*

Spruce, red—*Picea rubens*

Spruce, white—*Picea glauca*

Steeplebush—*Spirea tomentosa*

Sumac, staghorn—*Rhus typhina*

Sycamore—*Plantanus occidentalis*

Tamarack (American larch)—*Larix laricina*

Viburnums—*Viburnum spp.*

Walnut, white—see Butternut

Willows—*Salix spp.*

Winterberry (Black alder)—*Ilex verticillata*

Witherod (Wild raisin)—*Viburnum cassinoides*

Plants, Nonflowering

Algae, green—*Chlorophyceae* (family)

Chanterelles—*Cantherellus spp.*

Cliffbrake , slender—*Cryptogramma stelleri*

Clubmoss, bristly—*Lycopodium annotinum*

Clubmosses—*Lycopodiaceae* (family)

Diatoms—*Diatomaceae* (family)

Fern, cinnamon—*Osmunda cinnamomea*

Fern, crested shield—*Dryopteris cristata*

Fern, Green Mountain maidenhair—*Adiantum viridimontanum*

Fern, hayscented—*Dennstaedtia punctilobula*

Fern, interrupted—*Osmunda claytoniana*

Fern, lady—*Athyrium filix-femina*

Fern, maidenhair—*Adiantum pedatum*

Fern, male—*Dryopteris filix-mas*

Fern, marsh—*Thelypteris palustris*

Fern, New York—*Thelypteris noveboracensis*

Fern, ostrich—*Matteuccia struthiopteris*

Fern, royal—*Osmunda regalis*

Fern, sensitive—*Onoclea sensibilis*

Fern, serpentine maidenhair—*Adiantum aleuticum*

Ferns—*Eufilicales* (order)

Fir-moss, mountain (fir clubmoss)—*Huperzia appalachiana*
Fungi—*Fungi* (subdivision)
Horsetails—*Equisetaceae* (family)
Lichens—*Ascomycota* (division)
Moss, peat (sphagnum)—*Sphagnum spp.*
Mosses—*Bryophyta* (division)
Old-man's beard—*Usnea barbata*
Spleenwort, green—*Asplenium trichomanes-ramosum*
Spleenwort, narrow-leaved—*Athyrium pycnocarpon*
Spleenwort, silvery—*Deparia acrositicoides*
Wall rue—*Asplenium ruta-muraria*
Woodfern, marginal—*Dryopteris marginalis*
Woodfern, intermediate—*Dryopteris intermedia*

Mammals

Bat, big brown—*Eptesicus fuscus*
Bat, Indiana—*Myotis sodalis*
Bat, little brown—*Myotis lucifugus*
Bat, red—*Lasiurus borealis*
Bear, black—*Ursus americanus*
Beaver—*Castor canadensis*
Bison—*Bison bison*
Bobcat—*Lynx rufus*
Caribou, woodland—*Rangifer caribou*
Catamount (Eastern mountain lion)—*Puma concolor cougar*
Chipmunk, eastern—*Tamias striatus*
Cottontail, eastern—*Sylvilagus floridanus*
Cottontail, New England—*Sylvilagus transitionalis*
Coyote, eastern—*Canis latrans*
Deer, white-tailed—*Odocoileus virginianus*
Elk (Wapiti)—*Cervus canadensis*
Fisher—*Martes pennanti*
Fox, gray—*Urocyon cinereoargenteus*
Fox, red—*Vulpes fulva*
Hare, snowshoe (varying)—*Lepus americanus*
Lemming, southern bog—*Synaptomys cooperi*

Lynx—*Lynx canadensis*
Mammoth, woolly—*Elephas primigenius*
Marten—*Martes americana*
Mastodon—*Mastodon americanus*
Mink—*Mustela vison*
Mole, hairy-tailed—*Parascalops breweri*
Mole, star-nosed—*Condylura cristata*
Moose—*Alces alces*
Mouse, deer—*Peromyscus maniculatus*
Mouse, house—*Mus musculus*
Mouse, meadow jumping—*Zapus hudsonius*
Mouse, white-footed—*Peromyscus leucopus*
Mouse, woodland jumping—*Napaeozapus insignis*
Muskrat—*Ondatra zibethica*
Opossum—*Didelphis marsupialis*
Otter, river—*Lutra canadensis*
Pipistrel, eastern—*Pipistrellus subflavus*
Porcupine—*Erethizon dorsatum*
Raccoon—*Procyon lotor*
Seal, hooded—*Cystophora cristata*
Seal, ringed—*Pusa hispida*
Shrew, masked—*Sorex cinereus*
Shrew, northern water—*Sorex palustris*
Shrew, pygmy—*Microsorex hoyi*
Shrew, short-tailed—*Blarina brevicauda*
Skunk, striped—*Mephitis mephitis*
Squirrel, black—*Sciurus carolinensis*
Squirrel, gray—*Sciurus carolinensis*
Squirrel, northern flying—*Glaucomys sabrinus*
Squirrel, red—*Tamiasciurus hudsonicus*
Vole, boreal red-backed—*Clethrionomys gapperi*
Vole, meadow—*Microtus pennsylvanicus*
Walrus—*Odobenus rosmarus*
Weasel, long-tailed—*Mustela frenata*
Weasel, short-tailed—*Mustela erminea*

Whale, bowhead—*Balaena mysticetus*
Whale, finback—*Balaenoptera physalus*
Whale, humpback—*Megaptera novaeangliae*
Wolf, timber (gray)—*Canis lupus*
Wolverine—*Gulo luscus*
Woodchuck (Groundhog)—*Marmota monax*

Birds

Bittern, American—*Botaurus lentiginosus*
Blackbird, red-winged—*Agelaius phoeniceus*
Blackbird, rusty—*Euphagus carolinus*
Bluebird, eastern—*Sialia sialis*
Bobolink—*Dolichonyx oryzivorus*
Bobwhite, northern (Quail)—*Colinus virginianus*
Bufflehead—*Bucephala albeola*
Bunting, indigo—*Passerina cyanea*
Bunting, snow—*Plectrophenax nivalis*
Canvasback—*Aythya valisineria*
Cardinal, northern—*Cardinalis cardinalis*
Catbird, gray—*Dumetella carolinensis*
Chickadee, black-capped—*Parus atricapillus*
Chickadee, boreal—*Parus hudsonicus*
Cormorant, double-crested—*Phalacrocorax auritus*
Cowbird, brown-headed—*Molothrus ater*
Crosshill, red—*Loxia curvirostra*
Crossbill, white-winged—*Loxia leucoptera*
Crow, American—*Corvus brachyrhynchos*
Cuckoo, black-billed—*Coccyzus erythropthalamus*
Duck, American black—*Anas rubripes*
Duck, mallard—*Anas platyrhynchos*
Duck, ring-necked—*Aythya collaris*
Duck, wood—*Aix sponsa*
Eagle, bald—*Haliaeetus leucocephalus*
Egret, cattle—*Bubulcus ibis*
Falcon, peregrine—*Falco peregrinus*
Finch, purple—*Carpodacus purpureus*

Finches—*Fringillidae* (family)

Flicker, northern—*Colaptes auratus*

Flycatcher, alder—*Empidonax alnorum*

Flycatcher, great-crested—*Myiarchus crinitus*

Flycatcher, least—*Empidonax minimus*

Flycatcher, olive-sided—*Contopus borealis*

Flycatcher, yellow-bellied—*Empidonax flaviventris*

Gadwall—*Anas strepera*

Goldeneye, common—*Bucephala clangula*

Goldfinch, American—*Carduelis tristis*

Goose, Canada—*Branta canadensis*

Goose, snow—*Anser caerulescens*

Goshawk, northern—*Accipiter gentilis*

Grebe, horned—*Podiceps auritus*

Grebe, pied-billed—*Podilymbus podiceps*

Grosbeak, evening—*Coccothraustes vespertinus*

Grosbeak, pine—*Pinicola enucleator*

Grosbeak, rose-breasted—*Pheucticus ludovicianus*

Grouse, ruffed (Partridge)—*Bonasa umbellus*

Grouse, spruce—*Dendragapus canadensis*

Gull, herring—*Larus argentatus*

Gull, ring-billed—*Larus delawarensis*

Gyrfalcon—*Falco rusticolus*

Harrier, northern (Marsh hawk)—*Circus cyaneus*

Hawk, broad-winged—*Buteo platypterus*

Hawk, Cooper's—*Accipiter cooperii*

Hawk, red-shouldered—*Buteo lineatus*

Hawk, red-tailed—*Buteo jamaicensis*

Hawk, rough-legged—*Buteo lagopus*

Hawk, sharp-shinned—*Accipiter striatus*

Heron, black-crowned night—see Night-heron

Heron, great blue—*Ardea herodias*

Heron, green—*Butorides virescens*

Hummingbird, ruby-throated—*Archilochus colubris*

Jay, blue—*Cyanocitta cristata*

Jay, gray (Canada)—*Perisoreus canadensis*
Junco, dark-eyed—*Junco hyemalis*
Kestrel (Sparrow hawk)—*Falco sparverius*
Killdeer—*Charadrius vociferus*
Kingfisher, belted—*Ceryle alcyon*
Kinglet, ruby-crowned—*Regulus calendula*
Loon, common—*Gavia immer*
Meadowlark, eastern—*Sturnella magna*
Merganser, common—*Mergus merganser*
Merganser, hooded—*Lophodytes cucullatus*
Merganser, red-breasted—*Mergus serrator*
Mockingbird, northern—*Mimus polyglottos*
Moorhen, common—*Gallinula chloropus*
Nighthawk, common—*Chordeiles minor*
Night-heron, black-crowned—*Nycticorax nycticorax*
Nuthatch, red-breasted—*Sitta canadensis*
Nuthatch, white-breasted—*Sitta carolinensis*
Oldsquaw—*Clangula hyemalis*
Oriole, northern (Baltimore)—*Icterus galbula*
Osprey—*Pandion haliaetus*
Ovenbird—*Seiurus aurocapillus*
Owl, barred—*Strix varia*
Owl, great horned—*Bubo virginianus*
Owl, northern hawk—*Surnia ulula*
Owl, long-eared—*Asio otus*
Owl, northern saw-whet—*Aegolius acadicus*
Owl, eastern screech—*Otus asio*
Owl, short-eared—*Asio flammeus*
Owl, snowy—*Nyctea scandiaca*
Parula, northern—*Parula americana*
Pewee, eastern wood—see Wood-pewee
Phoebe, eastern—*Sayornis phoebe*
Pigeon, passenger—*Ectopistes migratorius*
Pintail, northern—*Anas acuta*
Plovers—*Charadriidae* (family)

Quail, bobwhite—see Bobwhite

Rail, Virginia—*Rallus limicola*

Raven, common—*Corvus corax*

Redhead—*Aythya americana*

Redpoll, common—*Carduelis flammea*

Redstart, American—*Setophaga ruticilla*

Robin, American—*Turdus migratorius*

Sandpiper, solitary—*Tringa solitaria*

Sandpiper, spotted—*Actitus macularia*

Sandpiper, upland—*Bartramia longicauda*

Sapsucker, yellow-bellied—*Sphyrapicus varius*

Scaup, greater—*Aythya marila*

Scaup, lesser—*Aythya affinis*

Scoters—*Melanitta spp.*

Shoveler, northern—*Anas clypeata*

Shrike, loggerhead—*Lanius ludovicianus*

Shrike, northern—*Lanius excubitor*

Siskin, pine—*Carduelis pinus*

Sparrow, house—*Passer domesticus*

Sparrow, Lincoln's—*Melospiza lincolnii*

Sparrow, Savannah—*Passaculus sandwichensis*

Sparrow, song—*Melospiza melodia*

Sparrow, swamp—*Melospiza georgiana*

Sparrow, American tree—*Spizella arborea*

Sparrow, white-throated—*Zonotrichia albicolis*

Starling, European—*Sturnus vulgaris*

Swallow, bank—*Riparia riparia*

Swallow, cliff—*Hirundo pyrrhonota*

Swallow, tree—*Tachicineta bicolor*

Swift, chimney—*Chaetura pelagica*

Tanager, scarlet—*Piranga olivacea*

Teal, blue-winged—*Anas discors*

Teal, green-winged—*Anas crecca*

Tern, black—*Chlidonias niger*

Tern, common—*Sterna hirundo*

Thrasher, brown—*Toxostoma rufum*

Thrush, Bicknell's—*Catharus bicknelli*

Thrush, gray-checked—*Catharus minimus*

Thrush, hermit—*Catharus guttatus*

Thrush, Swainson's—*Catharus ustulatus*

Thrush, wood—*Hylocichla mustelina*

Towhee, eastern (rufous-sided)—*Pipilo erythrophthalmus*

Turkey, wild (common)—*Meleagris gallopavo*

Veery—*Catharus fuscescens*

Vireo, red-eyed—*Vireo olivaceus*

Vireo, solitary—*Vireo solitarius*

Vireo, warbling—*Vireo gilvus*

Vulture, turkey—*Cathartes aura*

Warbler, bay-breasted—*Dendroica castanea*

Warbler, black-and-white—*Mniotilta varia*

Warbler, blackpoll—*Dendroica striata*

Warbler, black-throated blue—*Dendroica caerulescens*

Warbler, black-throated green—*Dendroica virens*

Warbler, Cape May—*Dendroica tigrina*

Warbler, chestnut-sided—*Dendroica pensylvanica*

Warbler, magnolia—*Dendroica magnolia*

Warbler, Nashville—*Vermivora ruficapilla*

Warbler, palm—*Dendroica palmarum*

Warbler, pine—*Dendroica pinus*

Warbler, Wilson's—*Wilsonia pusilla*

Warbler, yellow—*Dendroica petechia*

Warbler, yellow-rumped (Myrtle)—*Dendroica coronata*

Waterthrush, northern—*Seiurus novaboracensis*

Waxwing, cedar—*Bombycilla cedrorum*

Whip-poor-will—*Caprimulgus vociferus*

Wigeon, American—*Anas americana*

Woodcock, American—*Scolopax minor*

Woodpecker, black-backed (three-toed)—*Picoides arcticus*

Woodpecker, downy—*Picoides pubescens*

Woodpecker, hairy—*Picoides villosus*

Woodpecker, (northern) three-toed (ladder-backed)—*Picoides tridactylus*
Woodpecker, pileated—*Dryocopus pileatus*
Wood-pewee, eastern—*Contopus virens*
Wren, house—*Troglodytes aedon*
Wren, marsh—*Cistothorus palustris*
Wren, sedge—*Cistothorus platensis*
Wren, winter—*Troglodytes troglodytes*
Yellowthroat, common—*Geothlypis trichas*

Reptiles and Amphibians

Bullfrog—*Rana catesbeiana*
Cottonmouth, eastern (Water moccasin)—*Agkistrodon piscivorus*
Frog, green—*Rana clamitans*
Frog, leopard (meadow)—*Rana pipiens*
Frog, mink—*Rana septentrionalis*
Frog, pickerel—*Rana palustris*
Frog, striped (western) chorus—*Pseudacris triseriata*
Frog, wood—*Rana sylvatica*
Mud puppy—*Necturus maculosus*
Newt, eastern (red-spotted)—*Notophthalamus viridescens*
Peeper, spring—*Hyla crucifer*
Rattlesnake, timber—*Crotalus horridus horridus*
Salamander, blue-spotted—*Ambystoma laterale*
Salamander, dusky—*Desmognathus fuscus*
Salamander, four-toed—*Hemidactylium scutatum*
Salamander, Jefferson—*Ambystoma jeffersonianum*
Salamander, northern two-lined—*Eurycea bislineata*
Salamander, redback—*Plethodon cinereus*
Salamander, spotted—*Ambystoma maculatum*
Salamander, spring—*Gyrinophilus porphyriticus*
Skink, five-lined—*Eumeces fasciatus*
Snake, common garter—*Thamnophis sirtalis*
Snake, milk—*Lampropeltis triangulum*
Snake, northern ringneck—*Diadophis punctatus*
Snake, northern water—*Natrix sipedon*
Snake, rat (pilot)—*Elaphne obsoleta*

Snake, redbelly—*Storeria occipitomaculata*
Snake, smooth green—*Opheodrys vernalis*
Toad, American—*Bufo americanus*
Toad, Fowler's—*Bufo woodhousei fowleri*
Treefrog, gray—*Hyla versicolor*
Turtle, bog—*Clemmys muhlenbergi*
Turtle, common musk (stinkpot)—*Sternotherus odoratus*
Turtle, map—*Graptemys geographica*
Turtle, painted—*Chrysemys picta*
Turtle, snapping—*Chelydra serpentina*
Turtle, spiny softshell—*Alpone spinifera*
Turtle, wood—*Clemmys insculpta*

Fish

Bass, largemouth—*Micropterus salmoides*
Bass, smallmouth—*Micropterus dolomieui*
Bowfin—*Amia calva*
Bullhead, brown—*Ictalurus nebulosus*
Crappie, black—*Pomoxis nigromaculatus*
Dace—*Cyprinidae* (family)
Darters—*Percidae* (family)
Eel, American—*Anguilla rostrata*
Gar, long-nosed—*Lepisosteus osseus*
Lamprey, sea—*Petromyzon marinus* (class Agnatha)
Ling—*Lota lota*
Lungfish, African—*Protopterus spp.*
Muskellunge—*Esox masquinongy*
Perch, yellow—*Perca flavescens*
Pickerel, chain—*Esox niger*
Pike, northern—*Esox lucius*
Pumpkinseed (Sunfish)—*Lepomis gibbosus*
Salmon, Atlantic—*Salmo salar*
Salmon, landlocked (Sebago)—*Salmo salar*
Sculpins—*Cottidae* (family)
Shad, American—*Alosa sapidissima*
Sheepshead—*Aplodinotus grunniens*

Shiners—*Cyprinidae* (family)
Smelt, rainbow—*Osmerus mordax*
Sturgeon, lake—*Acipenser fulvescens*
Sucker, common—*Catostomus commersonnii*
Suckers—*Catostomatidae* (family)
Sunfish (Pumpkinseed)—*Lepomis gibbosus*
Trout, brook—*Salvelinus fontinalis*
Trout, brown—*Salmo trutta*
Trout, lake—*Salvelinus namaycush*
Trout, rainbow—*Salmo gairdnerii*
Walleye (Pike perch)—*Stizostedion vitreum*
Whitefish—*Coregonus clupeaformis*

Invertebrates
Arthropods—*Arthropoda* (phylum)
    Centipedes—*Chilopoda* (class)
    Crustaceans—*Crustacea* (class)
        Copepods—*Copepoda* (subclass)
        Crayfish—*Cambarus bartoni* and *Orconectes spp.*
        Shrimp, fairy—*Anostraca* (order)
    Insects—*Insecta* (class)
        Adelgid, hemlock woolly—*Adelges tsugae*
        Ant, carpenter—*Camponotus spp.*
        Ants—*Hymenoptera* (order)
        Backswimmers—*Notonectidae* (family)
        Bees—*Hymenoptera* (order)
        Beetle, arctic ground—*Nebria suturalis*
        Beetle, Colorado potato—*Leptinotarsa decemlineata*
        Beetles—*Coleoptera* (order)
        Beetles, bark—*Scolytidae* (family)
        Beetles, ground—*Carabidae* (family)
        Beetles, predaceous diving—*Dytiscidae* (family)
        Beetles, tiger—*Cicindelidae* (family)
        Beetles, whirligig—*Dineutes spp.*
        Boatman, water—*Corixidae* (family)
        Borers, wood—*Cerambycidae* and *Buprestidae* (families)

Brushfoots (butterflies)—*Nymphalidae* (family)

Budworm, spruce—*Choristoneura fumiferana*

Bugs—*Hemiptera* (order)

Bumblebees—*Apidae* (family)

Butterflies—*Lepidoptera* (order)

Butterfly, Baltimore—*Euphydryas phaeton*

Butterfly, bog copper—*Epidemia epixanthe phaedra*

Butterfly, cabbage—*Pieris rapae*

Butterfly, jutta arctic—*Oeneis jutta*

Butterfly, monarch (milkweed)—*Danaus plexippus*

Butterfly, mourning cloak—*Nymphalis antiopa*

Butterfly, spring azure—*Celastrina argiolus*

Butterfly, white admiral—*Limenitis arthemis arthemis*

Caddisflies—*Trichoptera* (order)

Crickets—*Orthoptera* (family)

Damselflies—*Odonata* (order)

Damselfly, black-winged—*Calopteryx maculata*

Darner, green—*Anax junius*

Dragonflies—*Odonata* (order)

Flea, snow—*Hypogastrura nivicola*

Flies—*Diptera* (order)

Flies, deer—*Tabanidae* (family)

Fly, black—*Simulium spp.*

Fritillaries (butterflies)—*Nymphalidae* (family)

Froghoppers (Spittlebugs)—*Cercopidae* (family)

Grasshoppers, long-horned—*Tettigoniidae* (family)

Grasshoppers, short-horned—*Acrididae* (family)

Hairstreaks (butterflies)—*Lycaenidae* (family)

Honeybee—*Apis mellifera*

Katydid—*Scudderia spp.*

Leafcutter, maple—*Paraclemensia acerifoliella*

Leafhoppers—*Cicadellidae* (family)

Mayflies—*Ephemeroptera* (order)

Midges—*Diptera* (order)

Mosquitoes—*Diptera* (order)

Moth, cecropia—*Hyalophora cecropia*

Moth, gypsy—*Lymantria dispar*
Moths, giant silkworm—*Saturniidae* (family)
Moths—*Lepidoptera* (family)
Moths, noctuid—*Noctuidae* (family)
Satyrs (butterflies)—*Satyrinae* (subfamily)
Sawflies—*Hymenoptera* (order)
Skippers (butterflies)—*Hesperiidae* (family)
Springtails—*Collembola* (order)
Stoneflies—*Plecoptera* (order)
Sulphurs (butterflies)—*Pieridae* (family)
Tent caterpillar, eastern—*Malacosoma americanum*
Tent caterpillar, forest—*Malacosoma disstria*
Thrips, pear—*Taeniothrips inconsequens*
Tortoise shells (butterflies)—*Nymphalis spp.*
Wasps—*Hymenoptera* (order)
Water bug, giant—*Belostomatidae* (family)
Water striders—*Gerridae* (family)
Millipedes—*Diplopoda* (class)
Spiders and Mites—*Arachnida* (class)
   Mites—*Acarina* (order)
   Spider, fish—*Dolomedes spp.*
   Spiders—*Araneida* (order)
Trilobites—*Trilobita* (class)
Brachiopods—*Brachiopoda* (phylum)
Bryozoans (Moss Animals)—*Bryozoa* (phylum)
Corals—*Coelenterata* (phylum)
Crinoids—*Echinodermata* (phylum)
Flatworms—*Platyhelminthes* (phylum)
Mollusks—*Mollusca* (phylum)
   Cephalopods—*Cephalopoda* (class)
      Snail, sea (fossil)—*Maclurites magna*
   Clams—*Pelecypoda* (class)
      Clams, fingernail—*Sphaeridae* (family)
      Mussels—*Unionidae/Margaritiferidae* (families)
         Mussel, zebra—*Dreissena polymorpha*
         Wedgemussel, dwarf—*Alasmidonta heterodon*

Snails and Slugs—*Gastropoda* (class)

Slugs—*Stylommatophora* (order)

Snail, land—*Succinea ovalis*

Sponges, freshwater—*Porifera* (phylum)

Worms, segmented—*Annelida* (phylum)

Earthworms—*Oligochaeta* (class)

Index

Only common names of plants and animals are given in the index. Scientific equivalents for these names are listed in Appendix IV, beginning on page 301. No entries are given from Appendixes II and III. An asterisk (*) indicates an illustration.

Archaic Period. *See* Native Ameri-
can(s)
Arctic: amphibians of, 137; birds, 72,
91, 95; and bogs, 183; and glaciers,
17, 37; mammals, 72, 83, 125;
plants, 70–73; tundra, 39, 69–70
Arethusa (Dragon's-mouth), 187, 301
Arlington, Vt., 98
Arrow-wood, 191, 304
Arrowhead, common (Duck potato),
172*, 173, 301
Arrowhead Mountain Reservoir, 158*
Arthropods, 95, 317
Artifacts, Native American, 44*
Asbestos, 29, 30, 61, 263
Ascutney, Vt., 157
Ash: black, 189; green, 189; for lum-
ber, 106; mountain, *see* Mountain
ash; white, 35, 37, 104, 198, 276;
scientific names, 304; "yellows,"
107
Aspen(s): as food for beavers, 117; as
food for grouse, 133; quaking
(trembling), 57, 133, 227; scientific
names, 304
Aster(s): of fields and farms, 227;
scientific names, 301; white wood,
110; whorled, 110
Atlantic Flyway, 177, 213
Atlantic Ocean: and anadromous fish,
209; formed, 7*, 8–9, 15; during
Pleistocene glaciation, 19, 22, 211
Australia, 15
Austria, 17

Backswimmers, 202*, 206, 317
Bacteria, 180
Barnard, Vt., 112, 113
Barre granite quarries, 11, 14, 28*,
34, 253, 255
Barton River, 253, 268, 273
Basalt, 4, 8, 12, 14, 60
Bass: largemouth, 206, 207, 278; sci-
entific names, 316; smallmouth,
160, 209, 278
Basswood (Linden), 35, 36, 37, 104,
304
Bat(s): big brown, 238; at brooks and
streams, 154; of fields and farms,

237, 238–39; hibernation, 122,
238–39, 260; Indiana, 239; little
brown, 238; migration, 239; red,
239; scientific names, 308. *See
also* Pipistrel
Bateaux, 81*
Batten Kill (river), 158, 253, 268
Bayberry, 191, 304
Beach gravel, 22
Beach heath, 22, 305
Bear, black: bountied, 122; breeding
season, 123; habitat, 121*,
122–23*, 192, 277; habits, 122;
hunted by Native Americans, 45;
population, in Vermont, 120, 122;
scientific name, 308; semihibernation, 122, 123, 125; taken for fur in
1700s, 52; travel corridors, 122*;
weight of, 120, 123
Bear Mountain, 263
Bear Pond, 96, 203, 279
Beaver(s): dams/ponds, 103, 117,
152, 191, 204*; near extinction,
116, 119; present population, 117;
protection of, 117; restoration,
117; riverbank, 163, 178, 198; scientific name, 308; trapped, 52
Beaver Pond (Bill Sladyk Wildlife
Management Area), 277
Bedrock (Vermont), 3–15*, 20–21,
27, 30, 200, 255–63
Bedstraws, 227, 301
Bee(s), 110, 241, 242, 317. *See also*
Bumblebee, Honeybee
Beech, American: of beech-maple
association, 35–37, 104; nuts (food
for wildlife), 115, 133; in old-
growth forests, 36; in presettlement forests, 106; scientific name,
304; stump sprouting in, 58; in
succession, 56
Beetle(s): bark, 140; diversity of, 40;
European bark, 107; ground, 40,
72, 243; as prey, 89, 139, 235; sci-
entific names, 317; tiger, 168;
whirligig, 206
Beggarticks, 227, 301
Bellows Falls, Vt., 78, 161, 162
Belvidere Mountain, 14, 29*, 61

Library of Congress Cataloging-in-Publication Data
Johnson, Charles W., 1943–
    The nature of Vermont : introduction and guide to a New England
environment / by Charles W. Johnson. — New and expanded.
    p.   cm.
    Includes index.
    ISBN 0–87451–856–3 (pbk.)
    1. Natural history—Vermont.   I. Title.
QH105.V7J63   1998
508.743—dc21
                                                          97–47154